Windows Server 2019 &

Installation Guide for S1

Nicholas Rushton, BA Hons.

Callisto Technology And Consultancy Services

© CTACS 2020

Table of Contents

COMMENTS & REVIEWS FROM OTHER PURCHASERS

You are in good company – many thousands of people have used guides from CTACS to help them setup their home and business networks. This is what purchasers of the *Windows Server* and *Windows Server Essentials* guides have written in their reviews:

"I haven't set up a Windows Server install in literally 20 years. The last server install I did was Windows 2000 Server. That said I found this book here on Amazon last week and thought it wouldn't hurt to try it out. I am SO THANKFUL I did. It literally covers everything a small business would need to setup in Essentials 2019 plus some more advanced options. I especially liked how easy it is read and understand & the included pictures are a great aid. I would like to thank the author for writing this book. It saved me all kinds of grief."
– VP

"This book was a lifesaver! It is a clear "how-to" manual for setting up a small network, with the perfect amount of depth for a networking beginner with a decent prior understanding of Windows 10. The instructions were clear, concise, easy to follow, and worked perfectly. I highly recommend this book to anyone who needs to set up a small business network with Windows Server Essentials!" – ML

"Basic and easy to understand for beginners step by step instructions on how to use Windows Server 2019 without complicated instructions" – JG

"Succinct and crystal clear. Easy to understand. I was quoted an outrageous amount to purchase and install a server for my small law office. I purchased a used Dell and this guide and I'm up and running for a fraction of the cost." – BSH

"I found this book to be very helpful, covers many topics well but doesn't get down so deep you don't know what they are talking about. I was able to setup my domain, file and printer servers and backups quite easily." – RS

"This book is the best for getting going quickly on the software. I had not used any server operating systems for several years, so the directions given here saved me a lot of headaches and I was up and running in no time. Some info is not exhaustive, but that is the point of this book. It keeps you from getting bogged down, but covers every major subject very well and gives recommendations for specific settings that really help." – DLM

"Great book! This led me step by step through setting up my new server. I have very little IT experience and have never worked with servers or networks before. Highly recommended this book to any neophytes like myself. Please do everything exactly as he suggests. The only problems I had was when I did not carefully read his instructions." - WDE

"Outstanding little book. Gets right to the basics to install and use Windows Essentials. Highly recommended." - A COBOL Guy

"If you are a small business IT provider, then you need this book." - King P

"Setting up my first server and this book is easy to follow, understand, and put into actual practice.
I highly recommend it to anyone setting up their first server." - CM

About the Book

The aim of this book is to take the reader through a typical installation of a small Microsoft Windows Server-based network, using Windows Server 2019 or Windows Server 2019 Essentials, which are substantially the same product and differ mainly in price, capacity and expandability. It is written for the following audiences:

- Someone who is new to Essentials 2019/Server 2019 and installing it for the first time
- Someone setting up Essentials 2019/Server 2019 in a small organization (business, non-profit, school, church, home office etc.)
- Someone wishing to learn the basics of Essentials 2019/Server 2019 and who wants a succinct, practical guide based on real world scenarios

This guide has been produced because Windows Server is not supplied with a proper manual and not everyone has the time or inclination to trawl through dozens of websites trying to find key information. There are very few books on Windows Server written for beginners and small businesses; the books that are available tend to be quite technical with hundreds and hundreds of pages and, whilst they may be useful as reference works for IT professionals, they can fall short as straightforward guides for simply getting a network installed and up and running in the minimum amount of time. In contrast, this book has been written according to the Goldilocks Principle: not too little information, not too much information, but just the right amount!

The approach is very much practical and hands on. It should give you a basic understanding of Windows Server/Essentials and help you setup a network that should meet your needs and indeed, many hundreds of people have done precisely that using this book and its predecessors.

However, it is not intended as a detailed description of all Window Server's many capabilities or as a reference manual and is not aimed at enterprise installations involving large numbers of servers and techniques such as virtualization. It assumes a reasonable working knowledge of Windows and the basics of networking. It is written in a friendly, "do-it-like-this" style, rather than with undue emphasis on theory and abstract topics, based in real world experience.

The roadmap on the next page below shows the structure of this guide. It is suggested that you work through Chapters 1 to 6 in sequence, as this will get your network up and running in the shortest possible time. Thereafter, work through Chapters 7 to 13 according to your interests and priorities.

About the Author

The author has worked in IT for over 35 years, on systems of all sizes and types throughout the world, from the largest companies to the smallest. Towards the end of the 1990's Microsoft released Small Business Server ("*SBS*"), which was the distant ancestor of today's Windows Server Essentials. Shortly thereafter he became involved with a number of business start-ups and SBS was an ideal fit in many cases. A lot of his professional interest since then has been with small businesses – including running several of his own – giving him a vast amount of experience on small business IT. He currently runs his own independent consultancy and is the author of over 20 networking guides, published through CTACS as eBooks and paperbacks.

We hope that you find this guide helpful and interesting. We pride ourselves on the accuracy of our guides and they are reviewed and updated several times a year. However, if you have any suggestions or have found areas for improvement, do let us know at *ctacs@outlook.com*. Please quote the date that is listed at the beginning of page 2 so we know which edition you have. Thank you.

A Quick Overview	Chapter 1: Introduction
Installing Windows Server	Chapter 2: Basic Installation and Configuration
Understanding Storage & RAID	Chapter 3: Storage
Setting up Shared Data Folders	Chapter 4: Shared Folders
Creating & Managing Users	Chapter 5: Users
Learn how to access the Server	Chapter 6: Connecting Devices to the Server
Configuring Backups	Chapter 7: Backups and Restores
Setting up Printers	Chapter 8: Printing
Connecting from Elsewhere	Chapter 9: Remote Access: VPN & Cloud Services
Controlling what happens	Chapter 10: Group Policy
Keeping the Server Healthy	Chapter 11: Housekeeping
Managing the Server with WAC	Chapter 12: Windows Admin Center
Making the Server do More	Chapter 13: Miscellaneous & Advanced Topics

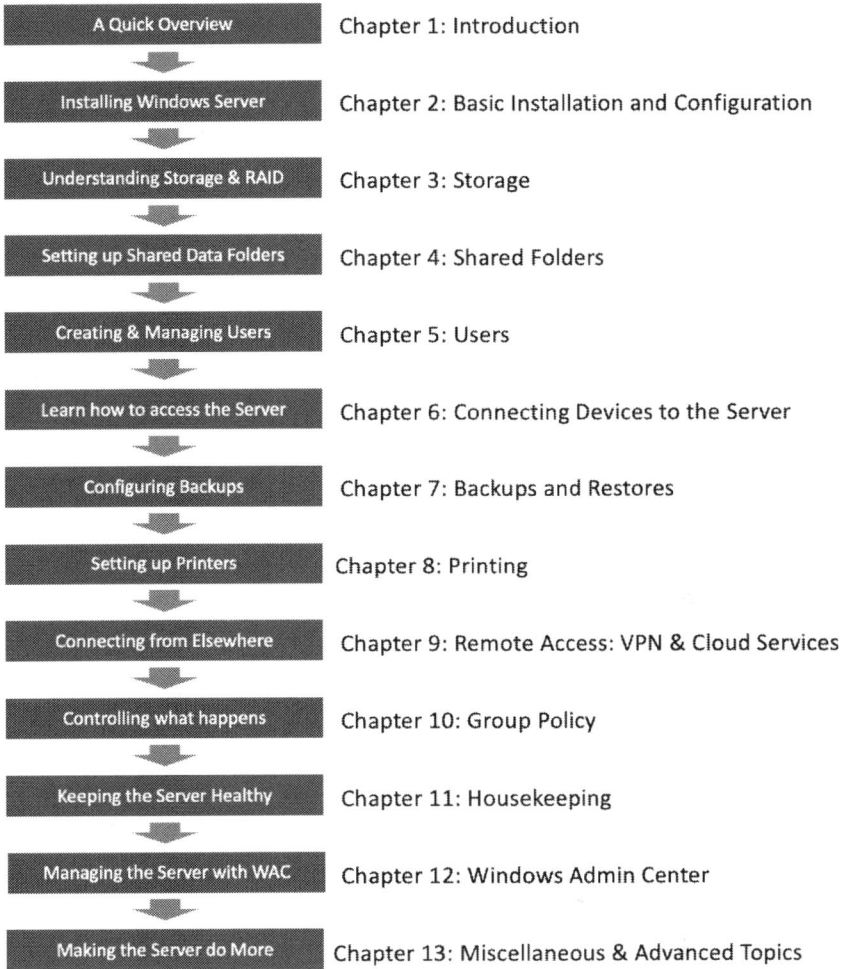

Figure 1: Roadmap for this guide

1

INTRODUCTION

1.1 What are Windows Server 2019 & Windows Server Essentials 2019?

Windows Server 2019 is the latest version of Microsoft's networking software for organizations of all sizes. With a legacy of more than 20 years, it is a mature, well-established and reliable platform and during that time it has evolved constantly, adding new functionality and capabilities and becoming easier to use and manage. In recent years, much of the focus in information technology has been on *cloud computing*, whereby data and applications are held externally and accessed over the internet. However, many organisations prefer to operate what Microsoft refer to as *on-premises computing*, whereby they own and run their own file server(s). There are several reasons for doing so:

- They wish to retain full ownership of their own data, keeping it fully under their own control. This may be because of security concerns, or a matter of simple preference.
- They may not have access to a sufficiently fast, reliable internet connection.
- The desire to avoid the ongoing subscription charges associated with cloud computing.
- There is a need to use one or more applications that require local processing and storage (for instance, a particular accounting or line-of-business package)

Windows Server is designed to address these requirements. It is available in three different variants; the variants reflect the different markets that Microsoft is targeting with the product and also reflect differences in licensing, capacity and functionality. They are as follows:

Windows Server 2019 Standard – this is the everyday version for business, education and other markets. A small business will typically have one or two physical file servers running Windows Server 2019 Standard, although a network could potentially comprise hundreds of servers and thousands of users.

Windows Server 2019 Essentials – this is a lower cost version but limited to a maximum of 25 users and restricted to a single file server in the network. Licensing works in a different manner; with regular Windows Server, it is necessary to purchase a separate license – called a Client Access Licence or CAL – for each user or device, which adds to the cost. With Essentials, there is no need for CALs.

Windows Server 2019 Datacenter – this is a higher capacity edition for larger organizations with multiple servers and/or locations and includes extensive support for virtualization and cloud-based computing.

This guide is focused on the first two editions, Windows Server 2019 Standard and Windows Server 2019 Essentials. As they are basically the same product, we will often refer to them simply as Windows Server or just Server. However, where there are any slight differences, these will be highlighted.

Essentials 2019 is significantly different than previous versions, such as Essentials 2016 and Essentials 2012 R2. In these versions, there were specific features designed to make them generally easier to configure, manage and operate than regular Windows Server, but with Essentials 2019 all of this has gone. Specifically, the following have all been removed: Windows Server Essentials Dashboard; Remote Web Access; Windows Server Essentials Connector; Launchpad; Backup for connected clients; Integration with Office 365. Essentials should be thought of as a low-cost variant of regular Windows Server, similar to the Foundation versions of Server than were available in the past.

1.2 A Typical Small Network

A typical small network or infrastructure is depicted below. The key components are:

Server - this is the heart of the network, which runs Windows Server and upon which the data is stored

Backup device – for example, an external USB drive connected to the server

Internet connection - this may be a separate router or an all-in-one wi-fi router

Switch and Wireless Access Point(s) – to provide expansion in larger networks

Printer(s) – may be networked or plugged into the server with a USB cable

Desktops PCs – running Windows Professional, connected using Ethernet or wirelessly

Laptops, tablets and smartphones – connected wirelessly

Whilst it may not match your own setup exactly, it should be broadly similar. Further information about the components is given underneath the diagram and/or in later sections of the guide.

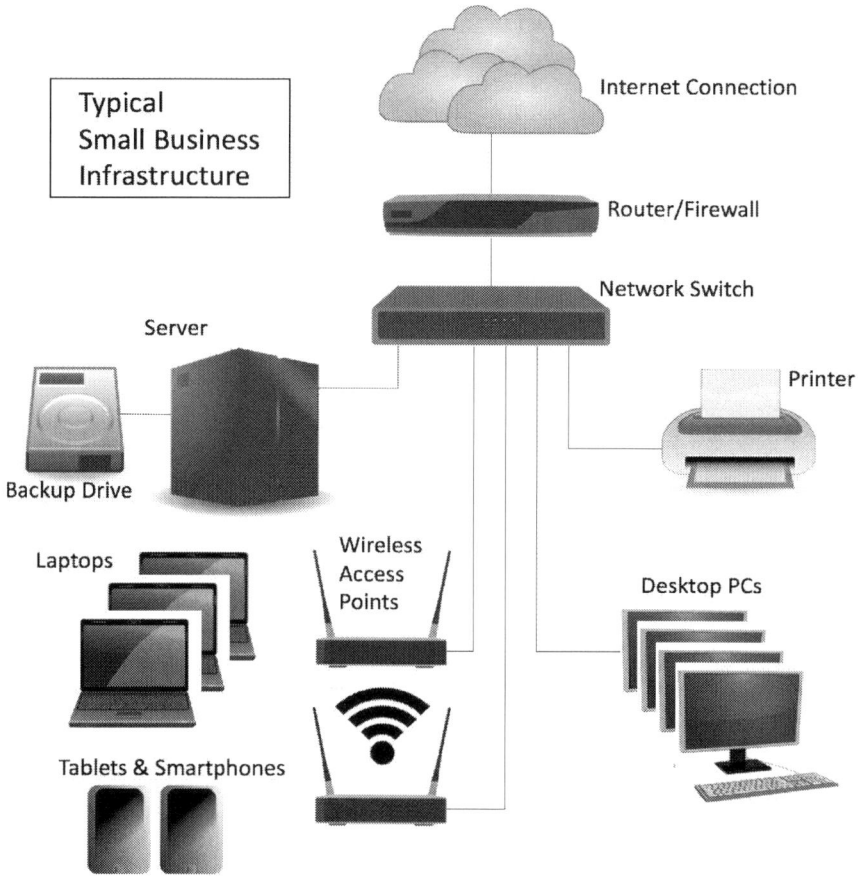

Typical
Small Business
Infrastructure

Internet Connection

Router/Firewall

Network Switch

Server

Printer

Backup Drive

Laptops

Wireless
Access
Points

Desktop PCs

Tablets & Smartphones

Figure 2: Typical small business infrastructure

1.3 The Server

Windows Server requires its own, dedicated server hardware, which may also be referred to as a *file server*. A server has some similarities to a regular desktop computer but is designed to hold multiple hard disk drives for additional storage and to be more reliable, as it is intended to be powered up continuously. The main suppliers of file servers include Dell, HP, Lenovo and Fujitsu; other brands are available, but you may wish to avoid obscure manufacturers and unbranded machines. File servers are not usually available in retail computer stores, but are obtained from specialist IT dealers or online. If you are learning about Windows Server and do not happen to have a spare server to hand, you can use virtualization software on most modern computers to run a copy in a closed environment (a good, free product that runs both on PCs and Macs is Oracle's *VirtualBox*). If you do not have a copy of the Windows Server software, you can download a fully-functional but time-limited evaluation copy from Microsoft, which is ideal for learning purposes.

Choosing a server can be daunting, particularly as it is not something that a small business is likely to buy very often (the typical replacement cycle for a server being around 5 years). Given the specialist nature of the topic, you may wish to seek professional advice if you are not knowledgeable in such matters. The following suggestions are guidelines only to help get you started:

- Spend as much as you can afford.
- In general, memory contributes more than processor power. So, you would usually be better off spending your money on more RAM rather than a marginally faster processor.
- Multiple disk drives are desirable as they enable increased capacity and performance. If you have at least two drives they can be configured to provide redundancy in the event of problems, using RAID or

Storage Spaces (for an in-depth look at storage, read chapter **3 STORAGE**).

- File servers should not be used with the regular hard drives found in desktop PCs and laptops. Instead, higher-quality drives with improved performance and increased reliability (improved MTBF or *Mean Time Between Failures*) are preferred. Such drives may have standard SATA interfaces or SAS interfaces (which are better, but may not be supported in low cost servers). Examples of such drives include: Seagate Enterprise Performance; Seagate Enterprise Capacity; WD Gold; WD Re. As might be expected, these hard drives are more expensive than desktop ones.

- Most servers have more than one network adapter. This enables them to share the workload, provide better throughput, or provide redundancy in the event of one adapter failing.

- Some servers have the option of redundant power supplies – if one fails then the other one takes over automatically. This is worth having.

- Servers are available in both tower format (similar to desktop PCs) and in horizontal rack format, for mounting in cabinets alongside other equipment such as communications equipment and network switches.

- Often the given base price for a server is for a bare-bones model and hard disk drives, memory and other features may have to be specified separately. Costs can add up and a complete system may be several times the initial headline price, so budget accordingly.

- Consider taking out a maintenance agreement at the time of purchase. These vary in service levels and price and your choice will depend upon your requirements, but generally they provide peace of mind and good value. The key decision point is: How long can you do without the server? It is possible to obtain maintenance agreements that provide an onsite presence within 4 hours.

For a very small business or other organization with less than ten staff, a suitable choice may be a *micro-server*. This is still a proper server rather than just a glorified PC, but in a small, low-cost form factor. The genre was largely invented by Hewlett-Packard and their ProLiant MicroServer series is very popular. An equivalent model from Dell is the T40. For a slightly larger organization – say up to 25 users or so – a standard entry-level file server is more appropriate. Beyond that, for users of Server 2019 Standard edition rather than Essentials, increasingly powerful servers are available that can service hundreds of users. The next stage is to use multiple servers, with the workload spread across them. As mentioned above, there are a number of vendors to choose from. Dell are a popular choice as everything can be conveniently ordered from their website in many countries.

Note that it is not necessary to purchase a monitor, keyboard and mouse for the server, as it can be operated without them in so-called *headless operation*. Consider borrowing them from another computer for the initial installation, as thereafter they are not required.

1.4 Switch and Wireless Access Points

The devices in a network are connected together using Ethernet cabling and wireless access points (WAPs). In a very small business, everything might link back to an all-in-one router or wireless router, whereas in a larger setup there may be a separate router and possibly a separate firewall. Ethernet switches and wire access points may be used to expand the network and provide greater capacity. The following points can be usefully observed:

- Use wired connections when possible, as performance is better than wireless
- Wired connections should be at least Gigabit speed. 10 Gigabit Ethernet (10GbE) is becoming more affordable and is better for linking the server to network switches and to desktop computers equipped with suitable network cards
- Wireless connections should be to 802.11ac or 802.11n standard
- Avoid domestic grade equipment. Spending more on professional or prosumer ("professional consumer") routers and switches should give better performance and reliability

1.5 Client Devices

By *client devices*, we mean desktop computers, laptop computers, tablets and smartphones. To connect to a Windows Servers-based network, the device needs to be running a version of Windows Professional or better, such as *Windows 10 Professional* or *Windows 7 Professional*. Older versions of Windows, such as XP and Vista, which are no longer generally supported by Microsoft, should not be used (although it is technically possible). Best practice is that all desktops and laptops are running the same version of Windows, rather than a mixture of versions.

Client computers running other operating systems, such as Windows Home editions, macOS or Linux, can be connected to Windows Server but in a limited, unofficial and unsupported manner and how to do so is covered in this guide.

Devices such as iOS or Android tablets and smartphones can likewise only be connected in a limited fashion.

2

BASIC INSTALLATION AND CONFIGURATION

2.1 Overview

Setting up a Windows server consists of several stages. The first one is to install the software and get it to the stage where it can subsequently be configured and customized to reflect the needs of your organization. This takes around 30-45 minutes and is the topic of this chapter.

2.2 Installing Windows Server

There are several techniques by which Windows Server can be physically installed onto the server. Read the descriptions below and choose the one which is most applicable to you:

Method 1: The Server software has been supplied on a DVD or USB. Go into the BIOS of the server and set it to boot from DVD or USB as appropriate. Accessing the BIOS varies according to the server brand, but is typically the F2 key on Dell and the F10 key on HP, for instance. Insert the DVD, connect an Ethernet cable to the main or only network adapter on the server and restart it.

Method 2: The server manufacturer has supplied a special start-up or management disk. This typically provides driver and RAID support for the server and may do some other configuration work. The usual process is to set the server to boot from CD/DVD as described above. Insert the disk, connect an Ethernet cable to the main or only network adapter on the server and restart it. The management software will run – this may take several minutes – but eventually you will be prompted to eject the disk and insert the main Windows Server DVD. The server may then restart.

Method 3: The Server software has been purchased pre-loaded on the server (this will generally be the Essentials version).
This does not mean that it is ready to use, just that what normally comes on the distribution DVD has already been copied to the server's hard drive, so the installation process can run from that.

Connect an Ethernet cable to the main or only network adapter on the server and start it.

Regardless of which method is used, a few minutes after starting the following screen is displayed. Check the settings, change them if necessary to reflect your preferred regional settings, then click **Next**:

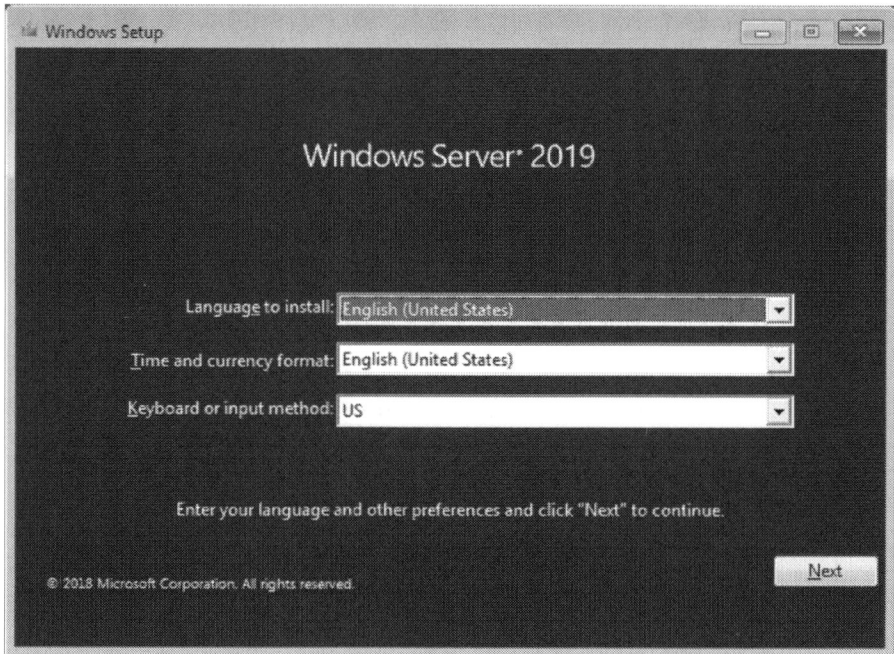

Figure 3: Adjust the regional settings if necessary

On the following screen click the **Install now** button. What happens next depends on which edition you are installing:

Windows Server 2019 Essentials
If you see a screen to enter your product key, do so (although if it is not to hand you can click **Skip** and do this after installation, as described in **13.2 Windows Activation**). On the screen after that, tick the box to accept the license terms and click **Next**.

Windows Server 2019 Standard

You will see a screen offering a choice of *Windows Server 2019 Standard* and *Windows Server 2019 Standard (Desktop Experience)*. You want the Desktop Experience option; with this, Windows Server will look like a regular version of Windows complete with Desktop, icons, Start menu and so on. With the other option the Windows graphical user interface ('GUI') is not installed and the server is more like an appliance or black box; this mode is more suitable for organizations that have many servers, used for specific roles rather than general purpose networking. So, choose **Windows Server 2019 Standard (Desktop Experience)** and click **Next**. Tick the **I accept the license terms** box on the following screen and click **Next**.

The installation now continues in the same way for both Essentials and Standard Editions.

On the following screen click the **Custom: Install Windows only (advanced)** box:

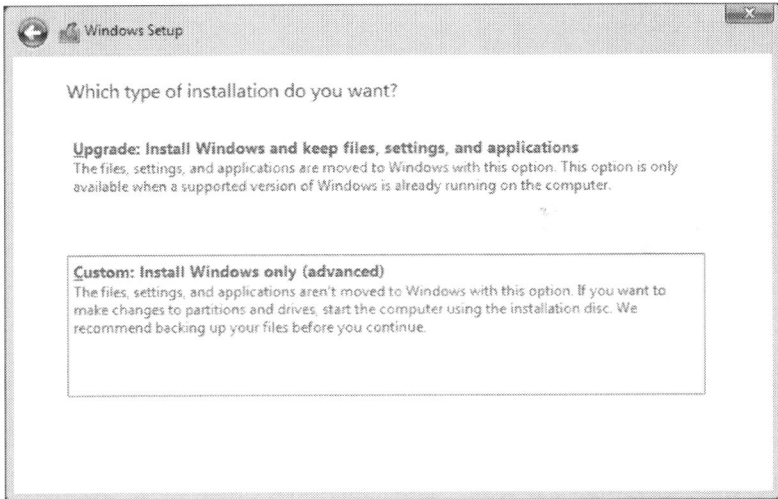

Figure 4: Choose the Custom option

A decision has to be made on where to install Windows (i.e. Windows Server/Windows Essentials). The options that appear here depend on what drives are in the server and how they are configured.

On a small system there may only be a single drive, in which case it is suggested that you split it into two partitions: a small one for the operating system and a larger one for data. A larger system might have two or more drives. On a RAID system, the drives may initially appear as a single drive. For a more in-depth look at storage, you might want to read chapter **3 STORAGE** before proceeding.

In this example there are two drives and Windows will be installed on the smaller one, with the larger one used for data. The Windows drive needs to be at least 60GB in size but larger is better. Note: only the drive that Windows is being installed upon will be formatted during installation – if there are any additional drives then it is suggested that they are formatted before proceeding. Also, some additional partitions may be created automatically at this stage, although these should be ignored as they have a special purpose and cannot be used for storage.

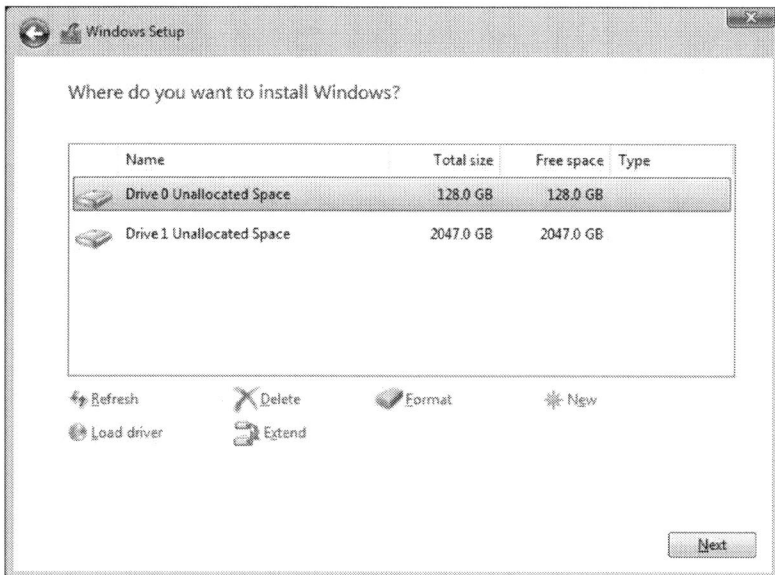

Figure 5: Choose a drive partition for Windows

Whilst the next stage runs, which typically takes around 10 minutes, the server will display a status screen and may restart several times. Upon completion, the following screen will appear, prompting you to create and confirm a password for the built-in *Administrator* account. Choose something non-obvious - a random mixture of letters, numbers and punctuation is best - and make a note of it as there is no way into the system if you forget it. Click **Finish**.

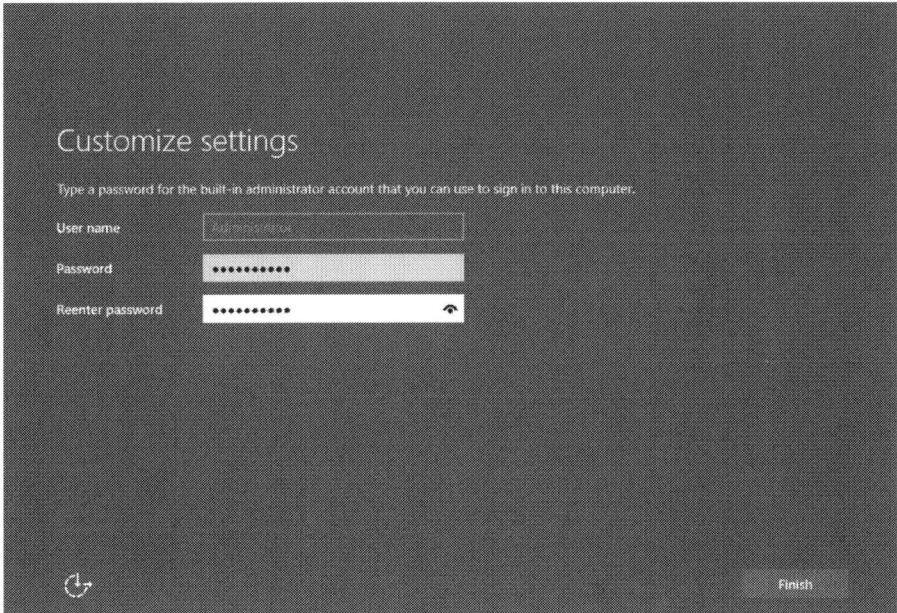

Figure 6: Specify a password for the Administrator

The server will prompt you to press **Ctrl+Alt-Delete** and login: do so as *Administrator*, using the password you just created. Following the first login, a message is displayed on the right-hand side of the screen asking whether the server should look for other devices on the network, including printers. It is very important that you choose **Yes**, otherwise Windows will be configured with a public rather than private networking profile and the network will not operate correctly:

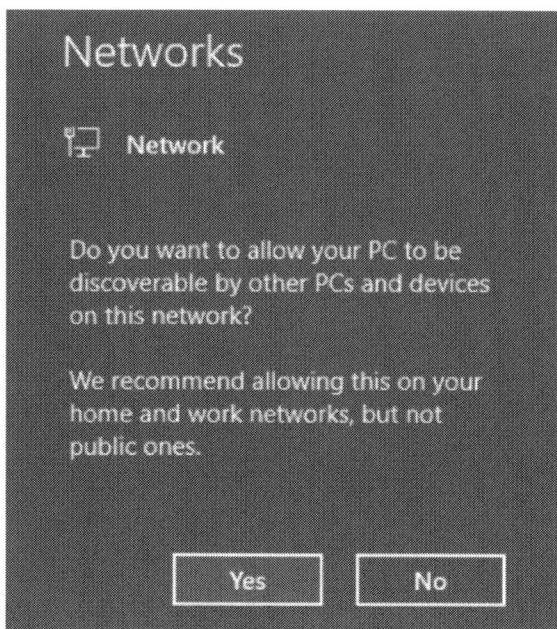

Figure 7: Networks notification screen

If you are installing Essentials, you will be presented with the Windows Desktop. However, if you are installing Standard, there will be a delay of about a minute and then the screen will clear to show *Server Manager*, which is used for configuring and managing many aspects of the server. We will return to Server Manager shortly; for now, close it, minimize it or press **Ctrl D** to show the Desktop.

If you are familiar with Windows 10, you will notice that Windows Server looks almost identical to it, which is not surprising as it is basically the same product but with additional features and capabilities for networking added and with some of the consumer features removed:

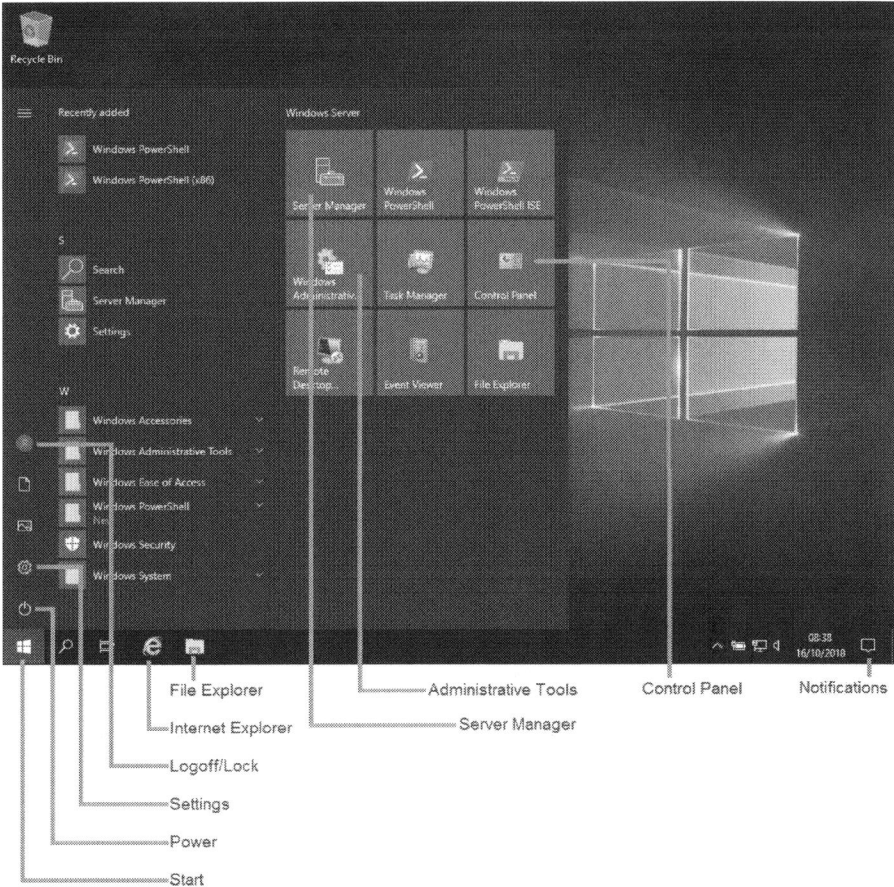

Figure 8: Windows Server User Interface

All of the programs on the system are available on the Start menu, organized alphabetically. The most recently added ones will appear at the top of the screen and also be marked as '*New*' in the alphabetic section. On the right-hand of the Start menu are tiles (icons) for a selection of commonly used items, including: *Server Manager*, which is used extensively and which will be introduced shortly; *Windows Administrative Tools*, which is a selection of useful tools and which can be viewed as a list or as icons; *Control Panel*, the traditional method of adjusting the settings on a Windows computer.

The Start menu can be customized to reflect your preferences. For instance, it can be resized and made larger or smaller. The individual tiles can be resized, removed, or added to the Taskbar on the bottom of the screen by right-clicking one and choosing the appropriate option. Additional tiles can be created: right-click on a program from the list on the left-hand side and choose **Pin to Start**.

In the bottom left-hand corner, above the Start button, are five small icons. The one at the bottom is *Power* and is used for shutting down or restarting the server, should that ever prove necessary (servers are generally left running 24x7). The next one up – which looks like a cogwheel – is *Settings* (strictly speaking, *Windows Settings*). Settings is the modern version of the Control Panel; it largely duplicates the functionality of the Control Panel and longer term will probably replace it entirely. The next two icons provide access to Documents and Pictures and are not commonly used on a server. The top icon is used for logging off from the server or locking the screen and should always be clicked for security purposes after you have finished working on the server. It is not widely known, but this list of mini-icons can be customized by right-clicking it. Another useful thing to know is that right-clicking the Start button brings up a menu of useful shortcuts for managing the system and is sometimes quicker than working through the Start menu, Server Manager or Settings.

On the Taskbar, to the right of the Start button, are several icons. The two most useful ones are *Internet Explorer* and *File Manager*. One curiosity is that the *Edge* browser, which is Microsoft's preferred browser for Windows 10, is not present in Windows Server.

On the right-hand side of the Taskbar is the *Notifications* icon; when the system needs to inform you of something a number appears on it, corresponding to the number of waiting messages; clicking the icon will then expand it, so you can read the messages. Many of the messages are actionable and you can click them to make something happen, which will usually take you to the appropriate area in *Settings*:

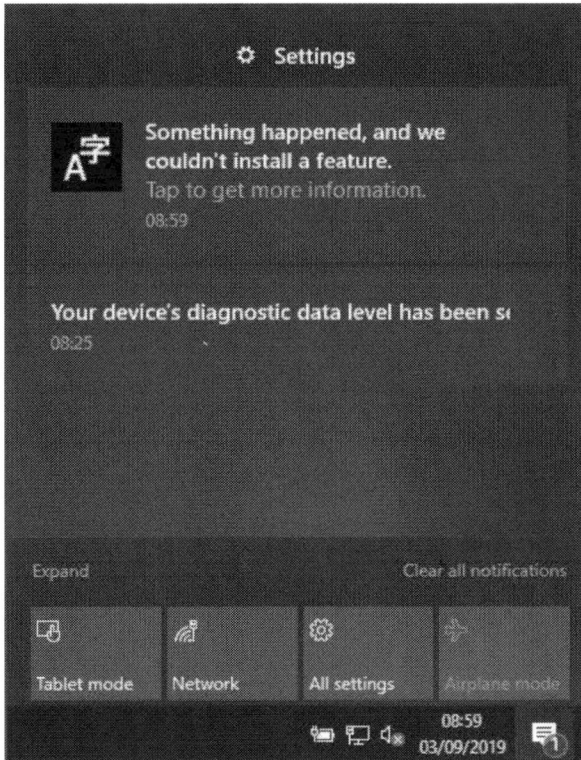

Figure 9: Notifications

2.3 Setting the IP Address

The first thing to do is set the IP address of the server. Every device in a network has a unique number within that network to identify it, known as the *IP address*. These numbers consist of four sets of digits and take the form *nnn.nnn.nnn.nnn*. Nearly all of the possible numbers are allocated to the internet for websites and other purposes and are known as *public IP addresses*. However, a small selection is available for internal or local area networks; these are known as *private IP addresses* and are invisible to the outside world. As these IP addresses are private they can safely be used by anyone without risk of duplication and the same numbers are used worldwide millions of times over. The three sequences which are available for private use are: *10.0.0.0* to *10.255.255.255*; *172.16.0.0* to *172.31.255.255*; *192.168.0.0* to *192.168.255.255*

Much of the equipment intended for use in small businesses and homes tends to be pre-set to use the *192.168.nnn.nnn* numbering scheme; for instance, internet routers hubs commonly have an address of *192.168.1.1* or *192.168.1.254* depending on brand. Although these addresses can be changed, there is rarely any need to and it is best not to do so unless one has a good understanding of the topic.

Devices such as computers and printers do not come with IP addresses already allocated; instead, they have to be configured with a suitable address and there are two ways of doing so: you can use *static IP addresses* or *dynamic IP addresses*.

With static IP addresses, it is necessary to visit each device and individually configure it. For instance, you might set the first PC to *192.168.1.101*, the second to *192.168.1.102*, the third to *192.168.1.103* and so on. You have to be careful to keep track of everything and above all make sure that there are no duplicates. If this sounds like hard work then that's because it is – you might get away with it if there are only a handful of computers, but beyond that it rapidly becomes unmanageable.

With dynamic IP addresses, the numbers are assigned automatically by a DHCP (*Dynamic Host Configuration Protocol*) server and it keeps track of everything. This is not usually a physical server like a file server, rather it is a piece of software. Most all-in-one routers of the sort used in small businesses and homes have DHCP server software built-in. If Windows Server detects one of these during the installation it will use it but, if it does not, it can be configured to provide its own DHCP service.

However, it is not really a choice of static or dynamic IP, as you need both. Some devices – servers and routers, for instance, work better with or require static addresses, plus they are often useful for printers. So, the principle is to allocate them static addresses but have the general-purpose computing devices – the desktops, laptops, tablets and smartphones – using dynamic addresses.

Regardless of whether the IP addresses come from a router or are supplied by Windows Server itself, it is a good idea to have a scheme to follow. As mentioned above, routers are commonly set to numbers such as *192.168.1.1* or *192.168.1.254*. The server should be set to an adjacent address. Printers and any specialized devices should be close by. The numbers allocated for computers, tablets and smartphones should be a contiguous block of numbers elsewhere, allocated dynamically by the router or other DHCP source. So, for instance, a typical setup might be as follows:

IP Address(es)	Role
192.168.1.1-192.168.1.49 special devices (static)	Use for printers and any
192.168.1.50-192.168.1.200 smartphones (dynamic)	Use for computers, tablets,
192.168.1.253	Windows file server (static)
192.168.1.254 (static)	Internet router/gateway

One implication of the above is that the network has a maximum of 255 devices in it, although this is unlikely to be an issue in a small network (and recall that Essentials is restricted to 50 devices in any case). In larger networks, *subnets* are used to expand the size of the network, but we will assume there is only one in use (it is commonly set to *255.255.255.0* in a small network).

Note: there are two 'flavors' of IP: TCP/IPv4 and TCP/IPv6. In this guide we are using the more common IPv4, as most people find it easier to deal with addresses such as 192.168.1.254 rather than something like, say, 3ffe:1900:4545:3:200:f8ff:fe21:67cf.

In our system, the internet router is on *192.168.1.254* and we have decided to set the server to *192.168.1.253*. The server will currently be running on a DHCP address that it is picking up from the router; to change it, right-click the **Start** button and choose **Network Connections** from the pop-up menu:

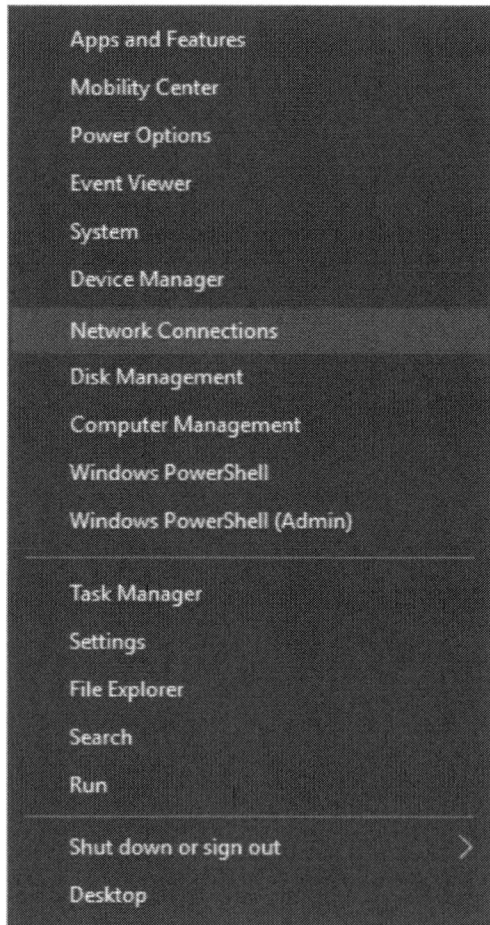

Apps and Features

Mobility Center

Power Options

Event Viewer

System

Device Manager

Network Connections

Disk Management

Computer Management

Windows PowerShell

Windows PowerShell (Admin)

Task Manager

Settings

File Explorer

Search

Run

Shut down or sign out

Desktop

Figure 10: Start button right-click menu

The *Network & Internet* section of Windows *Settings* is displayed – click **Change adapter options**. Right-click the first or only network adapter and choose **Properties**. Highlight **Internet Protocol Version 4 (TCP/IPv4)** and click **Properties**. Change it to use a specific IP address, in our case 192.168.1.253.

The *Subnet mask* should be 255.255.255.0 and the *Default gateway* is the address of the router. The *Preferred DNS* server should also be set to the address of the router, but it is not necessary to specify an *Alternate DNS server*.

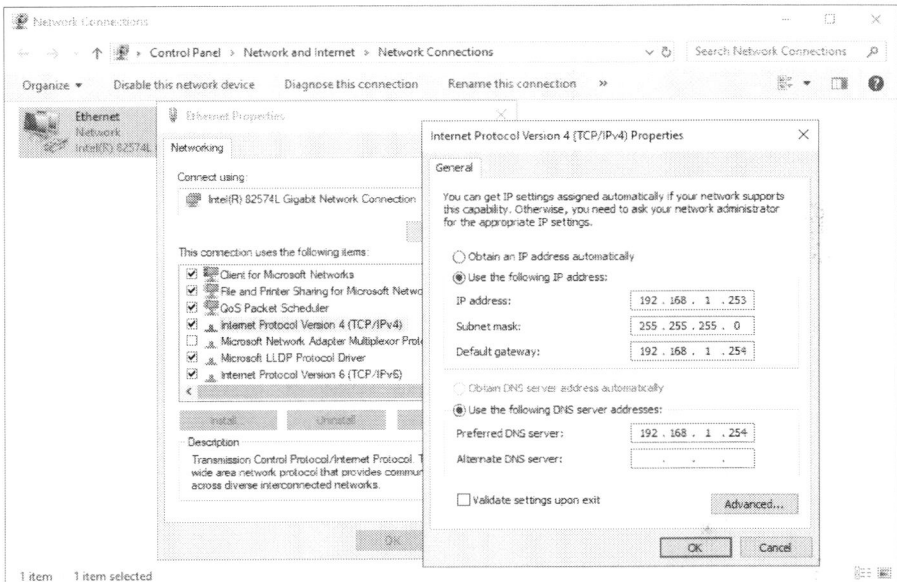

Figure 11: Specify the IP address of the server

Make the change, click **OK** and **Close.** Wait about 30 seconds for the adapter to pick-up the new IP address, close the *Network Connections* and *Settings* screens.

2.4 Naming the Server

Every computer in a network needs a unique device name. During installation, the server will have been assigned a seemingly random name e.g. WIN-24TQA9PT90E. Whilst the name does not affect the operation of Windows Server, it is better to change it to something more meaningful. In a small network with a single server or if you are using Essentials, you could simply call it *server*. However, if you are using Standard and have or intend to have multiple servers, then there will need to be a convention for naming the servers. This could be along the lines of *server01*, *server02*, *server03* and so on, or could be based on location (*newyork*, *london*, *delhi* etc.) or function (*accounts*, *sales*, *marketing* etc).

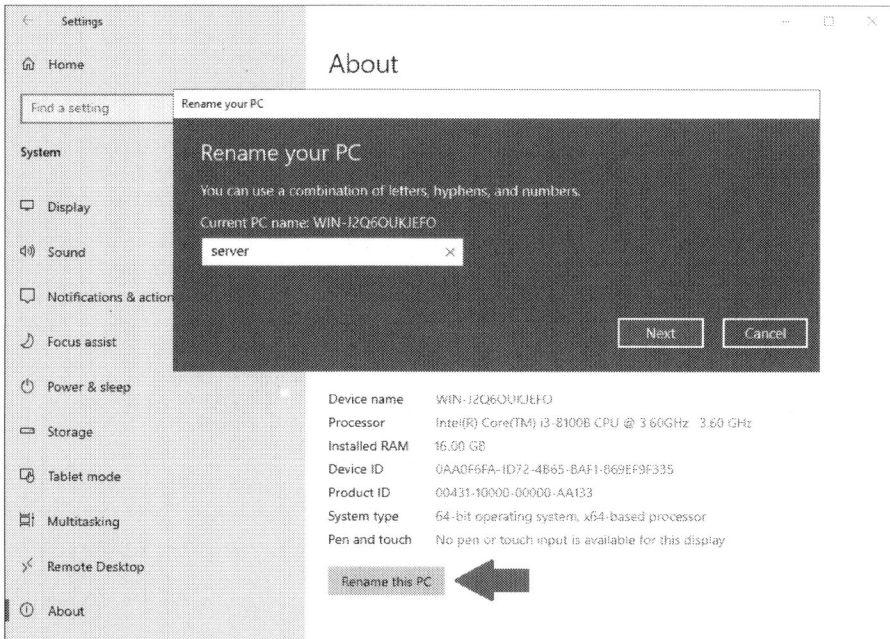

Figure 12: Renaming the server

To rename the server, go into **Start** > **Settings** > **System** > **About** and click **Rename this PC**. Type in the new name and click **Next**.

After a few seconds, you will be prompted to restart the computer, so click the **Restart now** button. In response to the prompt about why you are shutting down (sic) the computer, click **Continue** and the server will restart. When it has done so, login again as *Administrator*.

2.5 Server Manager

Much of the configuration of Windows Server is carried out using *Server Manager*, which can be found on the **Start** menu (if you are installing Standard Edition you will have briefly seen it already). In some respects, it behaves like a web site – notice the backwards and forwards buttons in the top-left hand corner, along with the refresh icon on the right-hand side – and also has many links to other components of Windows Server. When you launch it, you may receive a message regarding *Windows Admin Center*, a partial alternative to Server Manager, which can be ignored for now although we will return to it in Chapter **12. WINDOWS ADMIN CENTER** (you may wish to tick the **Don't show this message again** box):

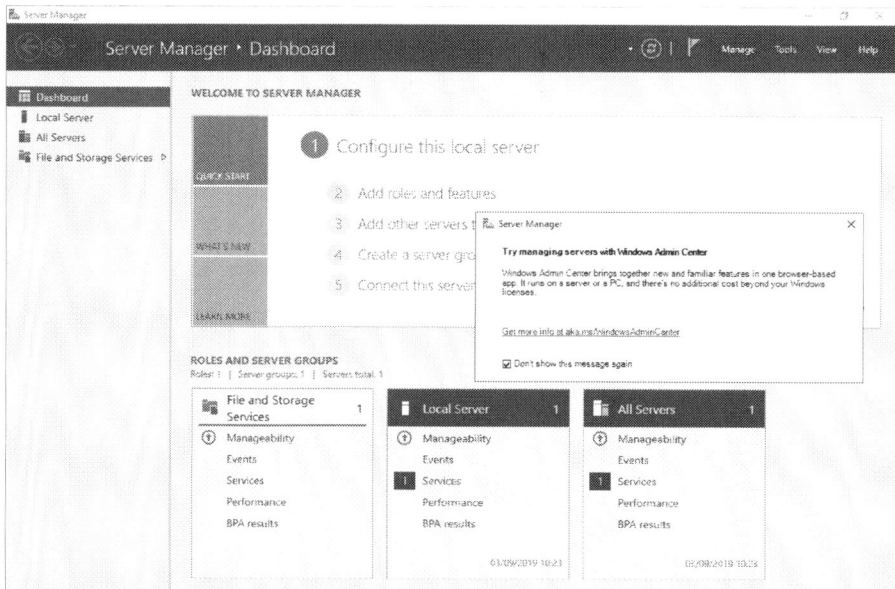

Figure 13: Server Manager Dashboard

2.6 Creating a Domain

A network comprises computers, users, shared storage areas and other resources. There needs to be a method for organizing these resources and advertising their availability, and this is the purpose of *Active Directory*. In very simple terms, the directory is a list of what is available on the network, in much the same way that a telephone directory is a list of people and businesses you can call; this collection of devices and resources is referred to as a *Domain*.

The domain is setup using Server Manager. Launch it from the Start menu, give it thirty seconds or so to refresh itself, then click **Manage** in the top right-hand corner followed by **Add roles and features**. The initial screen lists some pre-requisites but is not important, so tick the **Skip this page by default box** and click **Next**. On the subsequent screen, choose **Role-based or feature-based installation** followed by **Next**:

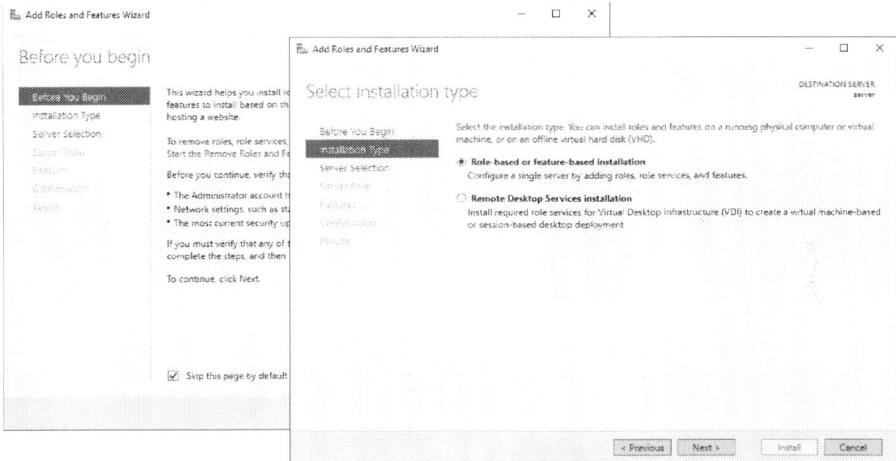

Figure 14: Add Roles and Features Wizard

On the following screen only one server should be listed - the one you are working on – although in a large organization with existing servers others may also be listed. Make sure the **Select a server from the server pool** option is marked and click **Next** to continue:

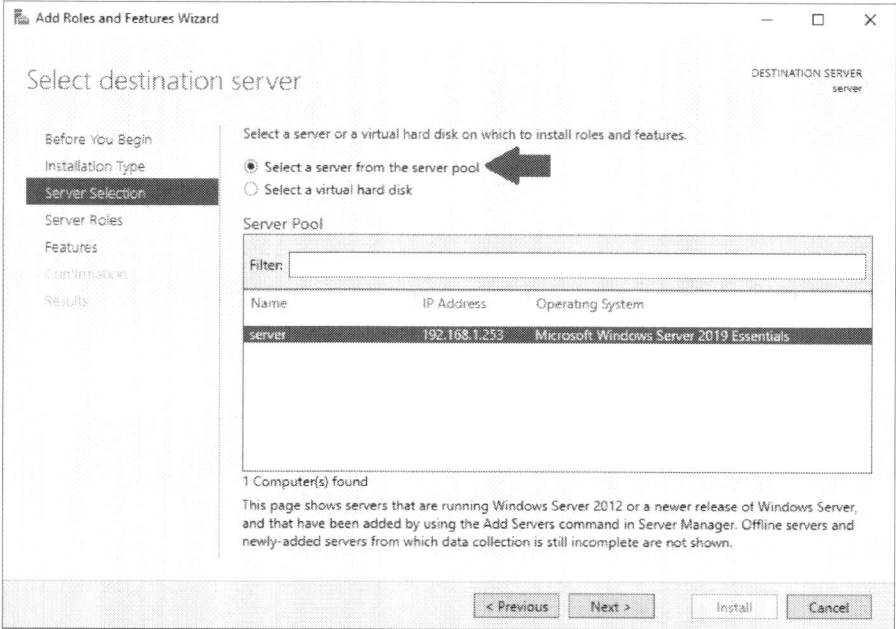

Figure 15: Select the destination server

There are a number of roles listed on the following screen. The ones that should be installed depend upon the role of the server; in a larger network with multiple servers the different roles can be shared out for reasons of performance and resilience, but in a small network with a single server then it will run everything required and hence matters are simpler. Accordingly, only the following roles need to be installed: *Active Directory Domain Services*; *DNS Server*; *File and Storage Services*. And of these, the latter one will already be in place.

Start by clicking on **Active Directory Domain Services**. The following panel immediately appears; the defaults are fine so just click the **Add Features** button:

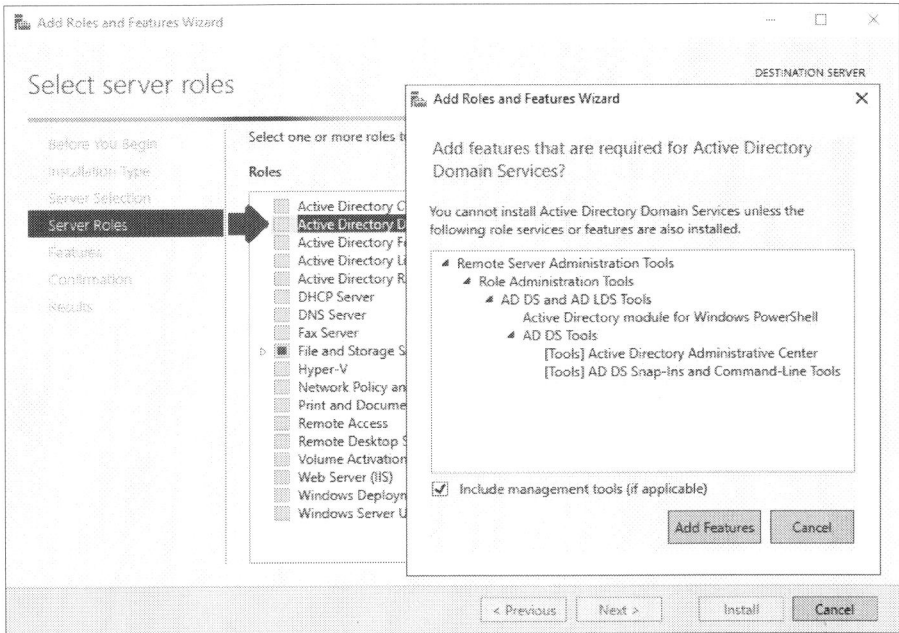

Figure 16: Prompt about adding features

You will be returned to the previous screen – click **Next**, **Next**, **Next**. Tick the **Restart the destination server automatically if required box**, acknowledge the message and click **Install**. It will take several minutes to install Active Directory, during which time an Installation progress screen will be shown. When installation is complete, the following screen is displayed; do not click *Close*, instead, click the link that reads **Promote this server to a domain controller**…

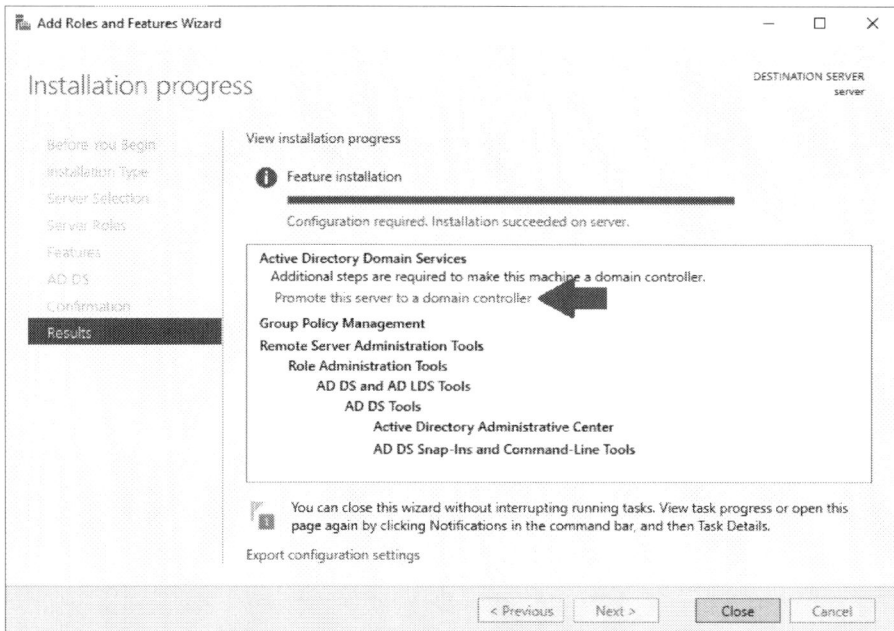

Figure 17: Installation of feature complete

…which will cause the *Deployment Configuration* panel to be is displayed.

*(Oops! Already hit the Close button by accident? Go into the main Server Manager screen. Looking at Server Manager, there will now be a new entry on the left-hand panel, marked AD DS, which you should click. On the resulting screen is a warning message that further configuration is required. Click where it reads **More…** and an additional panel appears. Click the link that reads **Promote this server to a domain controller**).*

Choose the **Add a new forest** option and specify a *Root domain name*. In large organizations with multiple servers and/or locations, it is common to use the internet domain name prefixed by some other information to identify the separate locations or functions e.g. *london.ctacs.co.uk, liverpool.ctacs.co.uk, washington.ctacs.co.uk*.

In a small organization with a single server e.g. when using Essentials, the domain name would commonly be the name of the organization with a suffix of *.local* added e.g. *ctacs.local* (people with prior experience of installing servers may be aware of some debate over the use of *.local* but we will stick with it here). Click **Next**:

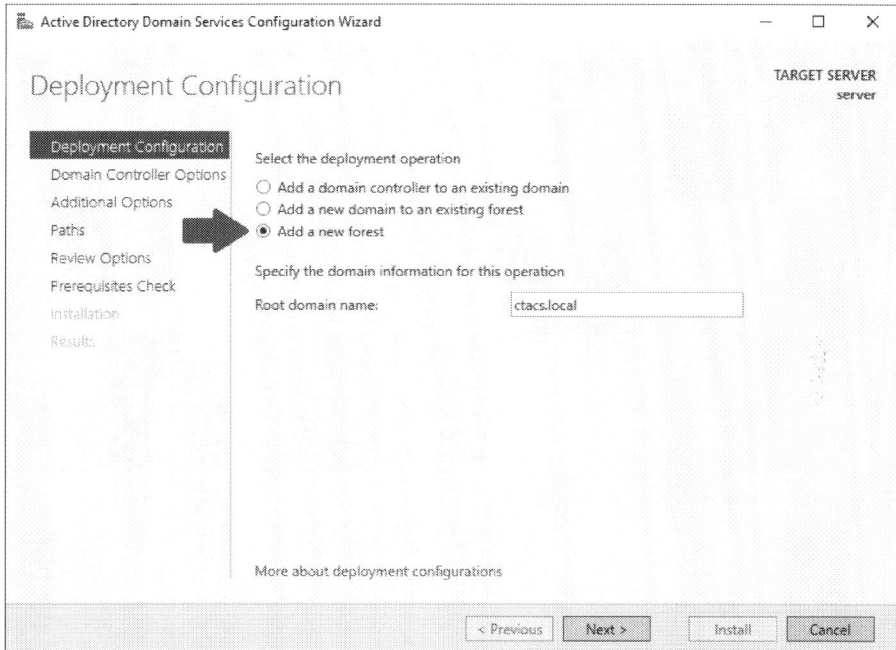

Figure 18: Specify options for the domain

After a short while the following screen is displayed. The **Forest functional level** and **Domain functional level** should both be set to *Windows Server 2016* as there is not a specific option for 2019 and it was the same in Server 2016 (alternative settings are available but would normally only be used if other, older versions of Windows Server were already in place in an existing, larger network). Leave the **Domain Name System (DNS) server** and **Global Catalog** boxes ticked. A password has to be specified; for convenience, you could use the same one as for the Administrator account (this is acceptable in a small network but would not be considered good practice in a large one). Click **Next**:

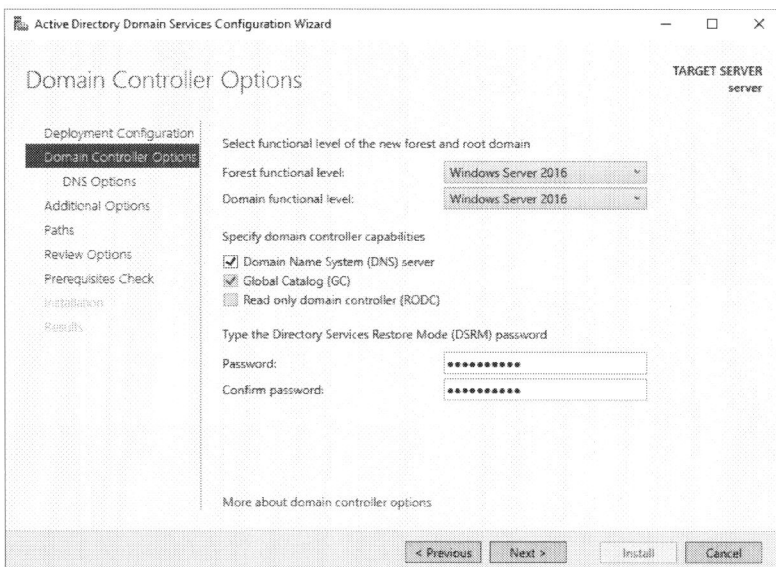

Figure 19: Domain Controller Options

On the next screen a warning may be displayed relating to DNS; a common cause of this is that you are using an all-in-one internet router that is providing DNS, in which case the message can be ignored for now by clicking **Next**:

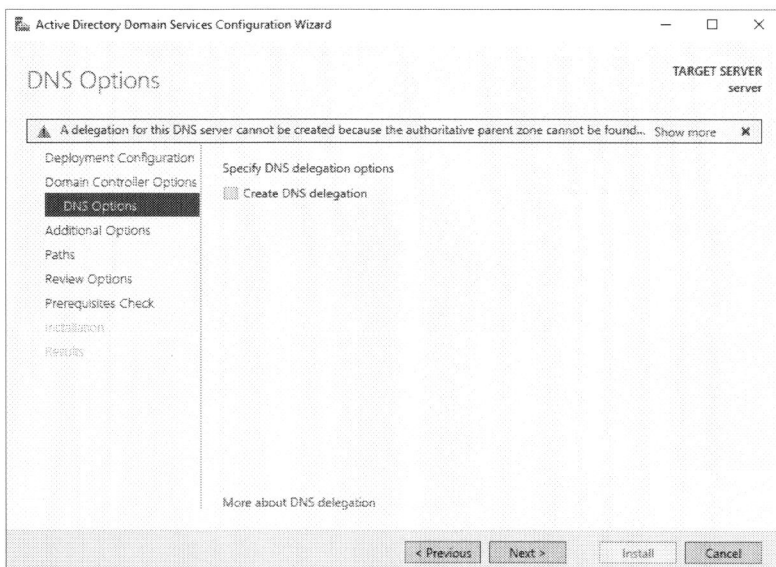

Figure 20: Message about DNS

The subsequent screen asks you to verify the *NetBIOS* name. This will be the same as the domain name you chose (minus the suffix) and usually you just accept it by clicking **Next.** The exception to this would be if it is more than 15 characters in length, in which case you would need to abbreviate it accordingly:

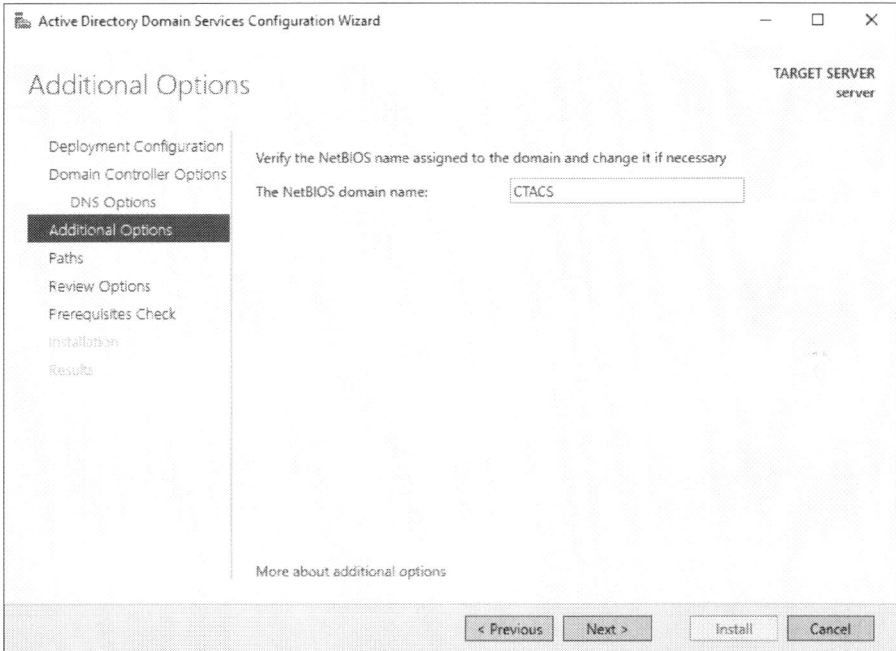

Figure 21: NetBIOS domain name

The following screen allows control over the location of the various files and logs associated with Active Directory. On a small system, there is no particular need to change this so just click **Next**; however, if the C: drive is very small (e.g. under 100 GB) then you should specify a more capacious drive by clicking on the 'three dots' box, as the logfiles can grow quite large:

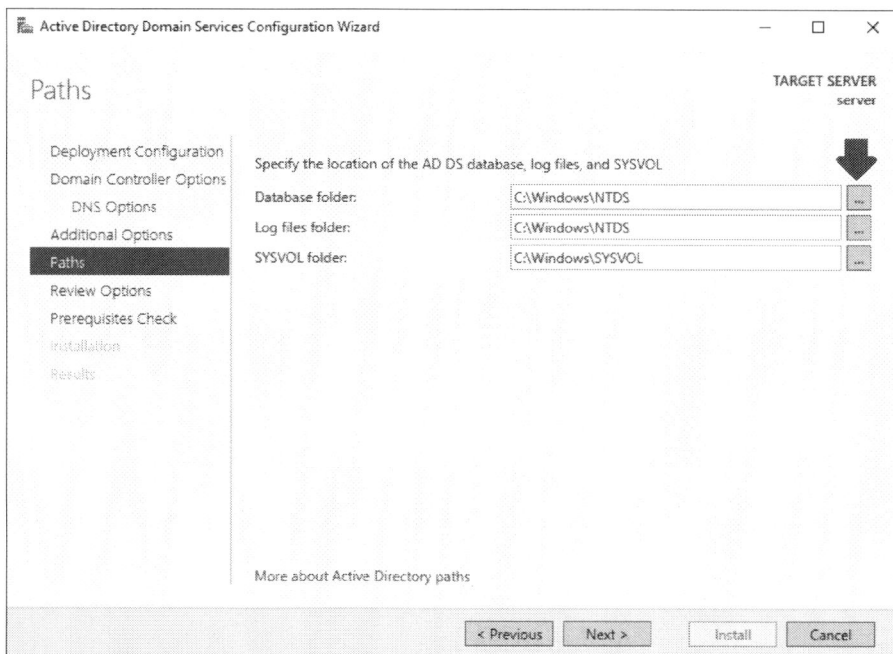

Figure 22: Active Directory paths

The subsequent screen is a review of the various selections and settings - click **Next**. The wizard first runs a *Prerequisites Check* - this may generate some warning messages which can be unsettling, but usually they are just theoretical or obscure issues or can be addressed subsequently. Provided the last entry in the results list reads *"All prerequisite checks passed successfully. Click 'Install' to begin installation"*, you can go ahead and do so. Click **Install** to begin the installation proper, which will run for several minutes and during which time a status screen is displayed and after which the server will restart. Again, there may be some warning messages, but these are inconsequential and do not require any actions. Log back in as Administrator.

What needs to be done next depends upon the local infrastructure. If the server is connected to an all-on-one router that provides DHCP services, which is typically the case in a small network, or is part of an existing network that already includes working servers, then you will shortly be able to continue with section **3 STORAGE**. However, if this is the *only* server and it is *not* connected through a router that provides DHCP, then it will be necessary to install the DHCP service on the server itself *before* continuing and how to do so is described in **13.9 Installing DHCP**.

3

STORAGE

3.1 Overview

Desktop and laptop computers usually have a single hard disk or solid-state drive, configured as one volume and commonly referred to as 'the C: drive' and upon which everything is stored. However, in a server there is usually a need for a greater amount of storage, plus that storage also has to be very reliable. Performance becomes a consideration too, as many people may be accessing the server simultaneously. The best way to address these issues is by using multiple hard drives and to configure them in special ways. However, there is no single one-size-fits-all solution for storage, as it depends upon the size, requirements and budget of the organization. There are four main options – *Two Drives*; *Single Drive*; *RAID*; *Storage Spaces* – and they are discussed separately below.

3.2 Two Disk Drives

A common approach is to have two drives in the server, one for the operating system and one for the data. This arrangement gives some performance benefits, as the drives operate independently, sharing the workload, plus the operating system and data are quite separate, which facilitates re-installations and upgrades. However, it still does not address the issue of reliability or protection: if the first drive failed, the system would be totally out of action; if the second drive data failed, all the data would be lost and you would be dependent on the integrity of the backup (the topic of backups is covered in **7. BACKUPS AND RESTORES**).

Figure 23: Using two disk drives

The first drive can be quite small; at the time of writing, the smallest readily available drives are 120GB SSDs, which are ideal although it is important to use a quality, enterprise device rather than a low-cost consumer part. However, if you plan on installing applications on the server, such as an accounting package or line-of-business application, then you might want something of greater capacity. The second drive, for the data, can be as large as you require or can afford.

3.3 Single Disk Drive

A server in a very small organization might only have a single physical hard drive, although this is not generally advised as in the event of it failing the server will be out of action until it can be replaced, plus the associated risk of data loss is high. If you are using a computer with a single hard drive, you can achieve some benefits of a two-drive system by dividing it into two volumes: one on which the operating system is installed (the C: drive) and one on which the organization's data is stored (the D: drive). The rationale here is that if the operating system ever needs to be re-installed or upgraded, then it can be done without directly affecting the data, plus it is also easier to manage and backup the data. The C: volume does not need to be huge – 60GB to 120GB is usually adequate and the remainder of the drive should be partitioned as the D: drive.

To partition a single drive, right-click **Start** and choose **Disk Management** to display this screen:

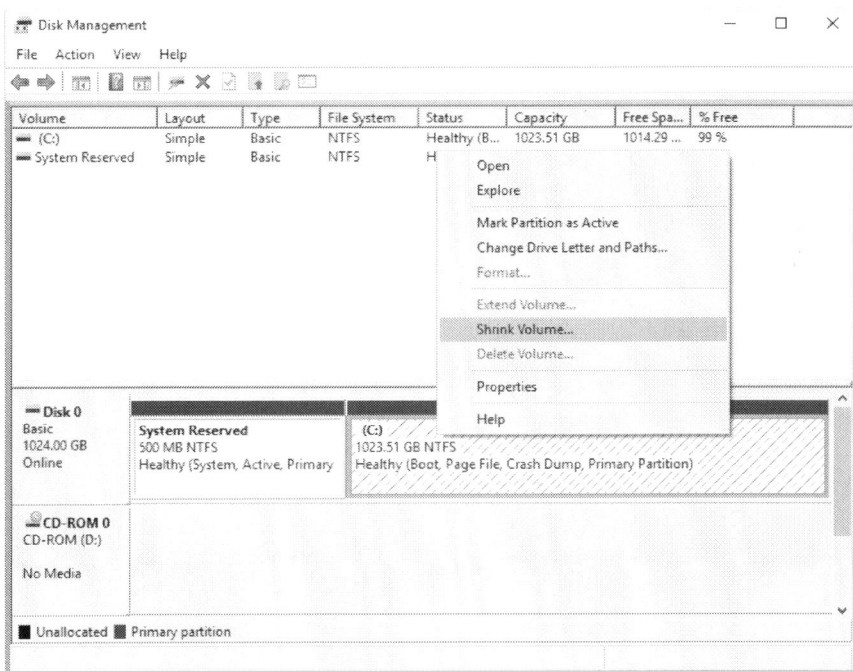

Figure 24: Disk Management screen

Right-click the C: drive and choose **Shrink Volume**. After a few seconds a panel appears advising by how much you can shrink C: in order to make some space for what will become our data volume. It defaults to the maximum permissible value, meaning you could choose to shrink by a smaller amount but not by a larger amount, although in practice you would normally accept what is being proposed by just clicking the **Shrink** button:

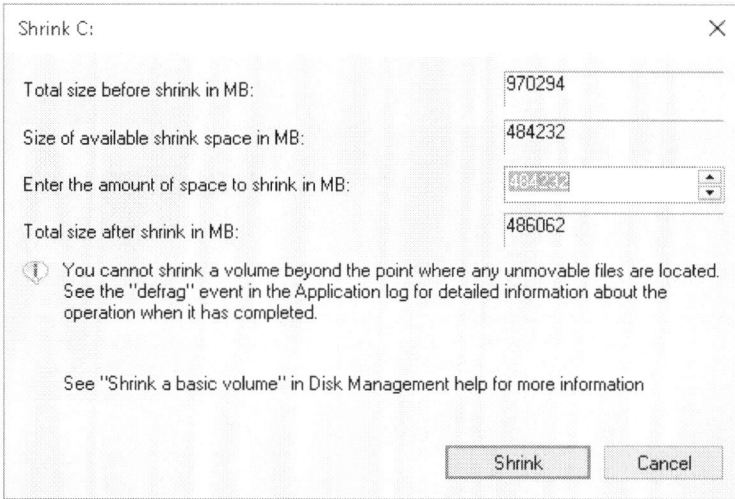

Shrink C:	×
Total size before shrink in MB:	970294
Size of available shrink space in MB:	484232
Enter the amount of space to shrink in MB:	484232
Total size after shrink in MB:	486062

ⓘ You cannot shrink a volume beyond the point where any unmovable files are located. See the "defrag" event in the Application log for detailed information about the operation when it has completed.

See "Shrink a basic volume" in Disk Management help for more information

Shrink · Cancel

Figure 25: Shrinking a volume

It may take a few moments to shrink the volume and when complete you will be returned to the previous screen. Right-click on the *Unallocated* area which has appeared and choose **New Simple Volume**:

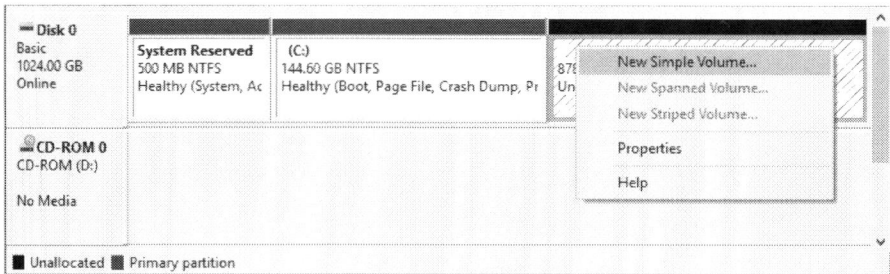

Figure 26: Choose New Simple Volume

The *New Simple Volume Wizard* will be invoked. Click **Next** on the first two panels. The third one is used for assigning a drive letter to the new volume; typically, in a single drive system it will propose E: as the new drive, on the basis that the main drive is C: and the DVD drive (if present) is D:, which is fine. Things could be different on your system, although it does not particularly matter what the new drive letter is. Click **Next**:

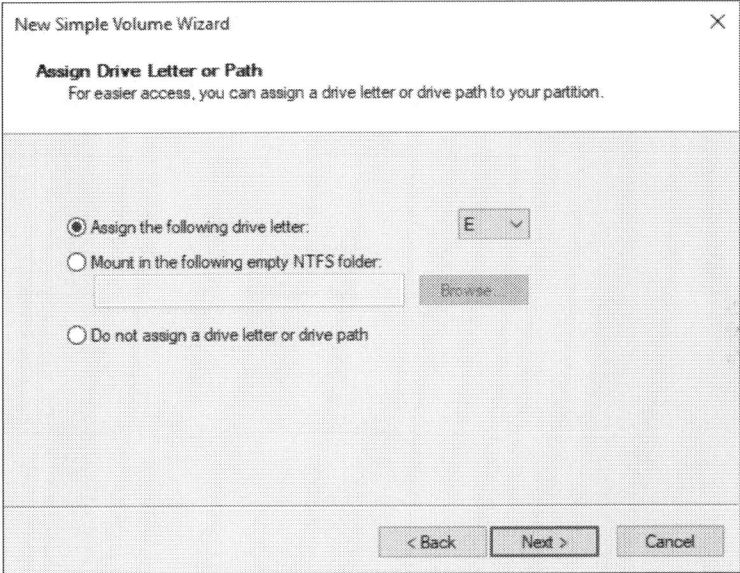

Figure 27: Assigning a drive letter

On the subsequent panel the defaults are fine, although you may optionally wish to change the *Volume label* to a more meaningful name, such as *Data*. Click **Next**:

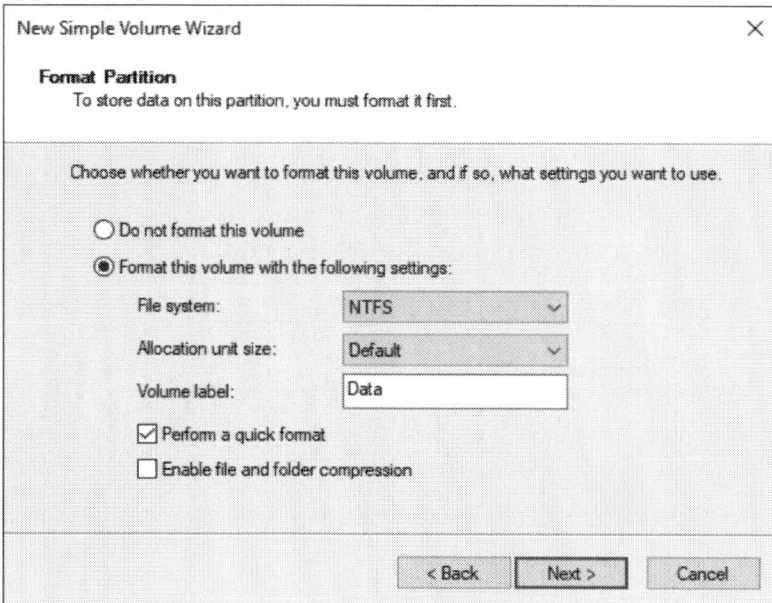

Figure 28: Format Partition

The final panel is just a summary screen – click **Finish**. The new volume may take a few moments to format and after it has done so a notification message will pop-up in the bottom right-hand corner of the screen, although it can be ignored. Close down the Disk Management screen.

3.4 RAID

RAID stands for *Redundant Array of Independent (or Inexpensive) Disks*. There are various types of RAID, referred to using a numbering system i.e. RAID 0, RAID 1, RAID 5 and so on. The idea is to improve reliability and performance by using multiple disks to provide redundancy and share the workload. The most common scenarios in small server systems are RAID 0, RAID 1, RAID 5, RAID 6 and RAID 10.

RAID 0 consists of two identical drives. When data is written, some goes on one drive and some goes on the other. As both drives are being written to or read simultaneously, throughput is maximized. However, as bits of files are scattered across the two drives, if one drive fails then everything is lost. Also, the speed of disk drives is not necessarily a bottleneck in many small network systems. For these reasons RAID 0 should not normally be used.

Figure 29: RAID 0 – Data striped across two drives

RAID 1 consists of two identical drives that mirror each other. When a file is saved, there are actually two separate but identical copies behind the scenes, one held on each drive, even though you can only see one as the mirroring process itself is invisible. If one of the drives fails, the second one automatically takes over and the system carries on without interruption. At the earliest opportunity, the faulty drive should be replaced with a new one; the system is then synchronized so it becomes a true copy of the remaining healthy drive, in a process known as 'rebuilding the array'.

In a RAID 1 system, the total usable storage capacity is half that of the total drive capacity installed. For instance, if a disk array has two 2 TB drives installed then the total amount of usable storage capacity is 2 TB rather than 4 TB.

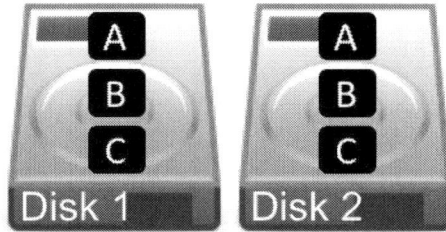

Figure 30: RAID 1 – Data mirrored across two drives

RAID 5 uses at least three but preferably four drives. Data is written across all the drives, along with what is known as *parity information*. The benefit of this is that the system can cope with the failure of any one single drive. RAID 5 is considered to offer a good combination of price, performance and resilience. Whereas a RAID 1 system loses 50% of the total drive capacity to provide resilience, RAID 5 typically loses only about 25%. For instance, if a disk array has four 2 TB drives installed then the total amount of usable storage capacity is 6 TB rather than 8 TB.

Figure 31: RAID 5 – Multiple drives with parity information

RAID 6 uses at least four but preferably five or more drives. It is similar to RAID 5, but uses two sets of parity information written across the drives. The benefit of this approach is that the system can cope with the simultaneous failure of two of the drives, thereby making it more resilient than RAID 5, but it loses more capacity in providing that resilience.

There may also be a performance hit compared with RAID 5, due to the additional parity processing. If a disk array has five 2 TB drives installed in a RAID configuration, then the total amount of usable storage capacity is 6 TB rather than 10 TB.

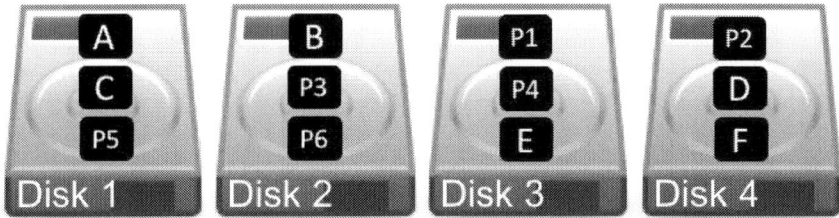

Figure 32: RAID 6 – Multiple drives with double parity information

RAID 10 (also known as RAID 1+0) combines RAID 1 and RAID 0 techniques. Requiring a minimum of four drives, it comprises a pair of RAID 1 mirrored drives, with data being striped across the pair in the way that RAID 0 operates. It thus combines both redundancy and performance, making it of particular interest where high throughput in needed, for instance in demanding applications such as video editing. The amount of available storage is half that of the total drive capacity e.g. a system with four 2 TB drives would give 4 TB of usable space.

Figure 33: RAID 10 – Simultaneous striping and mirroring

What to do? If you have a server with a single drive then the question of RAID does not arise; rather, you might want to look at section **3.3 Single Disk Drive**. If you have a server with two drives of identical capacity, you should consider using RAID 1 (and if they are not of identical capacity, then section **3.2 Two Disk Drives** will be more applicable).

If you have a server with three or four drives it should be configured for RAID 5 (or possibly RAID 10) and if you have five drives then use RAID 6.

It is important to note that RAID systems require a special controller and that these come in two types. Low-cost servers may have a so-called built-in RAID controller on the motherboard; these are sometimes referred to as 'software RAID' or 'embedded RAID' by manufacturers but are known colloquially as 'fake RAID' and are to be avoided as they can be prone to failures and data loss. Instead, a separate hardware RAID controller card should be purchased as this offers better performance and reliability. Just to further confuse matters, some manufacturers may implement true hardware RAID, but with the controller as part of the motherboard rather than as a separate card.

Special utility software is usually provided by the vendor for configuring the RAID, sometimes at the BIOS level when the server is booted. If this is not the case, then the array may initially appear as a single drive and the instructions in **3.3 Single Disk Drive** *might* be applicable. This utility will also assist in coping with drive failures and a process known as 'rebuilding the RAID', which is where a replacement drive is incorporated into the existing system. Many RAID systems also support the concept of a hot spare or redundant drive. This is a drive which is not normally used, but in the event of one drive failing it will automatically switch in and the rebuilding process will begin, rather than requiring a manual intervention.

One important thing to note is that a RAID system is **not** a backup system. It can help prevent data loss in the event of problems, but it is still important to make separate provision for backup. For instance, if the server was stolen or the premises went up in flames then the data would be lost regardless of whether and whatever RAID system was used.

3.5 Storage Spaces

Storage Spaces is an alternative to RAID and a standard feature available in Windows Server. It is designed to address three aspects of storage:

Firstly, on a Windows computer each hard drive normally has a separate drive letter to identify it. For instance, the first drive is the C: drive, the second is the D: drive, the third is the E: drive and so on. However, it is more convenient, particularly in a network, if drives can be pooled together to appear as a single large volume. This makes it easier to find things by removing the requirement to know upon which physical drive a particular file or folder is located:

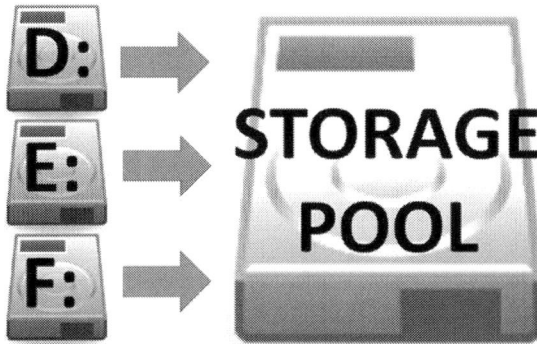

Figure 34: Storage Pool aggregates the hard drives

Secondly, like RAID, Storage Spaces provides a degree of protection against data loss in the event of a drive failing. Multiple copies of files are stored on different drives; if a drive fails then a copy from a different one is automatically used. The failed drive can then be replaced and added back to the storage pool. Finally, the pool can easily be added to in order to provide more storage space, without excessive disruption or reconfiguration. One important thing to note is that the drives can largely be of any type; for instance, external USB hard drives can be connected to the computer and added to the storage pool.

In some respects Storage Spaces is more flexible than RAID, as well as being cheaper to implement. There is a common perception that it is just a low-cost alternative to RAID; in fact, it is an extremely sophisticated feature and with additional capabilities of particular interest to corporate users, although in this example we will stick to the basics as more applicable to a small network.

In this example, the server had a single hard drive, upon which Windows Server was installed. Two further drives, each of 2 TB, have now been added and Storage Spaces will be used to join them together to create a larger, protected volume. These drives can be internal hard drives or external USB, USB-C or eSATA drives, although more commonly the former would be used.

First make sure that the new drives are being recognized: right-click **Start** and click **Disk Management**. There may be a message about having to initialize the new drives, but do not do so, just cancel and exit from Disk Management.

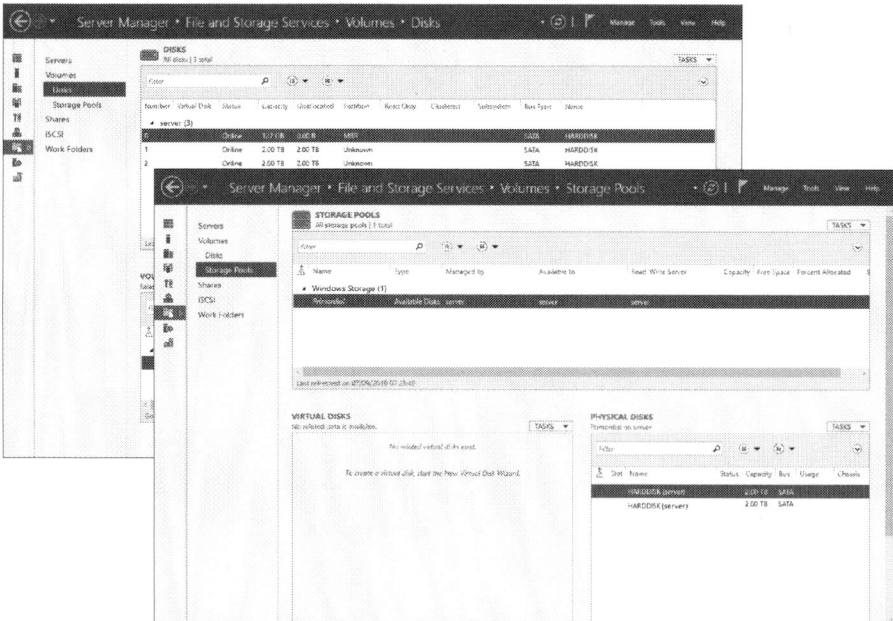

Figure 35: Server Manager Storage Pools

Go into **Server Manager** and click **File and Storage Services**. On the left-hand side panel, click **Disks** and confirm that all the hard drives are available; assuming they are, click **Storage Pools** – the initial screen should be listing a default storage pool, referred to as *Primordial*, plus the new drives should be listed in the *Physical Disks* section.

The screen is divided into three main panels: *STORAGE POOLS*, *VIRTUAL DISKS* and *PHYSICAL DISKS*. In the top-right hand corner of each panel is a dropdown labelled *TASKS*; click on TASKS for Storage Pools and click **New Storage Pool** to invoke the *New Storage Pool Wizard*. Click **Next** on the opening panel and on the second one enter a Name (e.g. *Data*), an optional *Description* and click **Next**:

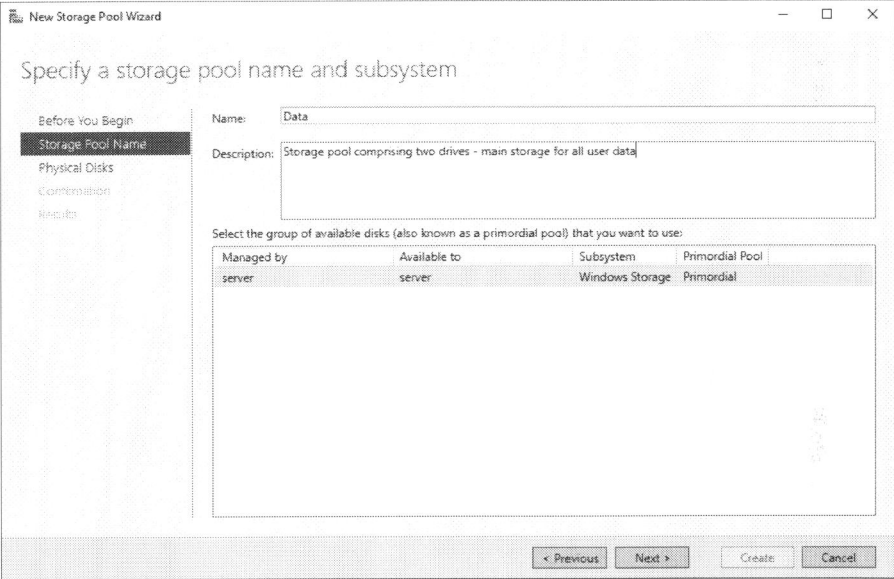

Figure 36: New Storage Pool Wizard

On the subsequent screen, tick the boxes for each disk to be used in the storage pool, followed by **Next**:

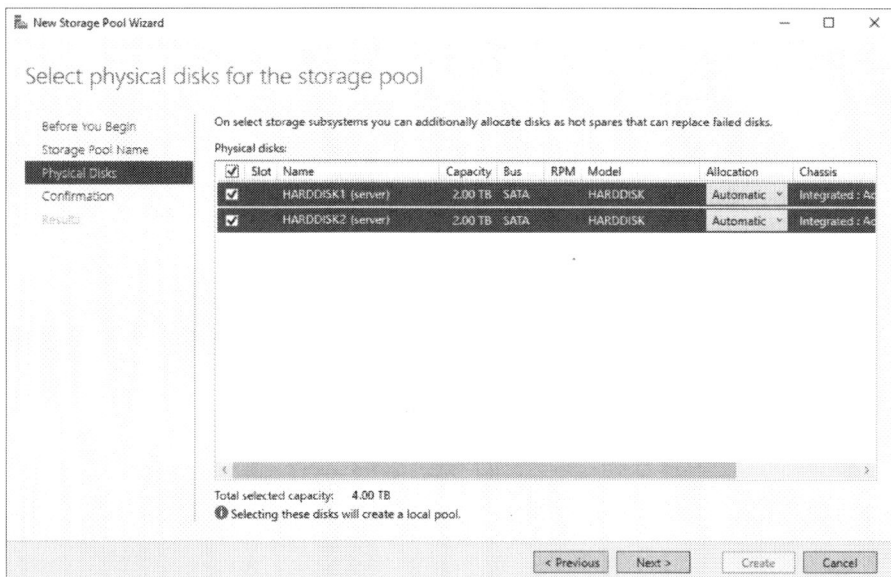

Figure 37: Select disks for the storage pool

A *Confirm selections* screen will be shown - click the **Create** button. After a short while the *Storage Pool Wizard* will complete - click **Close**:

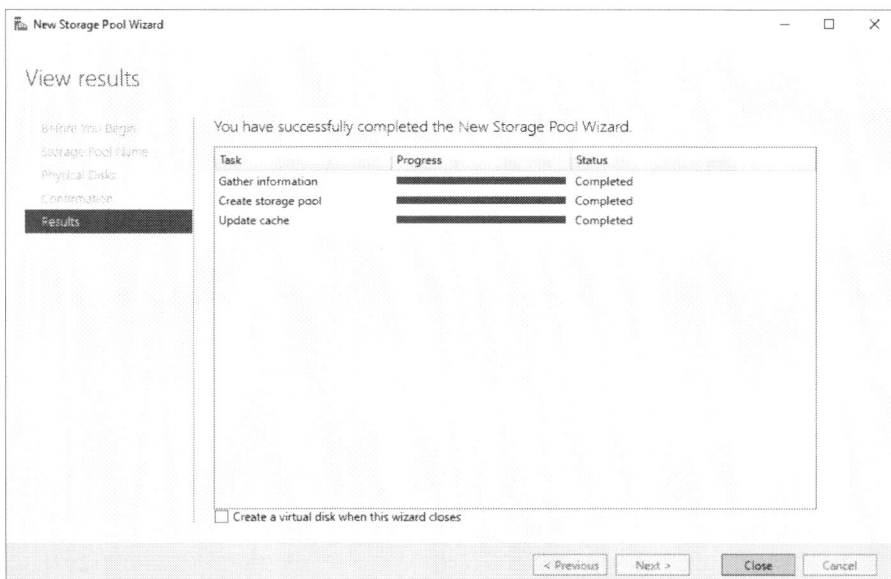

Figure 38: Completion of New Storage Pool Wizard

The next step is to create a *Virtual disk*. From the main *STORAGE POOLS* screen, in the VIRTUAL DISKS section, click the link that reads **To create a virtual disk, start the New Virtual Disk Wizard**. Select the storage pool from the pop-up screen and click **OK**. The *New Virtual Disk Wizard* will begin – click **Next** on the first screen. On the subsequent screen, specify the virtual disk name (e.g. *'Data'*) and an optional description, then click **Next**. The next screen is about something called *Enclosure resiliency*, which is unlikely to be used on a small system, so just click **Next**. The following screen appears:

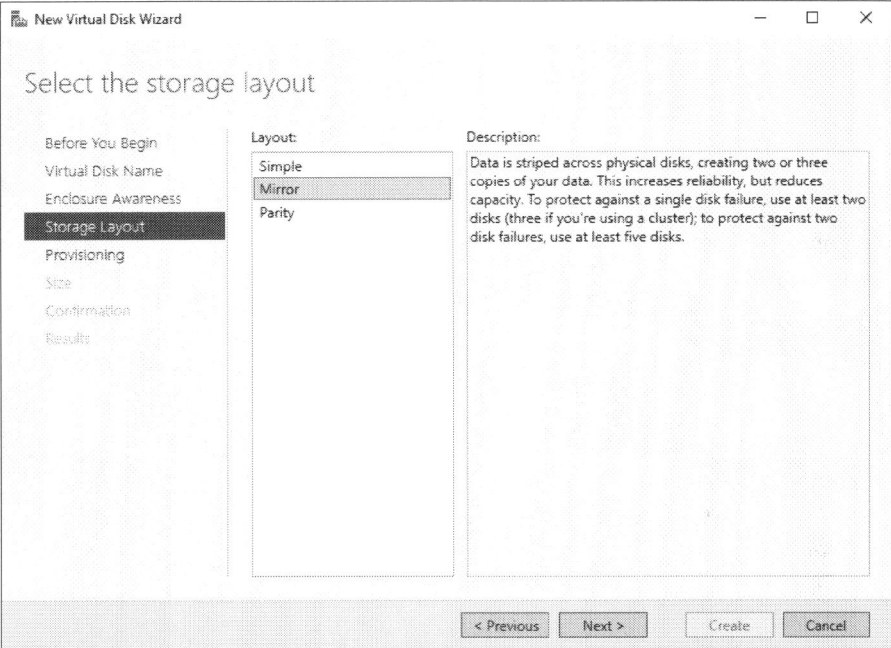

Figure 39: New Virtual Disk Wizard

There are three types of storage layout to choose from:

- *Simple* - in which the drives are aggregated to create a single large volume, analogous to RAID 0 or JBOD (*Just a Bunch of Disks*) in other computing environments
- *Mirror* – in which data is duplicated on each drive in order to provide redundancy, analogous to RAID 1 in

other computing environments. Requires at least two physical drives in the underlying Storage Space.

- *Parity* – here data is stored across all the drives. Additional information (known as *parity*) is used by the system, such that data is preserved in the event of drive failures, analogous to RAID 5 or RAID 6 in other computing environments. Requires at least three physical drives in the underlying Storage Space.

The amount of storage space available depends upon the option selected. In our example, we are using a pair of 2TB drives. If these are configured in Simple mode, then the total amount of storage is 4 TB; if configured in Two-way mirror mode then the amount of available storage is 2 TB. Make a choice depending on your requirements and the number of disks available, then click **Next**.

On the follow-on screen, there is a choice between *Thin* or *Fixed Provisioning*. This defines whether all the disk space is allocated at the beginning ("Fixed") or starts small and grows as required ("Thin"). In a small setup, you would generally choose **Fixed** (Thin Provisioning is of more interest in a larger network with many servers, typically sharing common disk space). On the next screen you can further specify the size of the virtual disk – choose the **Maximum size** option and click **Next**. A *Confirm selections* screen is displayed – click **Create**. After a short while, depending on the options chosen, a completion screen is shown. Note that the **Create a volume when this wizard closes** box should be ticked:

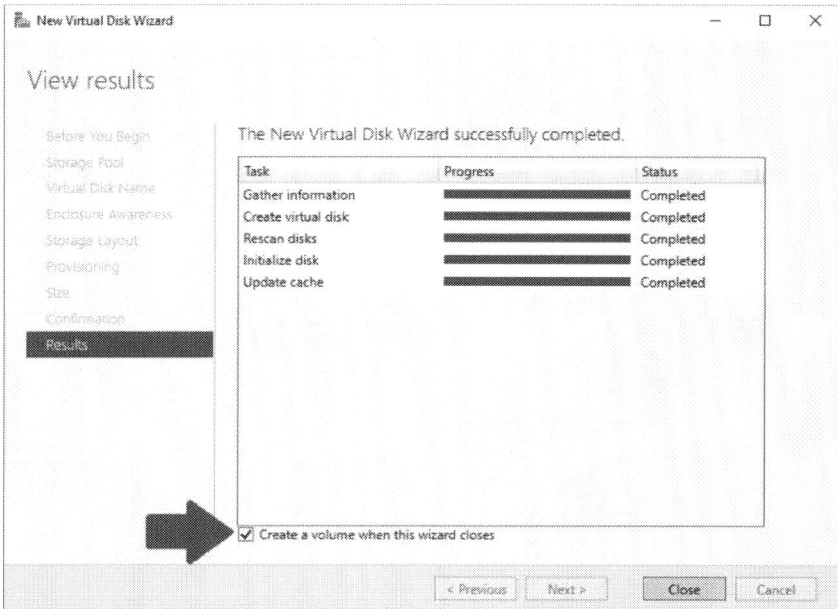

Figure 40: Virtual Disk Wizard completion screen

Click **Close** and the *New Volume Wizard* will duly commence. Click **Next** on the first screen. On the second screen highlight the newly created storage space and click **Next**:

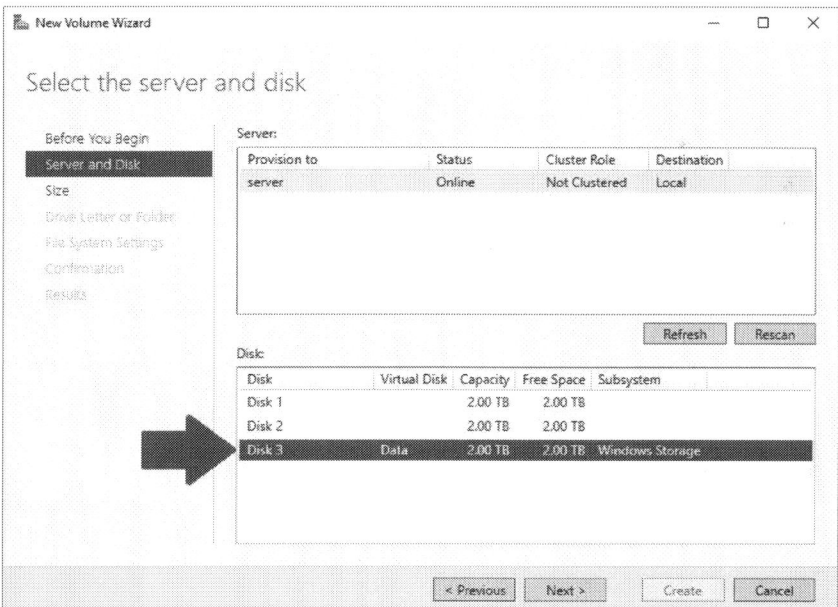

Figure 41: New Volume Wizard

The size of the volume can now be specified. Unless you have very specific reasons to do otherwise, make it as large as permitted and click **Next**:

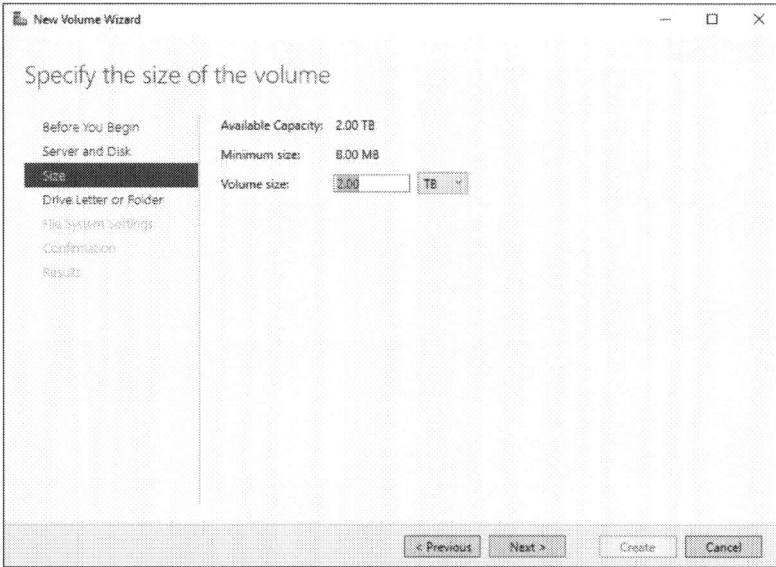

Figure 42: Specify the size of the new volume

On the subsequent screen, assign a free drive letter to the new volume. In this example, we will make it the D: drive.

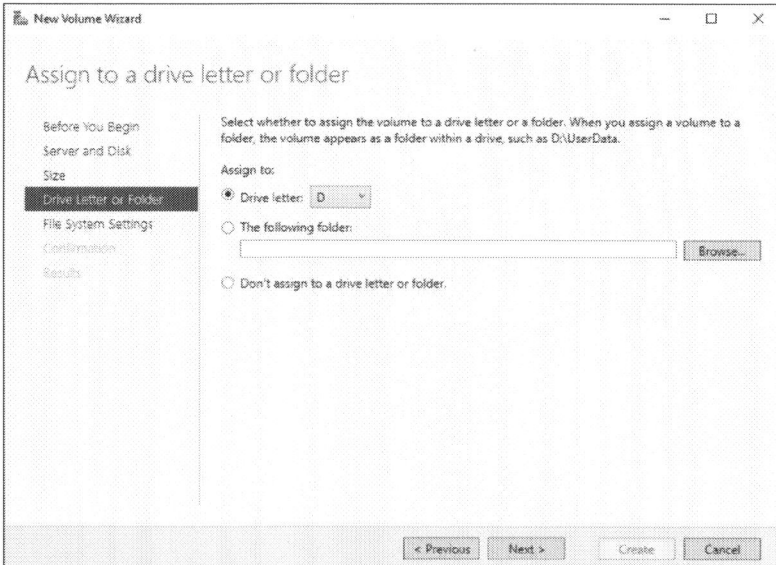

Figure 43: Assign a drive letter to the new volume

On the subsequent screen, check the *File System* type - you will usually want NTFS - and assign a *Volume label* e.g. 'Data'. Click **Next**:

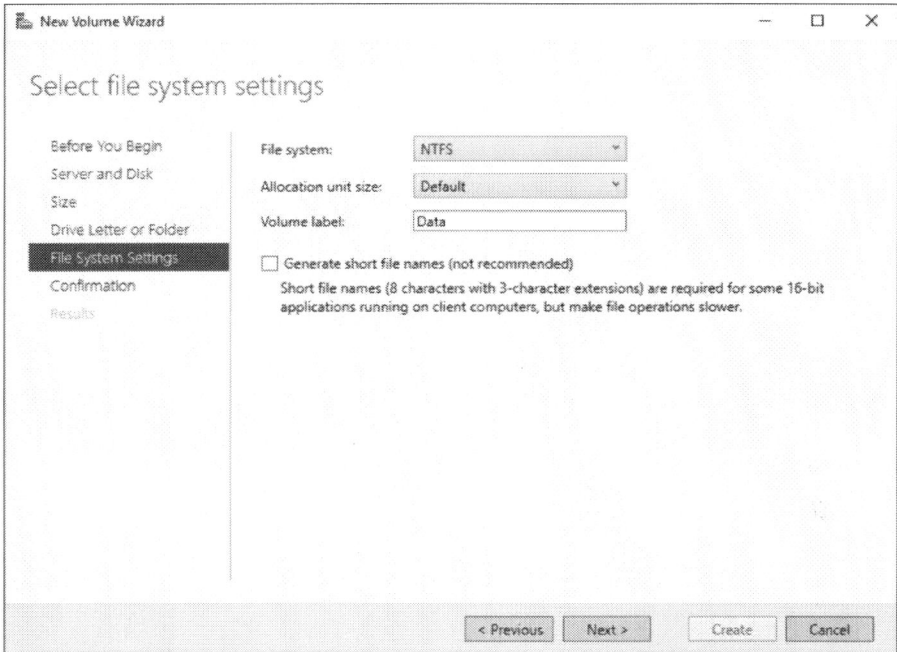

Figure 44: Select file system settings

A *Confirm selections* screen is displayed - assuming everything is satisfactory, click **Create**. After a while a completion screen is shown, the time for which depends upon the size of the drives and the options chosen. Click **Close** and exit from Server Manager. The new drive should now be visible in File Explorer.

4

SHARED FOLDERS

4.1 Overview

The main purpose of a network is to provide an environment in which users can store and share information. This is implemented by creating folders on the server, some shared and some private, then defining access rights to control who sees what. The structure of these folders will depend upon the requirements of the organization, but a typical arrangement might be: one or more shared folders that everyone has access to; folders for the different departments and functions within the business; individual private or 'home' folders for each user (analogous to the Documents folder on a PC). These folders are known as *network shares* or *shared folders*.

In our example we have two volumes, one for the operating system (the C: drive) and one for the data (the D: drive). On the data volume we will create the following structure:

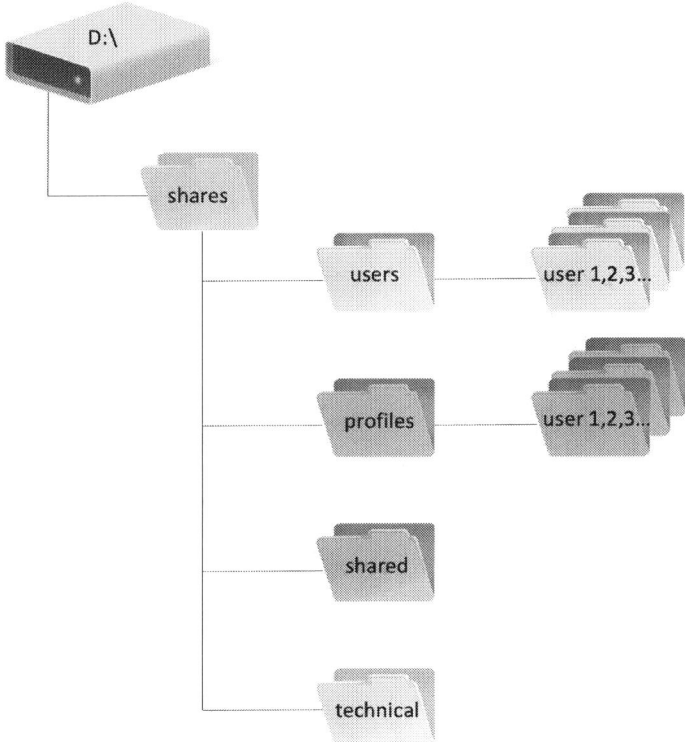

Figure 45: Example shared folders structure

The shared folders sit below a top-level one called *shares* that is created by Server Manager. The folders are used as follows:

Users - Holds the individual home folders for users

Profiles - Folder for holding user profiles (the purpose and use of profiles is discussed later)

Shared - Holds data that can be used by everyone in the organization

Technical - For use by the person(s) supporting the system and contains master copies of software, utilities, technical documentation and so on.

You can create as many folders as you require, with whatever names you wish, at whatever point. For instance, you might create additional folders for departments or teams or classes depending on the nature of your organization. It is suggested that some thought is given to the structure, to make it logical and sensible. However, you might wish to start using the template above.

Folders are created using Server Manager, as described in the next section. If you have worked with earlier versions of Windows Server, such as Windows Server 2003, 2008, 2012 or 2016, then you may be pleased to hear that the older techniques and tools for creating and managing shares are generally still available and work as expected. However, it is suggested that you acquaint yourself with and adopt the new methods of doing things; even though they may seem unfamiliar at first, they are well thought out and work well.

4.2 Creating Shared Folders

Go into **Server Manager**. In the left-hand panel click **File and Storage Services** followed by **Shares**. In the **SHARES** section click **TASKS** followed by **New Share** to start the *New Share Wizard*:

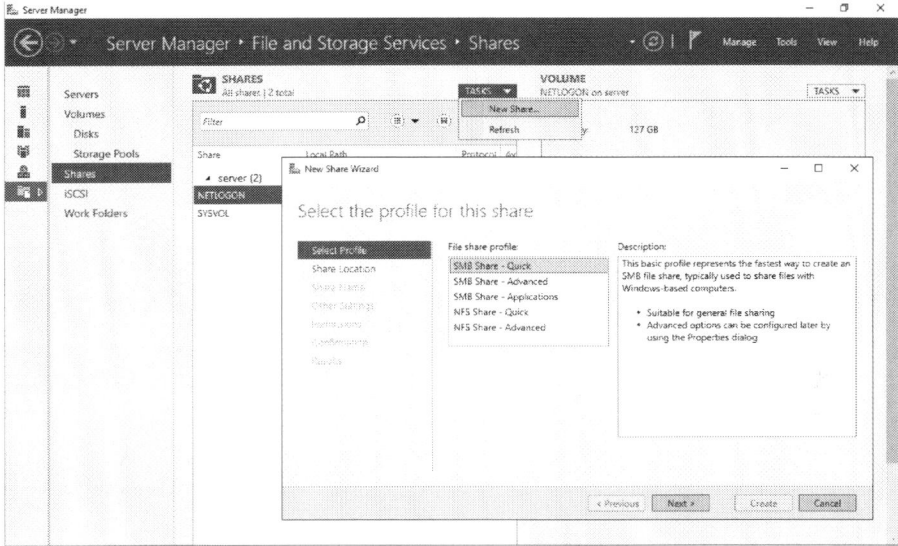

Figure 46: New Share Wizard

There are five types different 'profiles' for shares, in which the terms *SMB* relates to Windows PCs and *NFS* relates to computers running UNIX or Linux variants, although note that most devices, including Linux computers and Macs, also understand SMB:

SMB Share - Quick: the most commonly used option in a small network

SMB Share - Advanced: allows additional features to be specified and controlled

SMB Share - Applications: provides capabilities of relevance to corporate and larger environments

NFS Share - Quick: simple way of creating shares for UNIX/Linux computers

NFS Share - Advanced: additional features for UNIX/Linux computers

Choose **SMB Share – Quick** followed by **Next**. On the resultant panel explicitly specify the volume where the shared folder is to reside if there is more than one to choose from - in this example we are using the D: drive - and click **Next**:

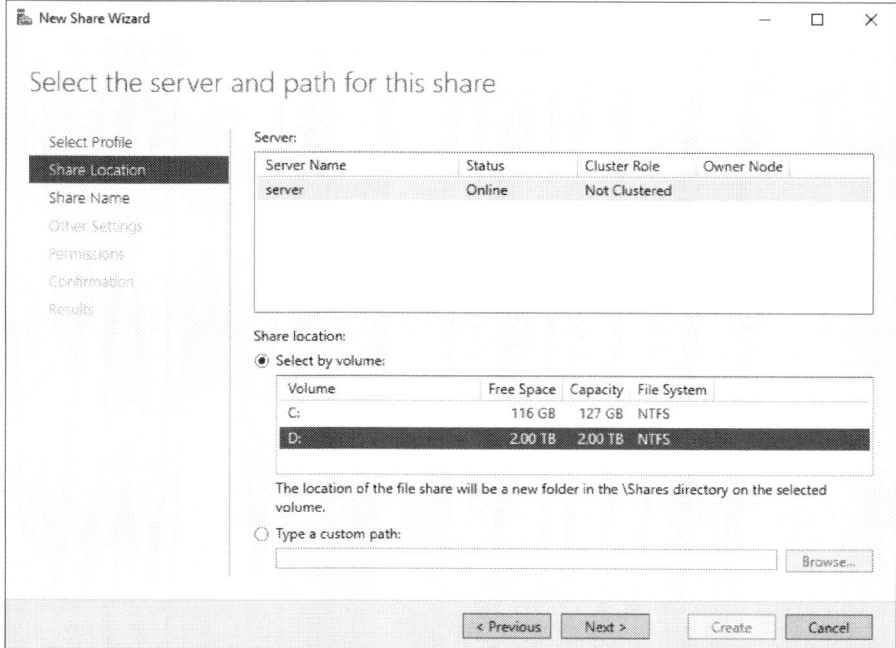

Figure 47: Specify the volume location for the share

On the follow-on screen enter a *Share name* of *users* plus an optional *Share description*. The wizard will fill-in the *Local path to share* as *D:\Shares\users* and the *Remote path to share* as *\\server\users*. Note that all shared folders sit below a folder called *Shares*, which the wizard creates automatically. Click **Next**:

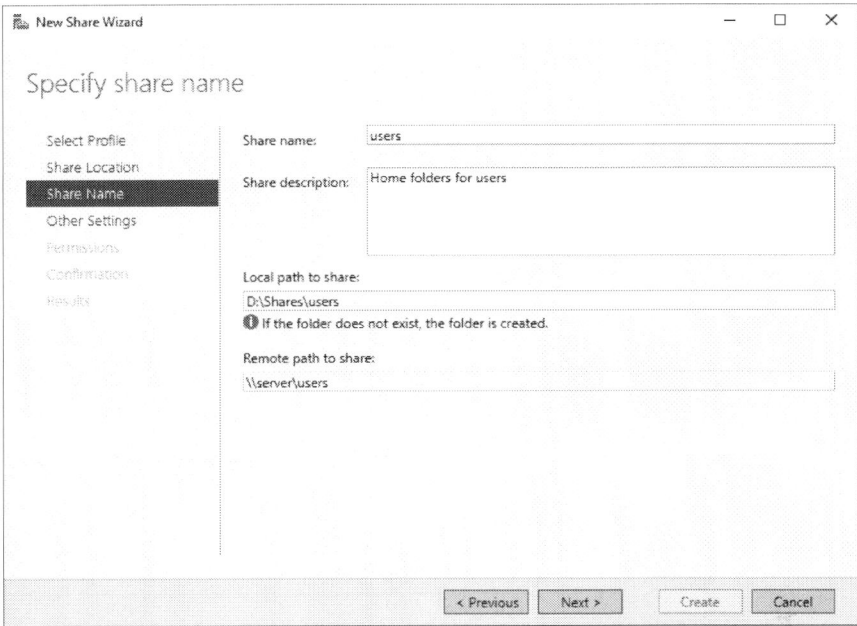

Figure 48: Specify the share name

On the next screen you would commonly leave all the boxes unticked. Click **Next**:

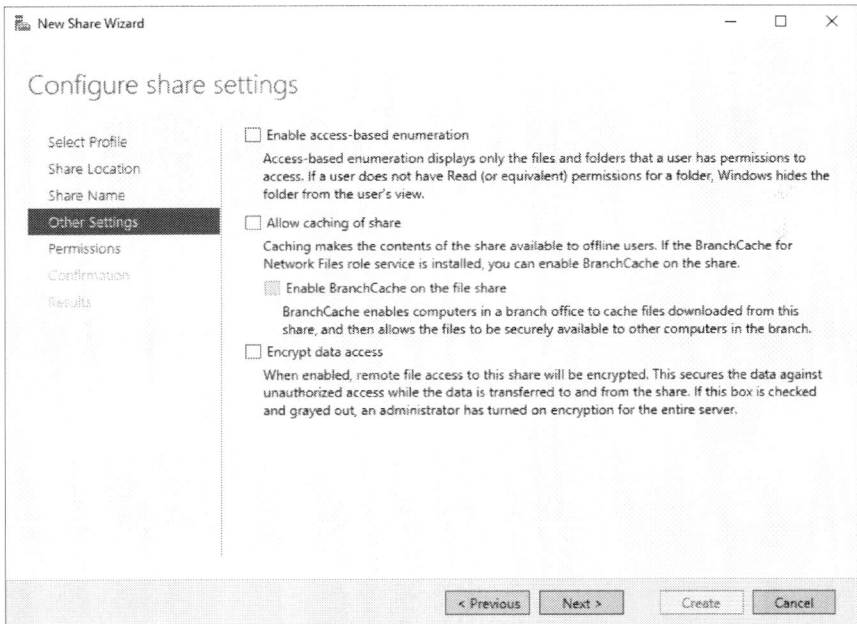

Figure 49: Configure share settings

The next screen defines permissions to control access. The default is that all users have complete control over this folder, which is fine for our purposes, so just click **Next**:

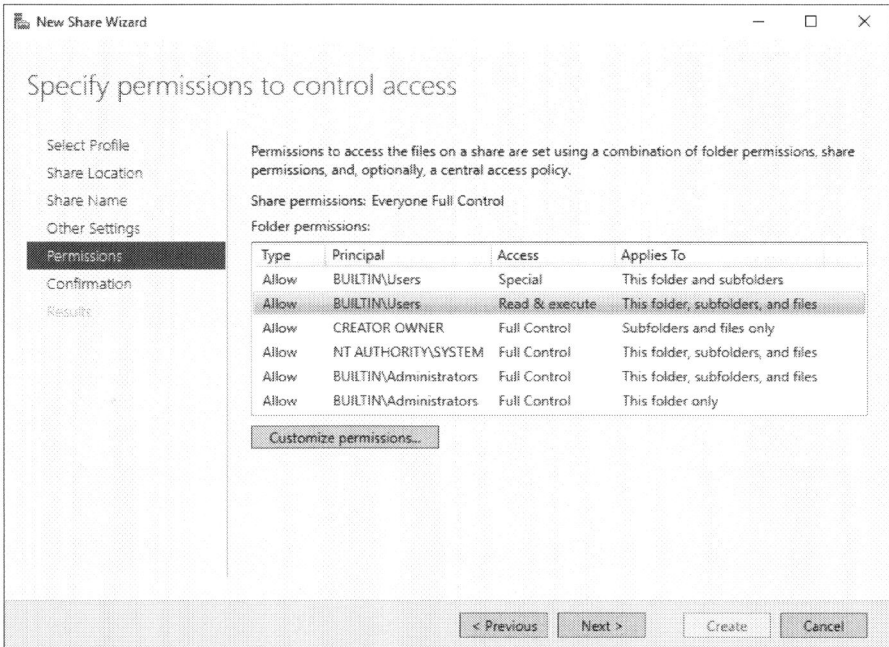

Figure 50: Specify permissions

The subsequent screen is for confirming the selections - press **Create** to continue. The share will be created in a few seconds – click **Close** on the resultant screen. You will be returned to the main Shares screen where the new share will be listed, alongside the two built-in ones of *NETLOGON* and *SYSVOL*.

Repeat the steps as described above and create another shared folder, this time explicitly called *shared*, which will act as a common area for all users to access.

Shared folders are normally visible to all users, but can be made hidden. The purpose of doing so is only partly related to security but is also to keep the overall system tidy and avoiding confusing users with a superfluous number of folders, as there may be dozens or even hundreds of shared folders on a network.

Shares are made hidden by placing a dollar sign ($) at the end of the share name. Repeat the steps described above to create a third shared folder and name the share *profiles$*.

Our fourth and final shared folder for now will be called *technical$*, also a hidden folder. This optional folder is for use by the person(s) supporting the system and contains master copies of software, utilities, technical documentation and other items of use to an administrator. Begin by creating it using the wizard as described above, only this time pause when you reach the *Specify permissions to control access* panel and click the **Customize permissions** button. On the resultant panel click the **Share** tab to show the following:

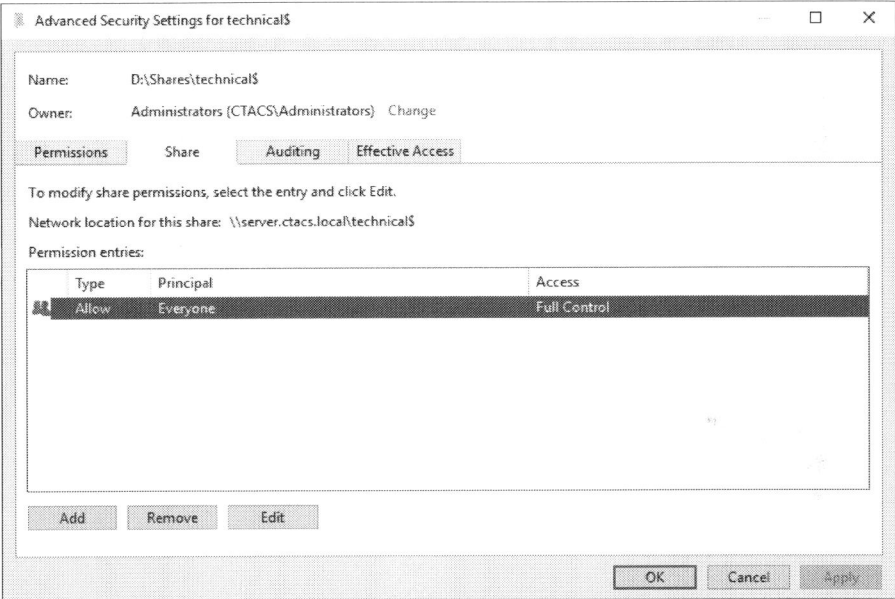

Figure 51: Advanced security settings

We wish to restrict this share to Administrators only. Highlight the current entry for *Everyone* and click **Remove**. Then, click **Add** and on the next screen click **Select a principal**. A panel pops up; in the field that reads *Enter the object name to select*, type in the name of the user(s), in this case *Administrators*. Click **Check Names** and the user name will become underlined. Click **OK**.

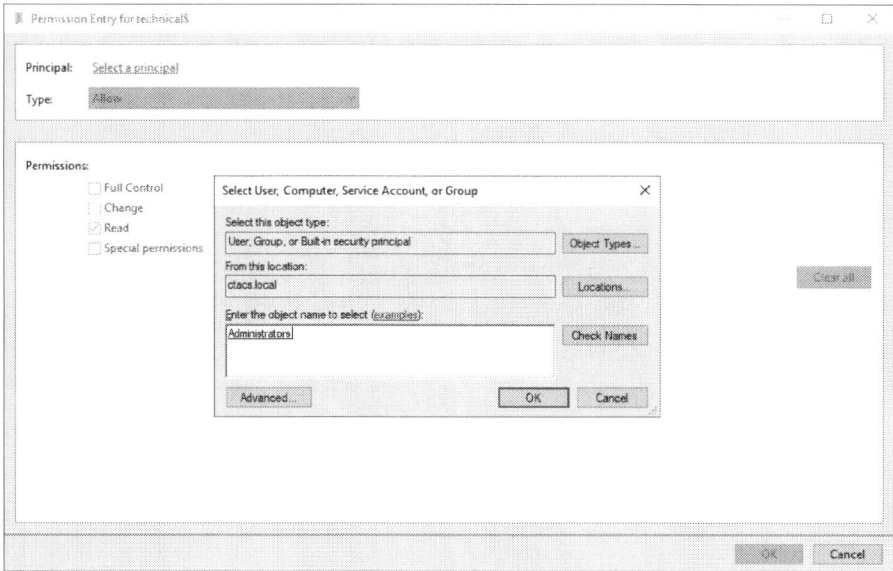

Figure 52: Select Administrators

On returning to the previous panel tick **Full Control** - the other boxes will then be filled automatically - followed by **OK**:

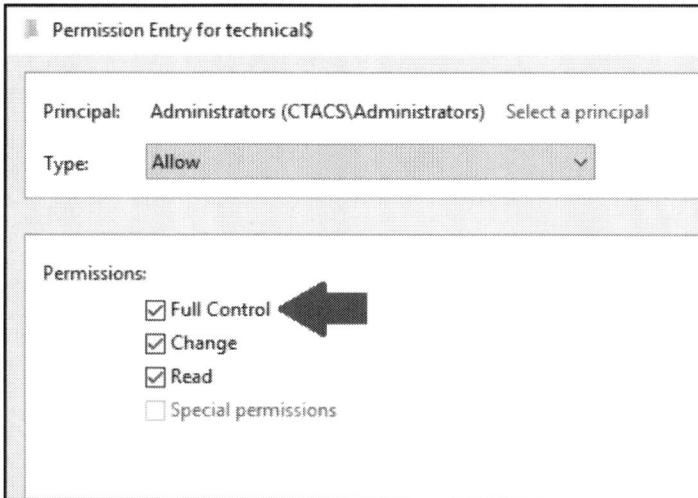

Figure 53: Specify permissions for Administrators

Returning to the previous panel, click **Apply**, **OK**, **Next**, **Create** to complete the creation of the share, followed by **Close**.

The share folders will now be listed in the main *Shares* screen. If it is ever necessary to subsequent modify a share, it can be done by right-clicking it and choosing one of the options from the pop-up menu:

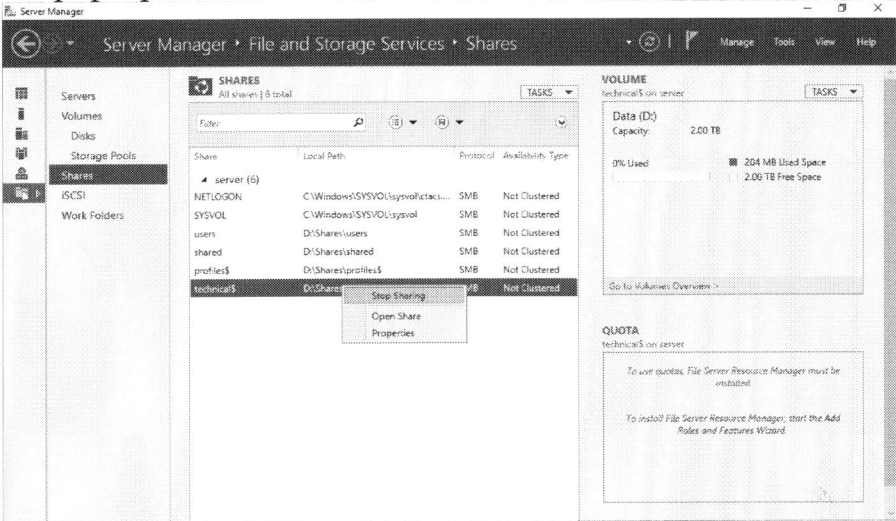

Figure 54: List of shares within Server Manager

Launch *File Manager* and the structure of the volume will appear along the following lines. Remember that such shared folders are of a special nature and have to be managed using Server Manager rather than File Manager.

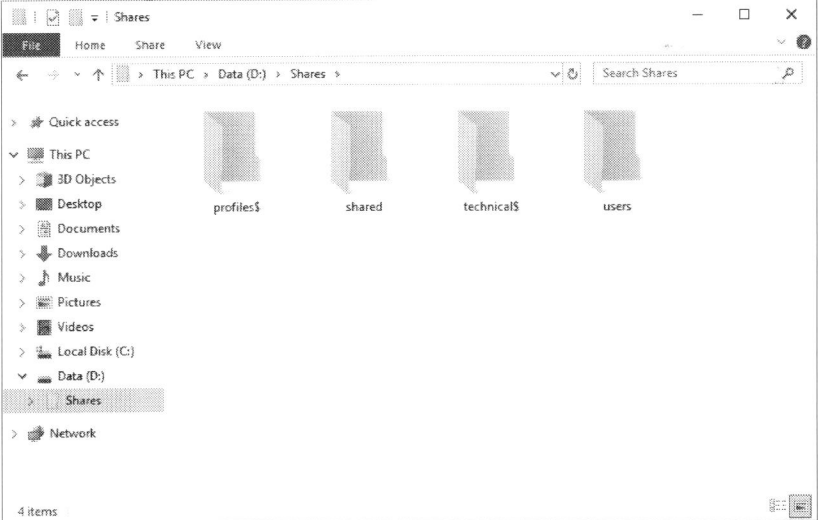

Figure 55: Listing of shares from File Manager

———

4.3 Loading Existing Data into Shared Folders

There may be a requirement to load data from existing computers or systems onto the server, into the new shared folders that have been created. There are a couple of ways to do so:

Method One: Wait until the network is up and running i.e. shared folders have been created, users have been defined, computers are connected and able to access the server. Then, connect from each computer and copy data from the user's folders to the appropriate folders on the server.

Method Two: Visit each individual computer and copy data from the user's folders to an external plug-in USB drive. Then, connect the USB drive to the server and copy it to the appropriate folders on the server. The advantage of this method is that it can be done before or in parallel with setting up the server.

Regardless of which method is used, an anti-virus/malware check should be run on the computers *before* copying any data. It is also a good idea to first review the data on the computers and prune (delete) any unrequired and duplicated data, rather than carry it forward to the new environment.

5

USERS

5.1 Overview

In order to access the server, each user needs an account. Before creating the user accounts, some thought should be given to a naming convention. As a general principle, aim for consistency. For user account names, two common conventions are to use the first name plus the initial of the surname, alternatively the initial of the first name plus the surname, although in some parts of the world other conventions might be more appropriate. In the case of particularly long names and double-barreled names it might be a good idea to abbreviate them. For example:

Name of person	User name	or	User name
Nick Rushton	nickr		nrushton
Mary O'Hara	maryoh		mohara
Ian Smith	ians		ismith
Amber Williams	amberw		awilliams
Daniela Petrova	danielap		dpetrova

Users are created and subsequently modified and managed using the *Active Directory Administrative Centre*.

5.2 Creating Users

Within *Server Manager*, click **Tools** in the top right-hand corner and choose **Active Directory Administrative Center** from the drop-down list. Alternatively click **Start > Windows Administrative Tools > Active Directory Administrative Center**. An *Overview* page is displayed; on the left-hand side of the screen click the domain name, which is *ctacs (local)* in our example, to display the following screen:

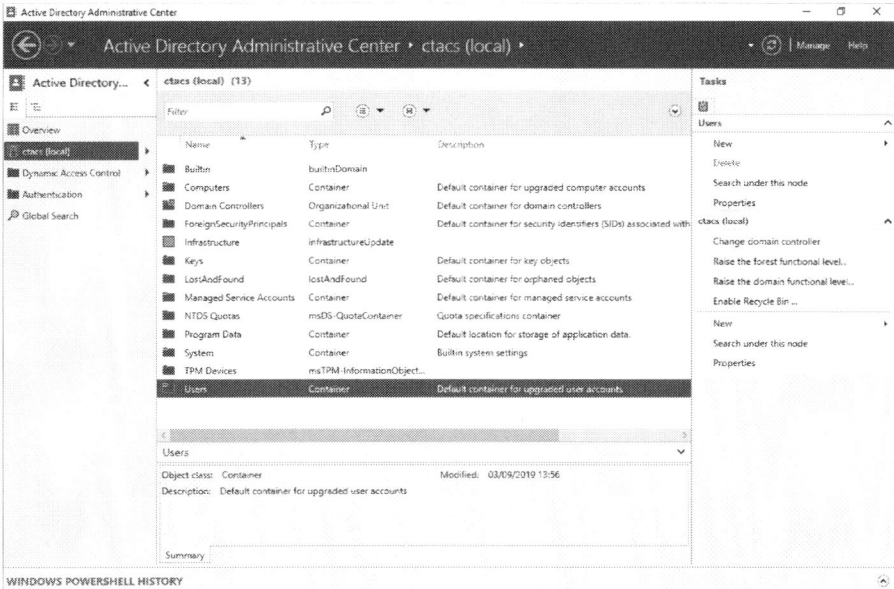

Figure 56: Active Directory Administrative Center

The screen comprises three main sections: the left-hand one can be thought of as a top-level menu or control area; the center one is the main work area, the contents of which vary depending on what has been selected on the left one; the right-hand section lists a number of tasks and its contents vary depending on what you are doing and where you are. In the above screenshot, the center panel is listing *Containers*. Containers are the different type of objects that exist in Active Directory and include *Computers* and *Users* amongst others.

By keeping objects in containers it makes them easier to manage and, in addition to the standard ones, you can create your own. For instance, double-clicking the *Users* container reveals that the system already contains a number of pre-defined special users and groups (although some of them are infrequently used, other than in larger networks) including *Administrator*. In a small network, when you create user accounts, it is suggested you place them in the *Users* container. But in a large organization, with hundreds or maybe thousands of users, you may wish to create additional containers first and place them in those, organized according to department or location, for instance.

If you are viewing the initial screen as shown above with Users highlighted, the right-hand panel will have a section under *Tasks* called *Users*. Click **New** followed by **User** and the following panel opens:

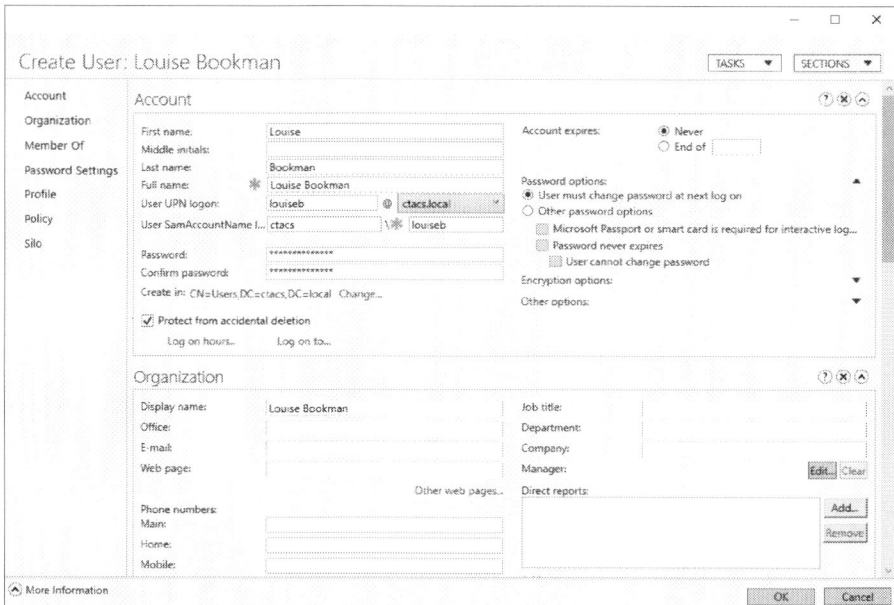

Figure 57: Create User

There are numerous fields; however, only a few are mandatory and these are highlighted with asterisks.

Enter the user's *First name* and *Last name*, which will then auto-complete the *Full name* field. Specify the *User UPN logon* – which is the actual logon name - in accordance with the naming convention you are following.

You need to specify and confirm a *Password* and this has to be what Microsoft defines as 'complex', which means: at least six characters in length; not the same as or includes parts of the user's name; contains a mixture of uppercase and lowercase letters, numbers and special characters (!, $, £, %). So, for example, the following passwords would be rejected…

louiseb (same as the user name, no numbers, no capitals, no special character)
Vega2 (too short, no special character)
washingtoN! (no numbers)

…but something like *mosCow!1917* would be fine.

If the password does not meet the criteria described above a message to that effect will be displayed at the bottom of the screen, in which case you should correct the password and try again. Whilst not generally recommended, it is possible to remove the requirement for complex passwords altogether and how to do so is described in section **10.6 Changing the Password Policy**.

It is suggested that you tick the **Protect from accidental deletion** box.

On the right-hand side of the form you would normally leave *Account expires* set to **Never**. However, if the user was, for example, a temporary employee or a student in a college you could specify a date upon which the account would automatically expire. Underneath it are some *Password options*:

User must change password at next log on – this is the default and is considered best practice. If instead you click *Other password options,* three other options become available:

Microsoft Passport or smart card is required for interactive log on – additional security that may be used in larger organizations

Password never expires and *User cannot change password* – useful when several people share an account and in some educational institutions

As can be appreciated, there are many other options on the form relating to the creation of users and some will be considered below or later on. However, what we have entered is sufficient to create the user so click **OK**.

5.3 Creating Users Using PowerShell

Some people are wary of working with PowerShell, but it is a very efficient way of performing some tasks and, particularly if you have multiple users to create, somewhat quicker than other techniques. The caveat is that the user accounts will be 'plain vanilla' and it will probably be necessary to later edit them or provide additional details using *Active Directory Administrative Centre*, but even so it can be a time saver.

Right-click **Start** and choose **Windows PowerShell (Admin)**. A box with a command prompt will open; type *net user username password /add /domain*.

For example: *net user laurar !zel892!ee# /add /domain*

When you have finished creating the users, type **exit** and press **Enter** to return to the system.

If you are an experienced user, you will probably realize that you could create a script or batch file that could be used to create multiple users at once.

As mentioned, the user details will need to be filled out using *Active Directory Administrative Centre* and you may find the technique described in **5.11 Editing Multiple Users Simultaneously** to be of some help.

5.4 Bulk Creation of Users

Note: this section is mainly relevant to Windows Server 2019 Standard only.

Creating users can be time consuming. In a small network this may not be an issue, but in an organization with hundreds of users it may well be. Fortunately, tools are available to bulk-create users. A free one comes with Windows Server; it is called *csvde.exe* and is located in the *C:\Windows\System32* folder. The basic principle is that a CSV file containing the names of the users and other information is first created in, for instance, Excel. In some instances, it might be possible to generate a suitable file from another application, such as a payroll, human resources system or school ledger. Or, if this is a replacement network, a list of user names can be exported from Active Directory on the old system and then imported into Active Directory on the new one using *csvde.exe*. However, the tool is basic and some effort is still required. Easier and more sophisticated commercial alternatives are also available.

5.5 Note for Users of Earlier Versions of Windows Server

If you have used earlier versions of Windows Server, you might like to know that the older tools for creating users are still available e.g. *Active Directory Users and Computers*, which can be located at **Server Manager > Tools > Active Directory Users and Computers** or by clicking **Start > All Apps > Windows Administrative Tools > Active Directory Users and Computers**. There are some differences between the old and the new methods, with the most noticeable one being that the multiple tabs of *Active Directory Users and Computers* have been replaced by a single 'one-stop-shop' form in the *Active Directory Administrative Center*.

5.6 Resetting a Password

There is sometimes a need to reset or change a user's password; for instance, they may have forgotten it or it has become compromised. There is no way to find out what a user's password is or was; the only thing that can be done in such situations is to reset it to something different. To do so, go into the *Active Directory Administrative Center*, click the domain name and expand the *Users* container. Click on the user's name to highlight it and a list of tasks for the user will be displayed on the right-hand side of the screen; alternatively, right-click the user's name to display the same list. Click **Reset password**. In the resultant dialog box specify and confirm the new password, then click **OK**.

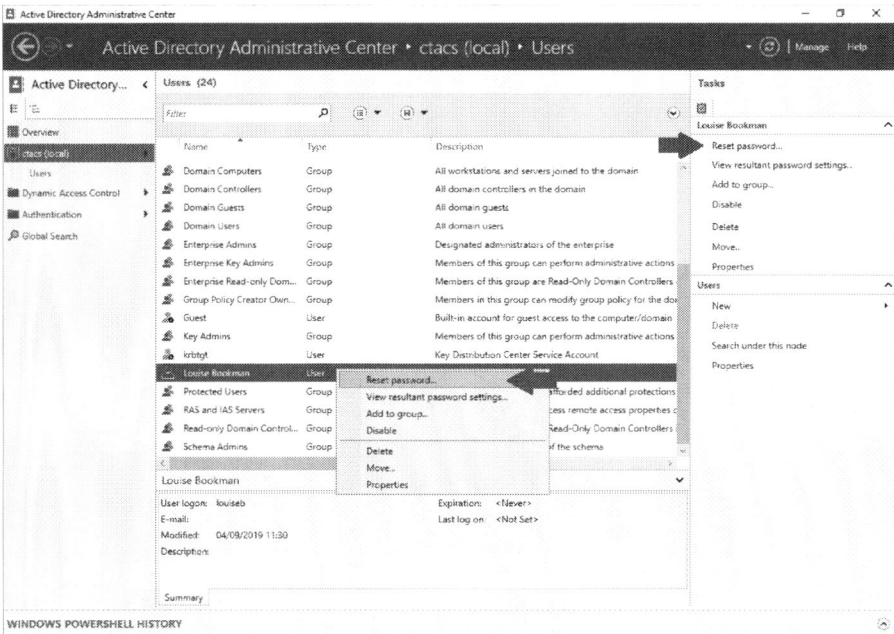

Figure 58: Reset password

5.7 Disabling an Account

When a user leaves the organization, their account should in the first instance be disabled to prevent it being used. It is preferable to do this rather than immediately deleting the account, as there may subsequently be a need to access it or the user may later return. Go into the *Active Directory Administrative Center*, click the domain name and expand the *Users* container. Click on the user's name to highlight it and a list of tasks for the user will be displayed on the right-hand side of the screen. Alternatively, right-click the user's name to display the same list. Click **Disable**. To re-enable the user, repeat the process and click **Enable**.

This technique is also useful when employees go on extended leave.

5.8 Deleting an Account

To delete an account, Go into *Active Directory Administrative Center* and drill-down to find the user as described above. Click on the user's name to highlight it and a list of tasks for the user will be displayed on the right-hand side of the screen. Alternatively, right-click the user's name to display the same list. Click **Delete**; a warning message is displayed – click **Yes** to continue.

To delete an account using PowerShell, right-click **Start** and choose **Windows PowerShell (Admin)**. A box with a command prompt will open; type *net user username /delete*.

For example: *net user laurar /delete*

When you have finished creating the users, type **exit** and press **Enter** to return to the system.

5.9 User Groups

In an organization with a small number of users, specifying who has access rights to folders is relatively easy to manage. But if there are more users it becomes more time consuming; for instance, you might have to specify the level of access for, say, a dozen. Such organizations are usually large enough that they contain departments or teams to carry out the different functions; for instance, there might be several people working in accounts, several in sales, several in marketing and so on.

To support these typical business structures, Windows Server features the concept of *groups*. A group consists of multiple users who have something in common within the organization, for instance they are all members of the same team. Access rights can be specified for a group, which means they then apply to all members of that group. If a new person joins the team they just have to be defined as a member of the relevant group, at which point they inherit all the relevant access rights.

To create a new group, launch *Server Manager* and go into *Active Directory Administrative Center*. Click on the domain name and from the list of *Builtin Tasks* on the right-hand panel choose **New > Group**. The following screen is shown. As when creating users, there are lots of possible options. But the only required ones are those towards the top of the screen. Enter the *Group name* and the *Group (SamAccountName)* and use the same value for both e.g. *marketing*. The *Group type* can be left with its default value of *Security* and the *Group scope* can be left with its default value of *Global* (the other options are not applicable if you are using Essentials). Click **OK**.

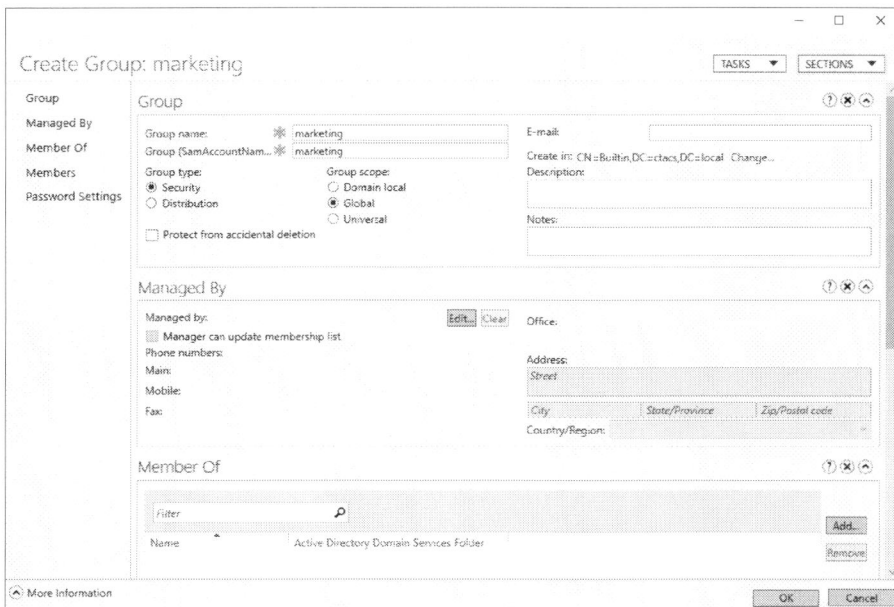

Figure 59: Creating a new Group

Having created the group, it now has to be populated with members (users) and there are two ways of doing so:

The first method is with the screen we have just used, either at the time of creating the group or by modifying it thereafter. Within the screen is a section titled *Members*; scroll down if necessary to find it and click the **Add** button. A small dialog box is displayed. Type in the name of the object, meaning the logon name of the user, and click the **Check Names** button. You do not have to type in the full name – just enough to make it unique. It will be validated and if found will then appear underlined. Click **OK** to add the user:

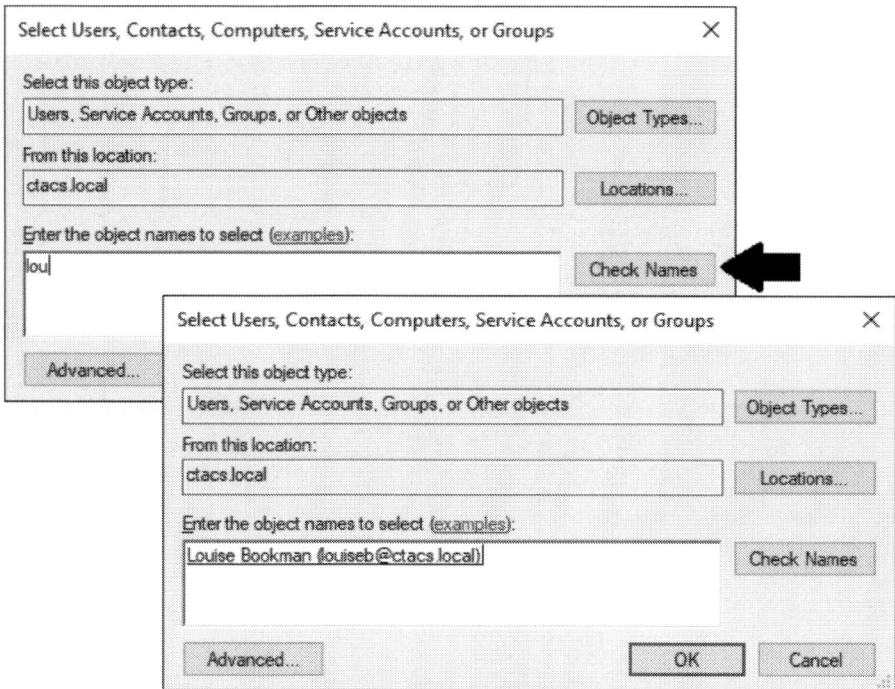

Figure 60: Selecting a user to add to a group

The second method is to display the list of users within the *Active Directory Administrative Center*. Right-click a user, click **Add to group...** and the same dialog box as above is displayed. However, this time type in the name of the group – *marketing* in our example - and click the **Check Names** button. It will be validated and if correct will then appear underlined. Click **OK**.

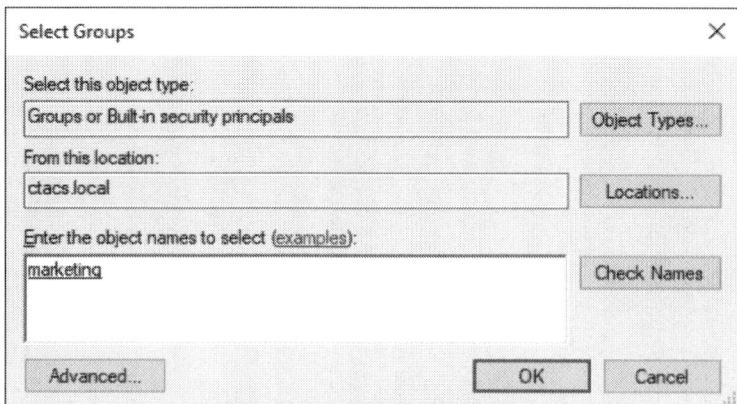

Figure 61: Selecting a group

—

5.10 Home Folders, User Profiles and Logon Scripts

Chapter 4 outlined a structure of shared folders for the system. To help make the network workable from a user perspective there are three, related mechanisms in the form of *Home folders*, *User profiles* and *Logon scripts*:

Home folders – each user can have a home or personal folder, where they can store data on the network that they can then access from any computer, but which they do not need to share with other people. In our design, these will reside under the shared *users* folder.

User profiles - a user profile is a collection of settings that personalize a computer for a particular user, including the desktop background (wallpaper), screen saver, sounds, toolbars and so on. Using a technique called *roaming profiles*, a user's profile is automatically picked up no matter which computer they login to, giving them a consistent, personalized environment.

Logon script – many users are accustomed to working with drive letters e.g. C: drive, D: drive and so on, and hence it is useful to be able to relate the shared folders to drive letters, in a process known as *drive mapping*. Logon scripts can be executed when a user logs on and are commonly used to map drives, plus can do other things as well.

Home Folders

Using *File Explorer*, navigate to the shared *Users* folder that we created earlier and now create individual folders within it for each user; the names of the folders must correspond **exactly** to the names of the users as created in section **5.2 Creating Users**. These are ordinary folders and can be created by clicking the *New Folder* icon on the *Home* tab of the *Quick Access Toolbar* or Ribbon, or by right-clicking and choosing **New > Folder**, or by pressing **Shift Ctrl N** simultaneously:

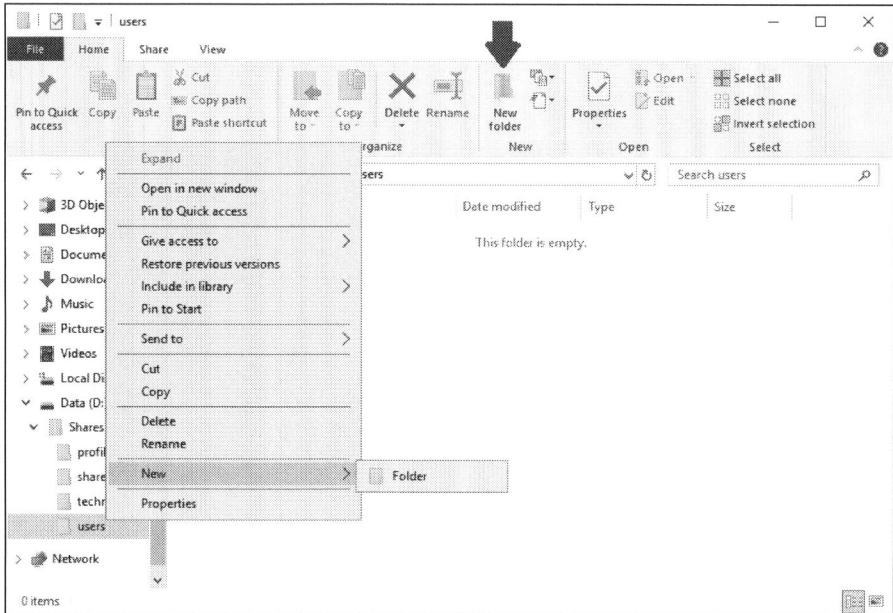

Figure 62: Create a new folder

The question of security needs to be considered. As things stand, any user can access any other user's home folder; in other words, the folders are *personal* but they are not *private*. In a very small business setting this might not be an issue, in which case you can skip to the next section. But if it is, then access to the home folders can be controlled and this is done as follows:

Right-click on a particular user's home folder and choose **Give access to > Specific people...** On the panel that appears enter the user's logon name and click **Add**. Alternatively, click the chevron on the drop-down (as indicated by large arrow in below illustration) and click **Find people**. Enter some of the user's name and click **Check Names** – if the user is found the name will be corrected and appear underlined, at which point click **OK**. Having added the user, click on **Permission Level** against their name and change it from *Read* to *Read/Write* and click the **Share** button.

After a few seconds, there will be a confirmatory message that the folder is now shared, which you can acknowledge by clicking **Done**. **Repeat** this step for all the users in turn, so that each user is sharing just their own individual folder:

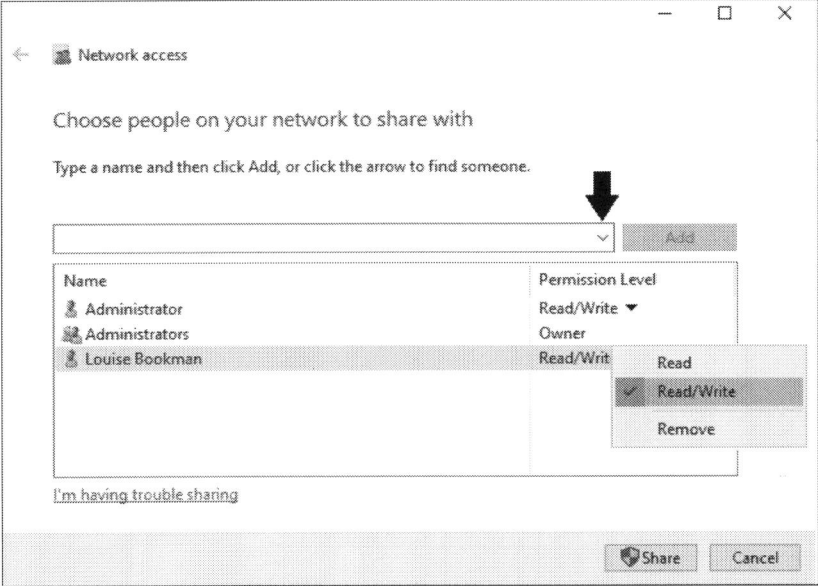

Figure 63: Specifying the permissions

User Profiles

As described above, a user profile is a collection of settings that personalize a computer for a particular user, so they have the same experience on whatever computer they use. One complexity is that because Windows clients have evolved over the years, profiles have had to evolve too, to keep track of the differences and consequently there are now several variants. Specifically, Windows XP used the original profile format; Windows Vista, Windows 7 and Windows 8 used V2 ('Version 2') profiles, plus there are some subtle variations between V2 profiles in Windows 7 and those in Windows 8. Windows 10 uses V5 ('Version 5' profiles). When a user connects for the first time, the profile folder is created automatically for that user, with a name based upon the username plus a possible suffix.

For instance, suppose *louiseb* logged on using Windows 7 computer, a profile named *server**profiles$**louiseb.v2* would be created. If she then logged on using a Windows 10 machine, a second profile named \\*server**profiles$**louiseb.v5* would be created. These can exist concurrently but note that the features they support vary (for instance, there are features in Windows 10 that have no counterpart in Windows 7). Best practice? If possible, have all the client computers in the organization running the same version of Windows, as suggested in **1.5 Client Devices**.

Logon Scripts
There are several techniques for creating logon scripts but the simplest method is via a *cmd* file (also known as a batch file). Using Notepad or another simple text editor, create two batch files named *user.cmd* and *admin.cmd* as shown below. These should be placed in...

C:\Windows\sysvol\sysvol\domainname.local\scripts

...where *domainname.local* is the name of the domain. This folder is automatically mapped by the server as a share called *NETLOGON*. It is assumed that you have called the server *'server'* – if this is not the case you will need to amend the scripts accordingly:

User.cmd script:
@echo off
: User logon script
net use s: \\server\shared /persistent:no

Admin.cmd script:
@echo off
: Admin logon script
net use s: \\server\shared /persistent:no
net use t: \\server\technical$ /persistent:no

The logon file now needs to be associated with the user accounts. Go into *Active Directory Administrative Center*, drill-down through the list of users and double-click one to display their details. Scroll down to the section called *Profile* and specify the *Profile path* and the *Log on script*. The Profile path takes the form *server**profiles$**%username%*; note the use of the *%username%*, which is a *system variable* that Windows Server will automatically associate with the user as they login. For general purpose users, the login script is *user.cmd* whilst for the Administrator it is *admin.cmd*. In the *Home Folder* area choose *H:* from the **Connect** drop-down and specify a value of *server**users**username* for it e.g. *server**users**aarong*. Click **OK**.

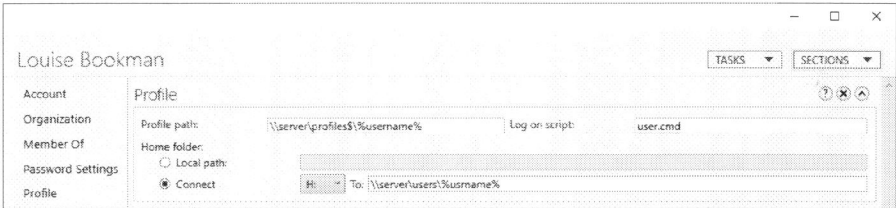

Figure 64: Specify user profile details

The effect of this is that when a user logs on they will have easy access to two network drives. The shared folder that everyone can see will appear as *S:* whilst their personal or home folder will appear as the *H:* drive. For the Administrator user(s), specify a logon script of *admin.cmd* rather than *user.cmd*, which will map the shared, home and technical folders.

Troubleshooting: if the home folder is not mapped or the profile does not appear to be working, explicitly specify the user's login name rather than the *%username%* system variable. For example, user *dpetrova* would have a profile path of *server**profiles$**dpetrova* and the H: drive would connect to *server**users**dpetrova*.

5.11 Editing Multiple Users Simultaneously

A useful time saver when assigning profiles to users is the ability to work with multiple users simultaneously. Go into *Active Directory Administrative Center*, locate the users and, holding down the Control key, click them one at a time to highlight them. Then, right-click one and choose **Properties** from the pop-up menu. A subset of the main screen but with four sections is displayed: *Account*; *Organization*; *Member Of* and *Profile*. Scroll down to **Profile** – this is the same dialog box as shown above but anything entered here will apply to all the selected users. It is thus a very fast way of assigning, say, the same logon script to many users at once.

6

CONNECTING DEVICES TO THE SERVER

6.1 Overview

Each computer in the organization needs to be connected to the server, a process also known as *adding it to the domain*. The key requirements are:

- The computer has to be running a Professional or better version of Windows, such as Windows 10 Professional or Windows 7 Professional with Service Pack 1.
- The latest Windows updates should first be applied to the computer.
- Each computer must have a unique name within the network to identify it. It is best to follow a scheme of some description: this could be as simple as PC01, PC02, PC03 etc., or one that relates to its location or function. To change the name of a Windows 10 computer: Right-click the **Start** button and choose **System** > **About**; under *Device specifications*, click **Rename this PC**; enter the new name and click **Next**. To change the name of a Windows 7 computer, go to **Control Panel** > **System** and click **Change settings** in the *Computer name, domain and workgroup* settings section.
- Make sure that the computer is linked to the network and has basic connectivity. It is preferable that it is wired; if you are working on a wireless laptop, temporarily use an Ethernet cable and plug it in.
- Logon to the computer as a local administrator or other user that has administrative rights.

Computers using Home or Starter editions of Windows cannot be added to the domain; however, see section **6.5 Connecting Computers with Home Editions of Windows** for a limited workaround. There are several different methods for connecting Macs – see section **6.6 Connecting Macs**. Linux computers can be connected in a limited manner, described in section **6.7 Connecting Linux Computers**.

To connect iOS tablets and smartphones, albeit in a limited fashion, see section **6.8 Accessing the Server from Tablets and Smartphones**.

—

6.2 Adding a Computer to the Domain

Connecting Windows 10 Clients to the domain

Note: it is recommended that the computer should have initially been setup to use a local account rather than an online Microsoft account.

Click **Start > Settings > Accounts > Access work or school.**

Click **Connect+**

On the resultant panel, ignore the email box and instead click the **Join this device to a local Active Directory domain** link at the bottom of the screen.

Enter your *Domain name* followed by the .local suffix e.g. *ctacs.local* in our example.

When prompted, enter the Administrator name and password for the domain. Do so and click **OK**.

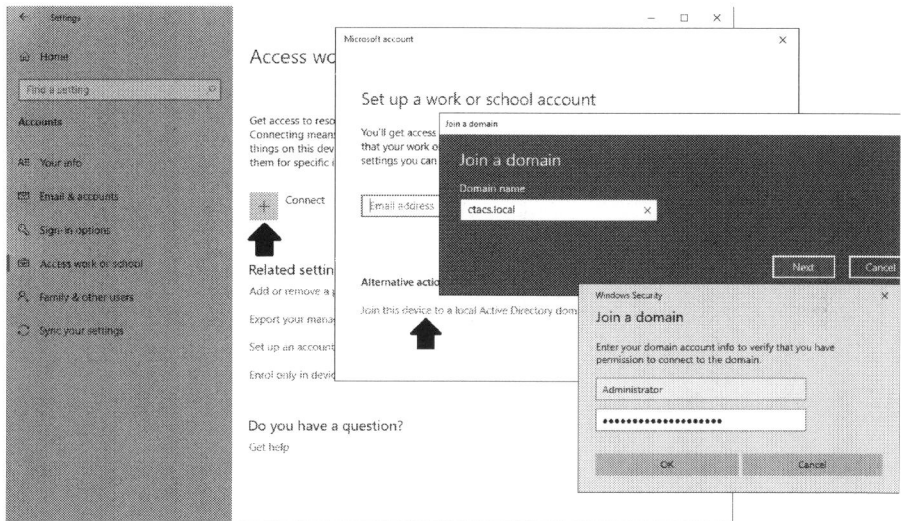

Figure 65: Adding Windows 10 computer to domain

An additional panel pops up, enabling you to add an account for the person who will be using the computer: ignore it by clicking **Skip**.

Follow the instructions to restart the computer.

Check that you can logon as Administrator. Note: you may need to choose Other user and specify the logon name as *domain \ Administrator* e.g. *ctacs \ Administrator*.

Connecting Windows 7 Clients to the domain

Click the **Start** button, right-click **Computer** and click **Properties.**

Under *Computer name, domain, and workgroup settings*, click **Change settings.**

System Properties are displayed. Make sure you are on the *Computer Name* tab.

Click the **Change** button.

In the *Member of* section, click on **Domain**. Enter the name of your domain, followed by the .local suffix (for example, *ctacs.local*).

You will be prompted to enter the Administrator name and password for the domain. Do so and click **OK**.

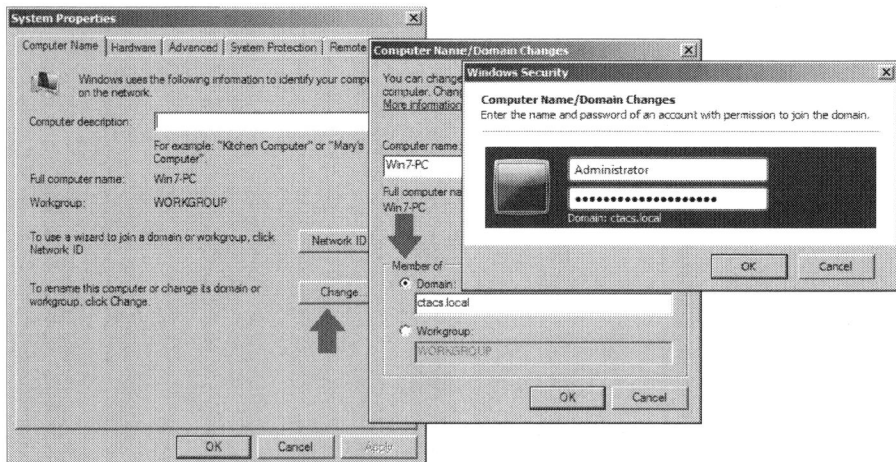

Figure 66: Adding Windows 7 computer to domain

After a short delay you will receive a 'Welcome to the domain' message.

Follow the instructions to restart the computer.

Check that you can logon as Administrator. Note: you may need to choose other user and specify the logon name as *domain\Administrator* e.g. *ctacs\Administrator.*

6.3 Removing a Windows Computer from the Domain

There is sometimes a need to remove a computer from the domain, for instance when it is being decommissioned or replaced. Very rarely, an existing computer may develop problems connecting to the server and sometimes the solution is to remove and then add it back to the domain.

To remove a Windows computer that is connected to the domain, go into **Control Panel** and click **System** followed by **Change Settings**. On the **Computer Name** tab, click the **Change** button. The computer will currently be a member of the domain. Click **Workgroup** and enter a name for it – it can be anything you wish but the usual convention is to call it *Workgroup.* Click **OK**. You may have to enter administrative credentials and restart the computer when prompted.

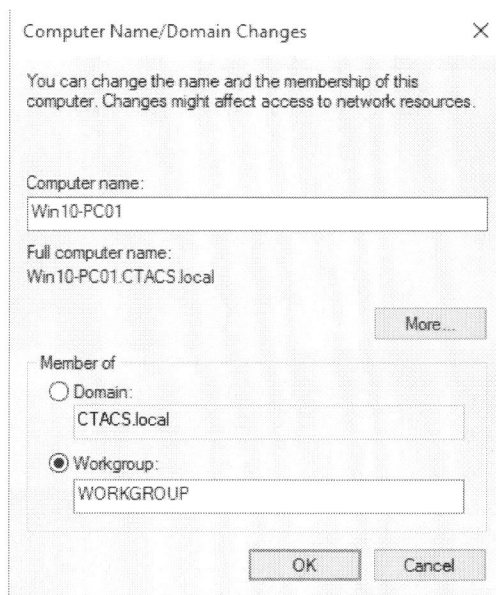

Figure 67: Computer Name/Domain Changes

6.4 Troubleshooting DNS Settings with All-in-One Routers

In a small organization, internet connectivity is frequently through an all-in-one router that also provides DHCP and DNS services; however, Windows Sever itself also provides DNS as a consequence of running Active Directory. This can cause problems with DNS, such that computers on the network cannot 'see' each other. Attempting to join a computer to the server may result in failure, with a message to the effect that "a domain controller cannot be found":

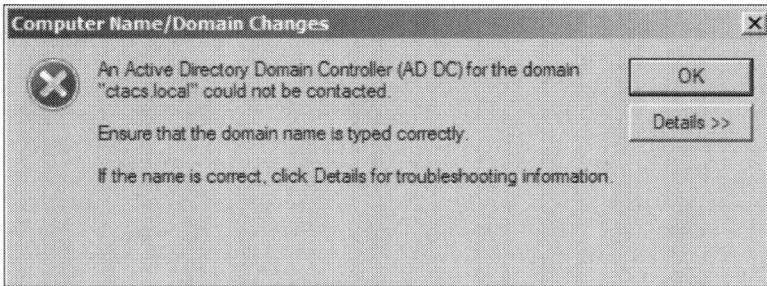

Figure 68: DNS-related error

The easiest fix for this is to explicitly force the client computers to point first to the server for DNS (which will find local resources) and only then to the router (which will find internet resources). To do so, go into the network adapter settings for each PC. For Windows 7: **Control Panel > Network and Sharing Center > Change Adapter Settings**. For Windows 10: right-click **Start > Network Connections > Change adapter options**. Right-click the network adapter, choose **Properties**, highlight **Internet Protocol Version 4 (TCP/Ipv4)** and click **Properties**. Click **Use the following DNS server addresses** option: for the **Preferred DNS server** specify the IP address of the file server; for the **Alternate DNS server** specify the IP address. Click **OK** and **Close**.

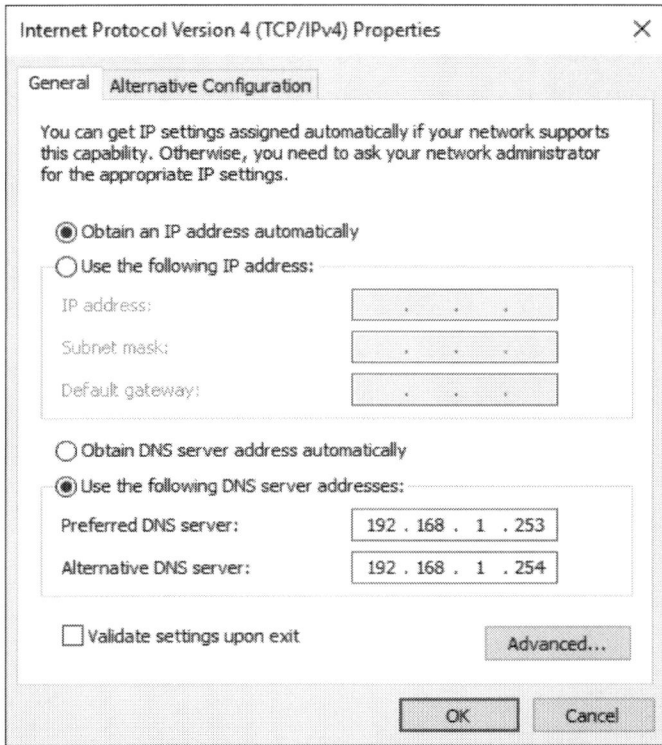

Figure 69: Manually specify the DNS servers

6.5 Connecting Computers with Home Editions of Windows

In theory, only computers running recent versions of Windows Professional or better can be connected to Windows Server. However, it is feasible to connect computers running Home Editions of Windows from Windows XP upwards, albeit in a simplified fashion. It will be possible to access the shared data folders, but not take advantage of the specific features that Windows Server offers in terms of control and management.

To connect a computer running a Home Edition of Windows, click **Start** (or right-click **Start** in Windows 10) and choose **Run**. Alternatively, hold down the **Windows key** and the **R key** simultaneously. In the dialog box that appears, type *server* or \\ followed by the IP address of the server (e.g. *192.168.1.253*). The user will be prompted to enter their user name and password; if they are the only person that uses that particular computer tick the **Remember my password** or **Remember my credentials** box:

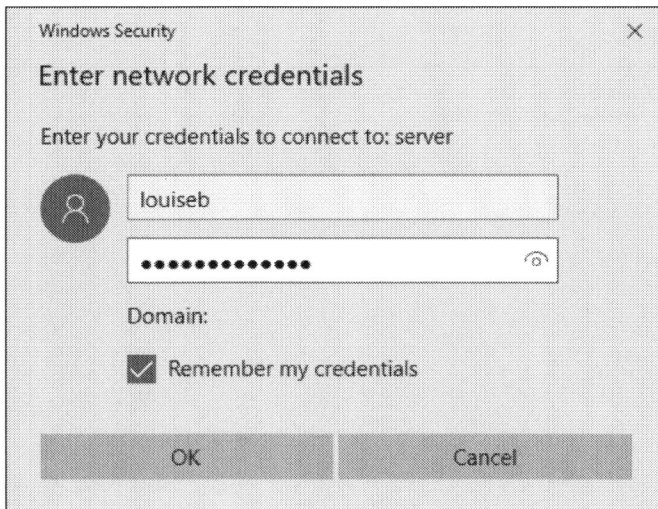

Figure 70: Enter the user name and password

A list of shared folders on the server will be displayed:

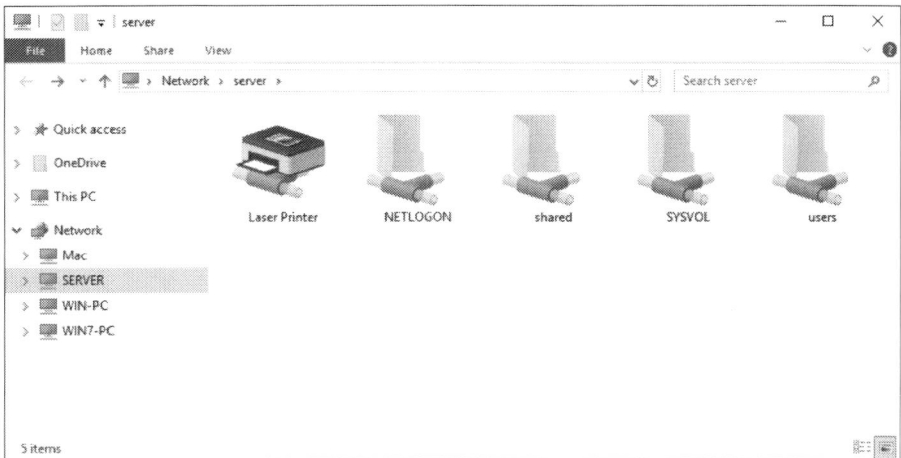

Figure 71: List of network folders

The user can work with any of the folders to which they have been granted access. To access their home folder, they should double-click the *Users* folder then double-click the folder that has their user name. Note that although they can see the names of other people's home folders, they will not be able to access the contents because of security restrictions.

6.6 Connecting Macs

Most organizations using Windows Server will be working with Windows client PCs. However, many organizations will also have some Macs as well, perhaps to meet specialized requirements or simply through preference and these can be connected to the network using a variety of techniques: they can be added to the domain; they can be equipped with Windows and connected in exactly the same way as the organization's other Windows PCs; they can be connected in a simplified manner as workgroup computers.

Adding to the Domain

Login as a user with local admin rights on the Mac. To prevent possible DNS issues, ensure that both the server and the router have their IP addresses entered on the Mac's network adaptor: **System Preferences > Network > Advanced > DNS**. Then, go into **System Preferences > Users & Groups**.

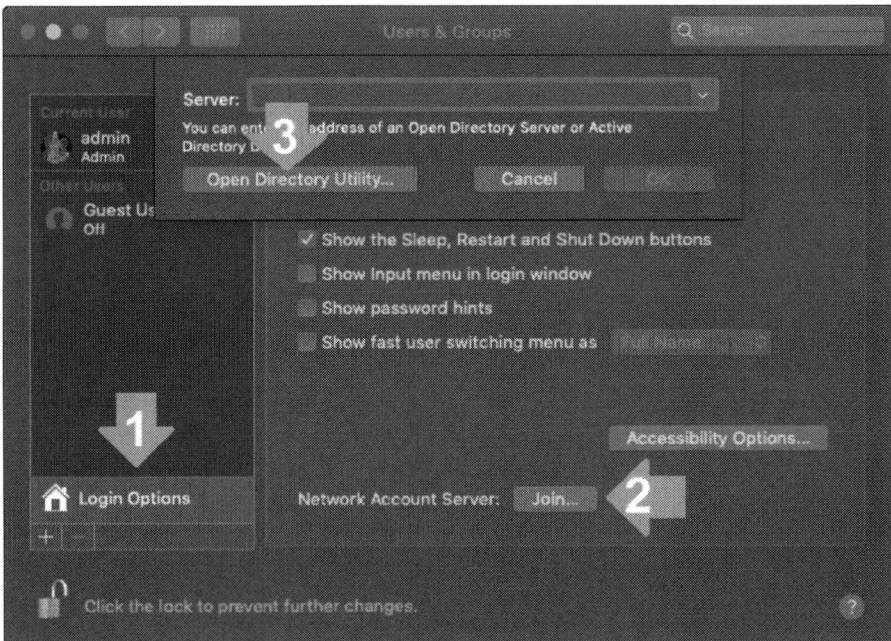

Figure 72: Login Options

106

Open the padlock – you may need to provide details of a user with administrative rights. Click **Login Options** then click the **Join** button next to *Network Account Server*. On the pop-up panel click **Open Directory Utility**:

On the *Directory Utility* panel, open the padlock by providing admin credentials and clicking **Modify Configuration**. Highlight **Active Directory** and click the mini pencil icon to make changes. Type in the name of the Active Directory Domain and click **Bind**. Note: you may be prompted to enter the local admin credentials numerous times during this process.

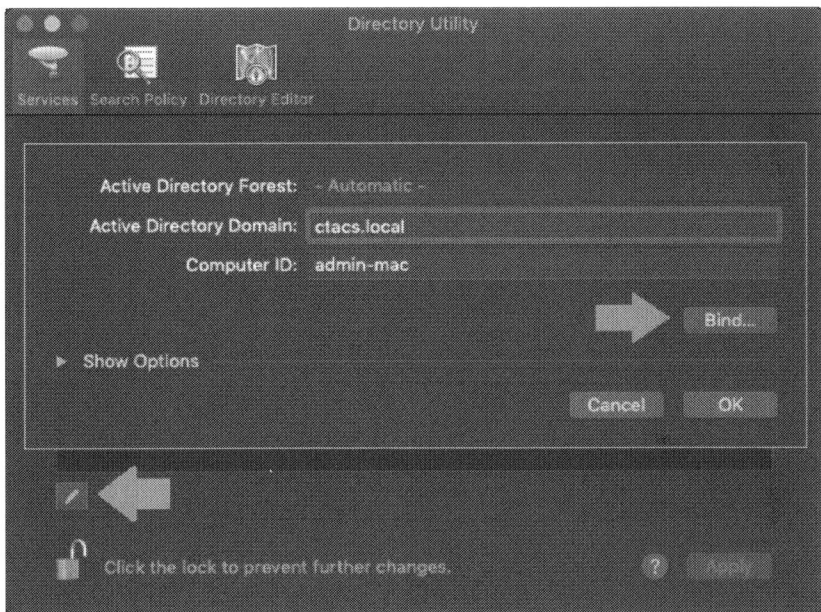

Figure 73: Enter details of the domain

Enter the logon credentials for the administrator of the server and click **OK**:

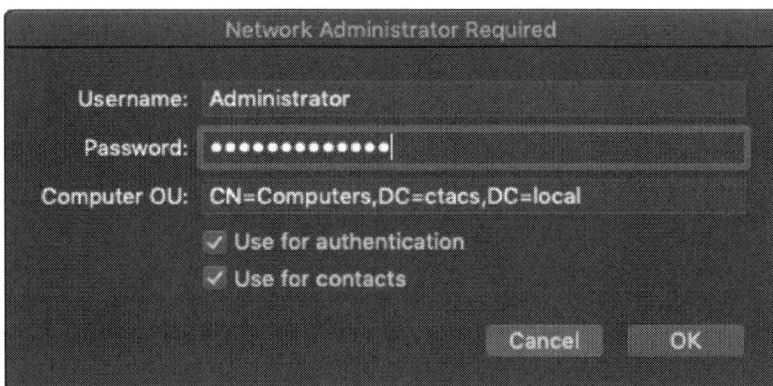

Figure 74: Enter details for the domain administrator

After a short while you will be added to the domain.

Whilst this method works on a technical level, it does not actually do very much and the support from both Microsoft and Apple has been described as 'lukewarm'.

Running Windows on the Mac

All modern Macs can run Windows in addition to macOS, thus enabling them to connect and behave exactly the same (from a networking perspective) as a regular Windows PC. If this is done, the Mac is then added to the domain using the technique detailed in section **6.2 Adding a Computer to the Domain**.

There are two methods of running Windows on a Mac:

Boot Camp: Apple's Boot Camp utility is a standard component of macOS, located in the **Applications > Utilities** folder. The Boot Camp Assistant partitions the Mac's hard drive, allowing a copy of Windows to be installed. At startup time, macOS or Windows can then be selected. There are two limitations: firstly, only one operating system at a time can be used. For instance, if the computer is running Windows and you want to use macOS, then it is necessary to restart it. Secondly, only the most recent versions of Windows (8, 8.1 and 10) are supported on modern Macs, although older machines may be able to use Windows 7 with earlier versions of Boot Camp.

———

Virtualization Software: This enables the Mac to operate as normal under macOS and run a separate copy of Windows in its own self-contained window at the same time, as though it was just another application. This is particularly useful where a user prefers to work predominantly in a Mac environment, but also needs to connect to the Windows server. The copy of Windows can be any version – none of the restrictions imposed by the Boot Camp method apply. Virtualization software is available from several sources: a well-regarded commercial program is *Parallels* from the company of the same name, whereas a free alternative is *VirtualBox* from Oracle.

Whichever method is used, a licensed copy of Windows still has to be obtained and used for the installation. This needs to be a Professional edition or better.

Connecting as a Workgroup Member

Rather than connect to the domain in the 'proper' way, Macs can be connected as Workgroup members, analogous to the manner in which computers running unsupported versions of Windows can be, as described in section **6.5 Connecting Computers with Home Editions of Windows**. The technique is as follows:

From Finder click **Go** followed by **Connect to Server** (or use **Command K** as a shortcut). On the resultant dialog box enter *smb://* followed by the name of the server or its internal IP address e.g. *smb://server* or *smb://192.168.1.253*. Click **Connect**:

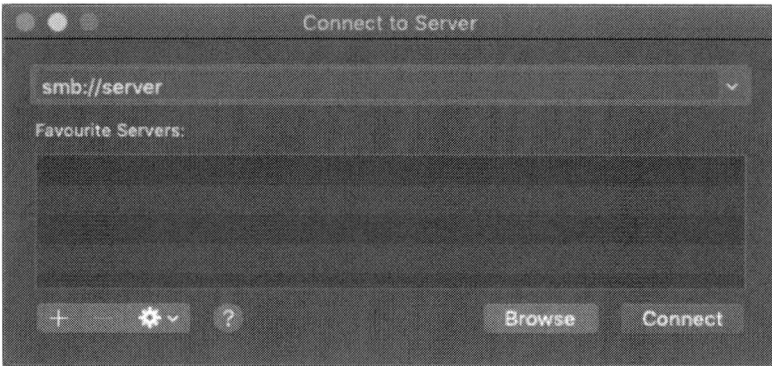

Figure 75: Enter the name or address of the server

You will be prompted for details of a Registered User; enter the user's name and password (as defined on the server) and optionally tick the **Remember this password in my keychain** box:

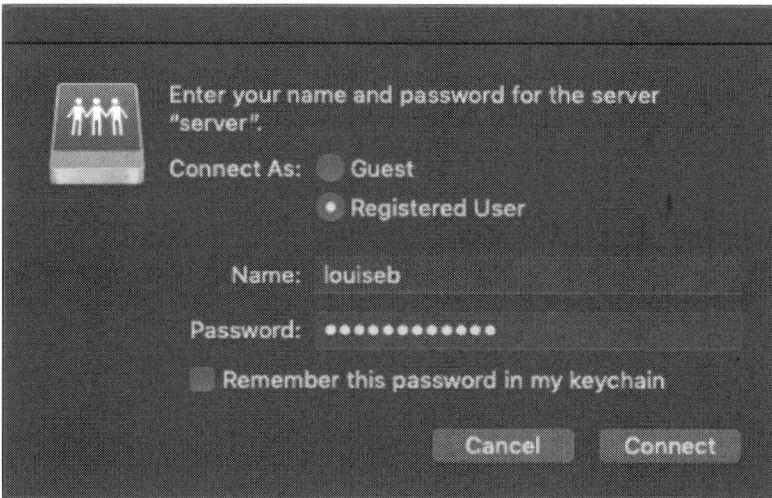

Figure 76: Enter the user's name and password from the server

A list of available shared folders (*volumes*) is displayed. Choose the volume to mount and click **OK**; or, to mount multiple volumes in one go, hold down the **Command key** and click on the required folders in turn. Note that all the shared folders on the server are listed, including ones not normally accessed by users and to which they may not have permissions:

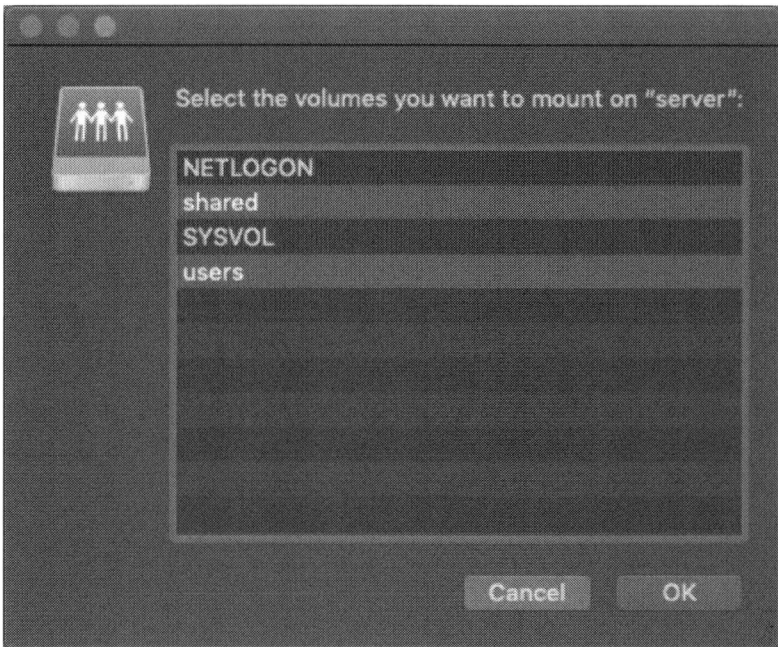

Figure 77: Select the volume(s) to mount

An icon for each mounted volume will be placed on the desktop and its contents will be displayed. From here the files and folders can be used in the normal way.

6.7 Connecting Linux Computers

Most Linux distributions do not come with the native capability to connect to Windows Server. However, Linux PCs can be connected as Workgroup members, in much the same way as computers running unsupported versions of Windows can as described in section **6.5 Connecting Computers with Home Editions of Windows**. This is possible because Linux distributions include support for the SMB filing system used by Windows networking; this is usually built-in or can be added by downloading what is commonly described as a Samba client. In this example, we are using the popular Ubuntu Linux distribution.

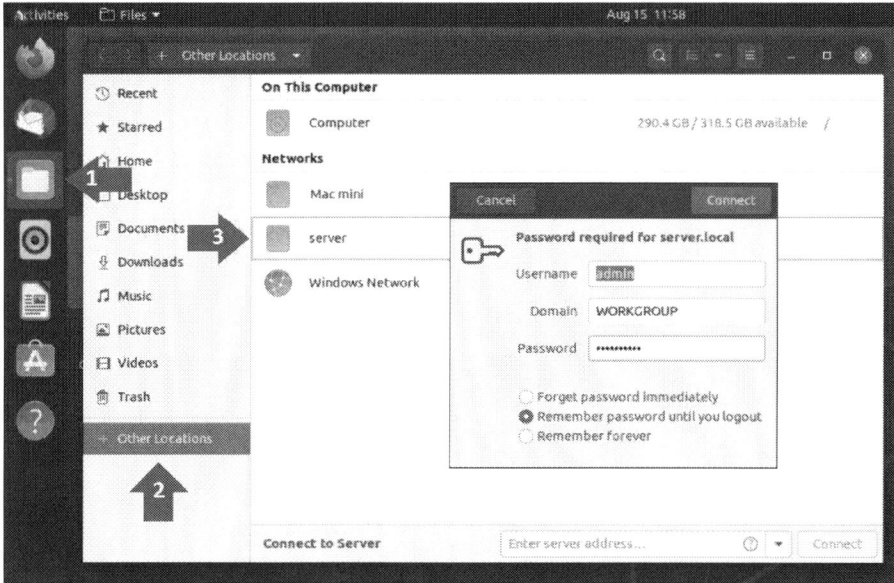

Figure 78: Enter the address of the server

Click on the **Files** icon, followed by **Other Locations**. The server should be listed under the Networks section; click on it and on the resultant panel, enter the user's name and password as defined on the server and click **Connect** (the *Domain* field can be ignored).

The shared folders on the server will be listed. To access one, double-click it. You may be prompted to provide the username and password again, in which case do so. The folder will then open and you can use the files in the standard manner.

6.8 Accessing the Server from Tablets and Smartphones

Tablets and Smartphones do not usually have the capability to connect to a Windows Server domain; rather, they connect as workgroup devices, in much the same way as computers running unsupported version of Windows can be and with similar functionality, as described in **6.5 Connecting Computers with Home Editions of Windows**. Three options are described below.

Files App (iOS)

The Files App is an integral part of recent version of iOS. Having launched it, click the three-dot menu at the top of the and tap **Connect to Server**:

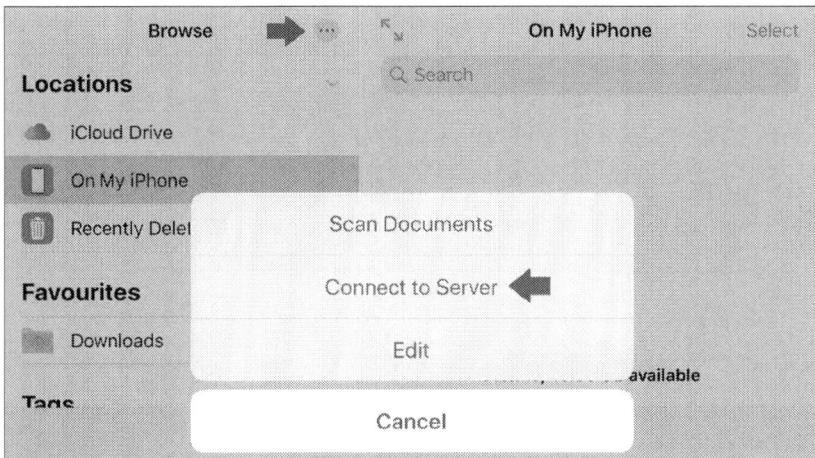

Figure 79: File App on iPhone/iOS 13

On the subsequent panels: enter the name of the server or its IP address and click **Connect**; choose the **Registered User** option; enter the name and password of a user that has previously been defined on the server and click **Next**:

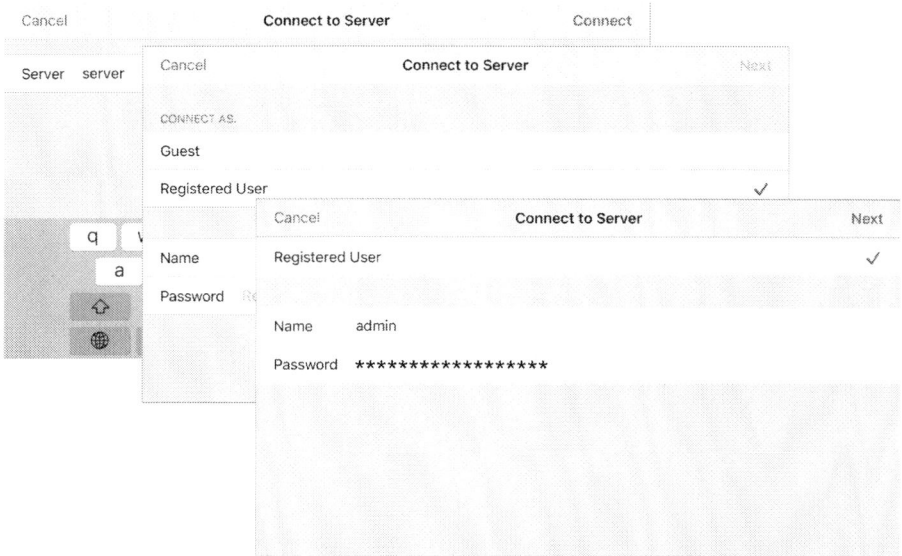

Figure 80: Connecting to the server

After a few seconds, you should be connected to the server, from where you can navigate through the file system to locate folders and files:

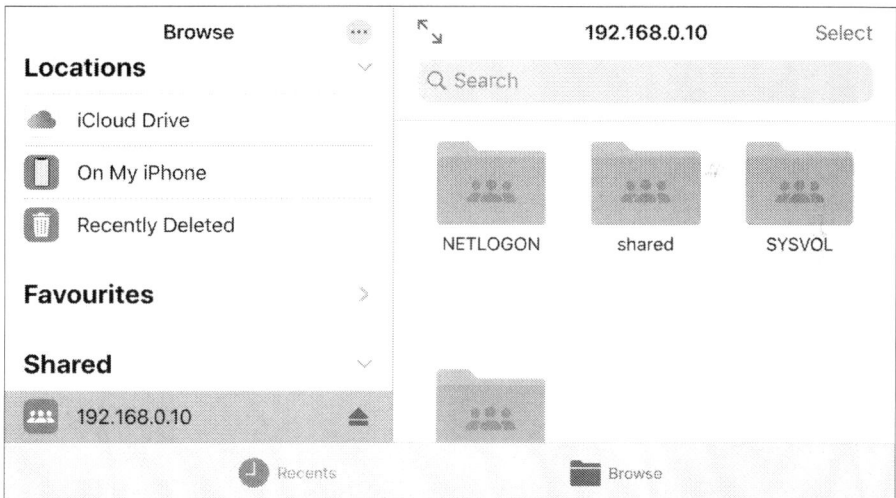

Figure 81: Viewing files and folders on the server

File Browser (iOS)

As an alternative to Apple's Files App or for older versions of iOS, *File Browser* from Stratospherix is a good way of accessing folders and files on the server. This is a commercial product but is inexpensive (less than $10 US equivalent). It is not specifically designed for Windows Server, rather it is a generic tool for accessing most computer systems.

To use, enter the IP address of the server along with a valid user name and password. The user can work with any of the folders to which they have been granted access. To access their home folder, they should double-click the *Users* folder then double-click the folder that has their own user name. Note that they can see the names of other people's home folders, but will not be able to access them because of security restrictions. Files can be viewed, but not edited.

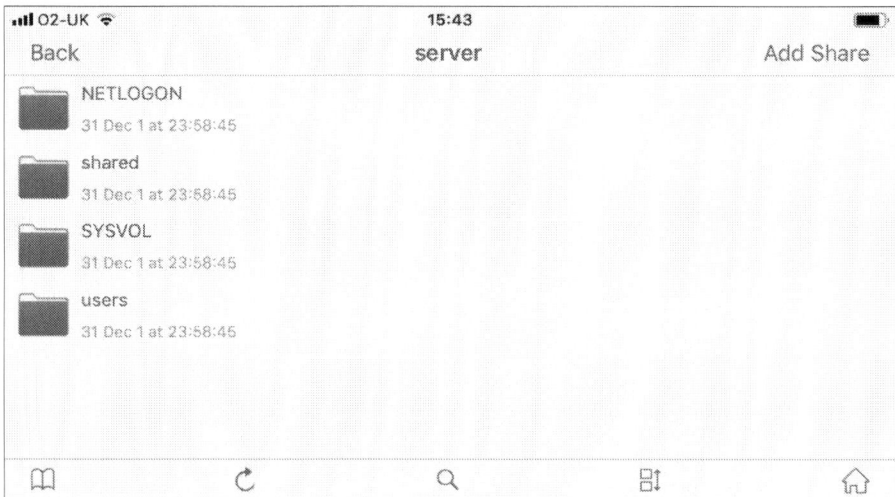

Figure 82: File Browser from Stratospherix running on iPhone

ES File Explorer (Android)

For Android tablet and smartphone users, ES File Explorer is a popular file manager. Although most people use it for exploring and managing the file system on their device, it also understands SMB-based network systems, such as Windows Server. The basic app is free; it includes advertisements, but it is possible to upgrade to remove them if they are considered intrusive, plus add further features.

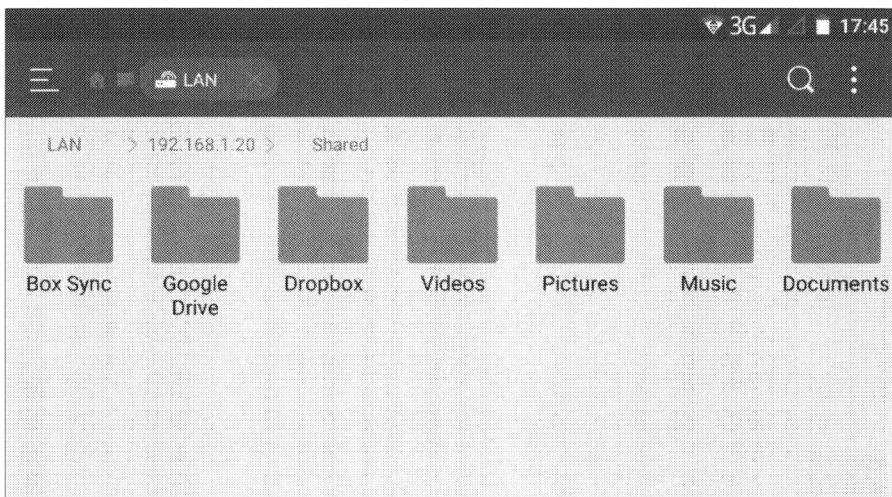

Figure 83: File Explorer running on Android phone

7

BACKUPS AND RESTORES

7.1 Overview

The importance of backing up data on a regular basis, in order to cope with the problems that can arise with computers, cannot be over-emphasized. Potential problems include: deleting files by accident; malware infections; data corruption; computer failure; equipment being lost or stolen. In general, the value of data far outweighs the value of computers; for instance, around half of businesses that have a serious data loss subsequently cease trading within twelve months, plus there may be statutory requirements to retain and able to produce certain data in some parts of the world. The assumption to follow is that it is a question of *when* rather than *if* data will be lost at some point, which is when the backups will be needed.

The best strategy is to aim for a *3-2-1 solution*, which means there are at least three copies of the data, they are held in at least two different formats, at least one copy is held offsite, away from the premises. This system of having multiple backups to multiple places ensures that there is always a fallback in the event of problems. For instance:

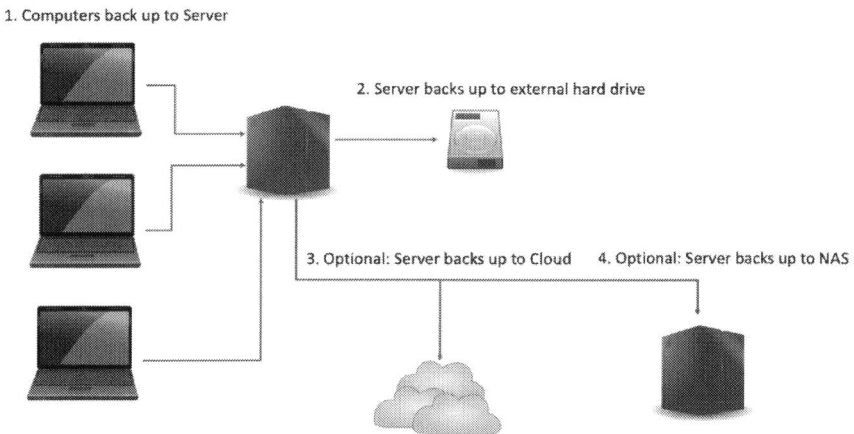

Figure 84: Multi-tiered approach to backups

The computers in the office are backed up to the server. The server in turn is backed up to a local external hard drive. Optionally, the server or at least the most important data are backed up to a Cloud-based service. For an extra level of protection, the server could also be backed up to a NAS (network attached storage) device located elsewhere in the premises:

Backups are carried out using Windows Server Backup, which will meet the needs of many small businesses. However, alternatives are available for those who require additional capabilities e.g. tape backup, backing up virtual machines, archiving, cloud backups, cross-platform compatibility and so on. Many are available and examples of popular products include: *Veritas Backup Exec*; *Acronis Backup*; *NovaStor NovaBACKUP*; *Cortex IT Labs' BackupAssist*. Most of these offer free trials so you can determine their suitability.

7.2 Configuring Backups for the Server

Backups are performed using *Windows Server Backup*. In the case of Essentials it is pre-installed, but with Windows Server Standard it has to be installed manually: go into **Server Manager** and click **Manage** followed by **Add Roles and Features**. Choose **Role-based or feature-based installation**, click **Next**, select the server on the following screen and click **Next**. Click **Features** on the left-hand panel and select **Windows Server Backup** from the middle one, followed by **Next**. On the subsequent screen click **Install**. The installation will only take a minute or two; when complete, click **Close**.

To launch *Windows Server Backup*, go into **Server Manager** and click **Tools** followed by **Windows Server Backup**. On the left-hand panel, click **Local Backup** and the screen will appear as follows:

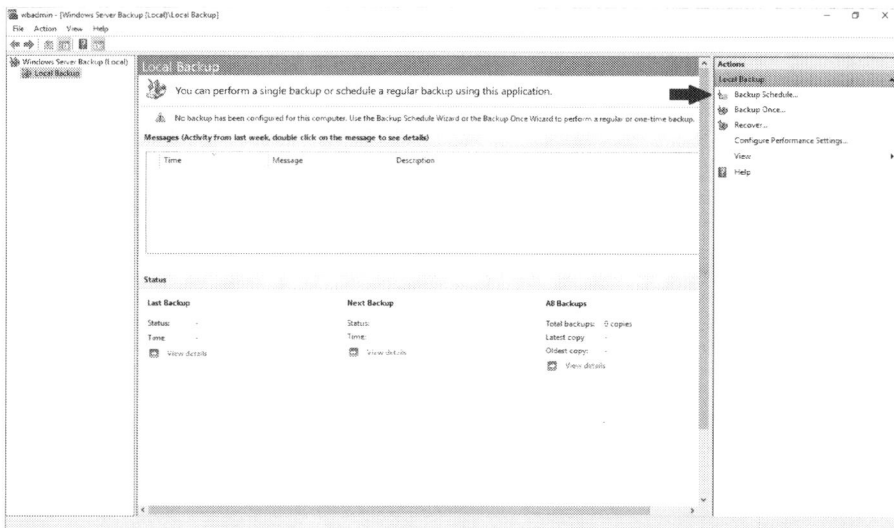

Figure 85: Windows Server Backup console

Backups can be run as and when required or, more usefully, scheduled to run on a regular basis. To setup a scheduled backup, click **Backup Schedule** on the right-hand of the screen, listed under *Actions* and which will start the *Backup Schedule Wizard*. Click **Next** on the Getting Started screen.

121

On the subsequent screen, there is a choice between a *Full Server (recommended)* or *Custom* backup. As the name implies, the former backs up absolutely everything whereas the latter allows greater control over what is backed up. We will choose **Full Server (recommended)**.

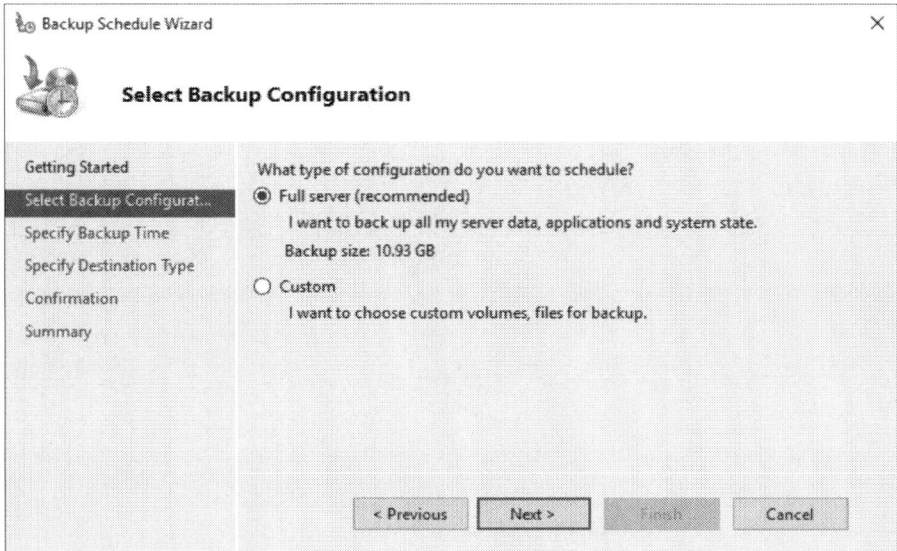

Figure 86: Select Backup Configuration

Click **Next** and a screen to specify the backup time is then shown:

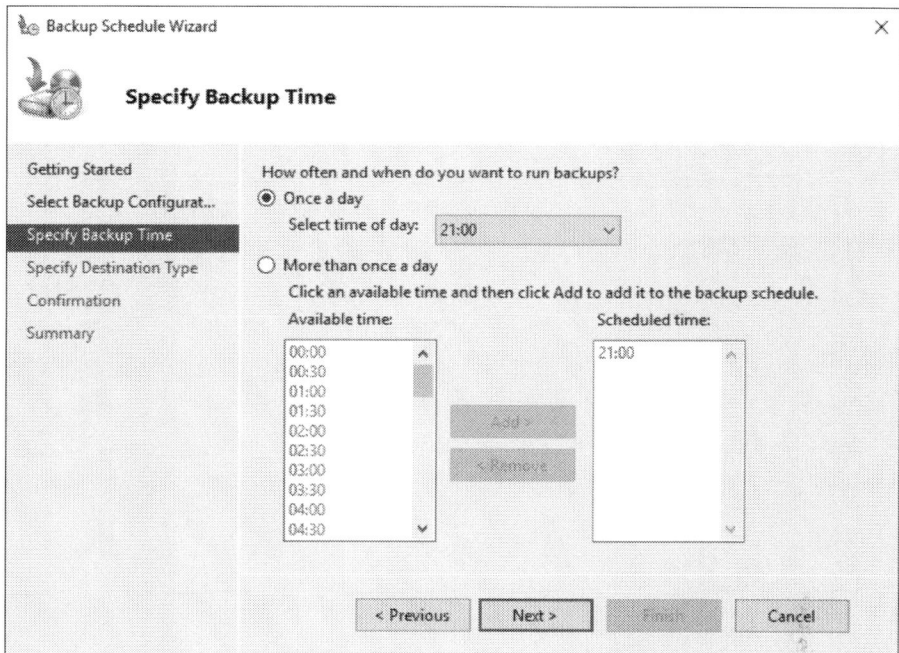

Figure 87: Specifying the Backup time

The default of a daily backup performed at 21:00/9:00pm will be suitable for many organizations, else can be changed using the drop-down. As a general principle, the backup should be scheduled to run outside of normal working hours or at least during a quiet time, as it can impact server performance. However, it is possible to have the backup run more frequently if needed; this might be more relevant with a custom backup, when a specific volume or folder needs backing up more regularly. Click **Next**.

The destination of the backup is specified on the subsequent screen. Usually the first option – **Back up to a hard disk that is dedicated for backups (recommended)** – is used, although we will also consider another option later. Make sure the external backup drive is connected at this point.

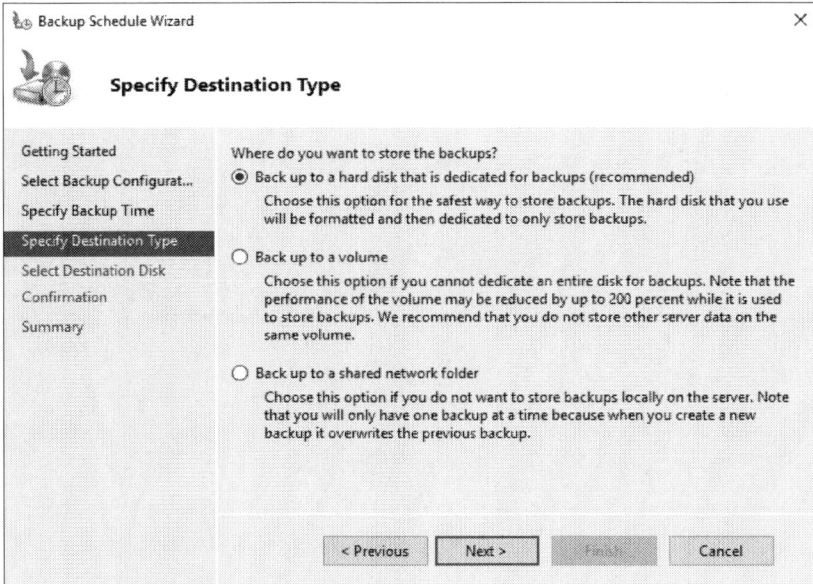

Figure 88: Specify the destination type for the backup

Click **Next** to show this screen:

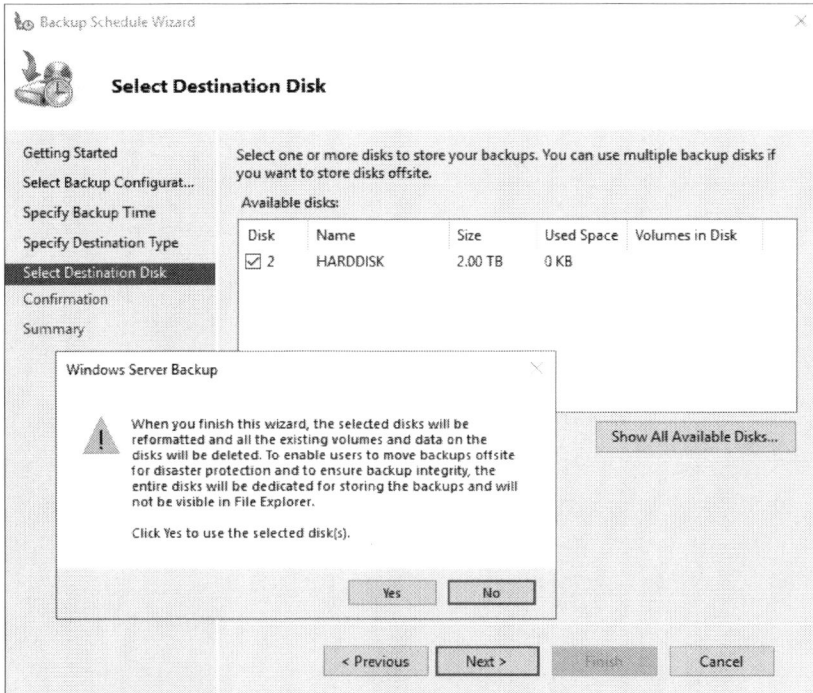

Figure 89: Specify the destination disk for the backup

Tick the external drive to be used. If no drives are listed, wait 10-15 seconds then click the **Show All Available Disks** button. Having selected the drive, click **Next**. If the drive is not already formatted, there may be a message to that effect and you will need to click **Yes** to format the drive and continue.

The backup program might detect that the external drive will be *included* within the backup rather than used as a separate backup drive, which you do not want as it would be backing up itself to itself! If the following message is received, click **OK** to fix the problem:

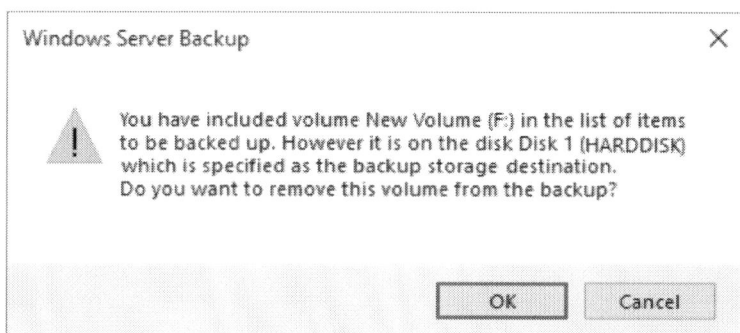

Figure 90: Backup warning message

There may be a warning message about formatting. Backup disks use a special file system that is not visible to regular Windows and hence it is not possible to plug a backup disk into a standard Windows computer and read it like a normal drive once it has been formatted for backup purposes. Click **Yes** to the message then click on **Finish** on the Confirmation screen that follows:

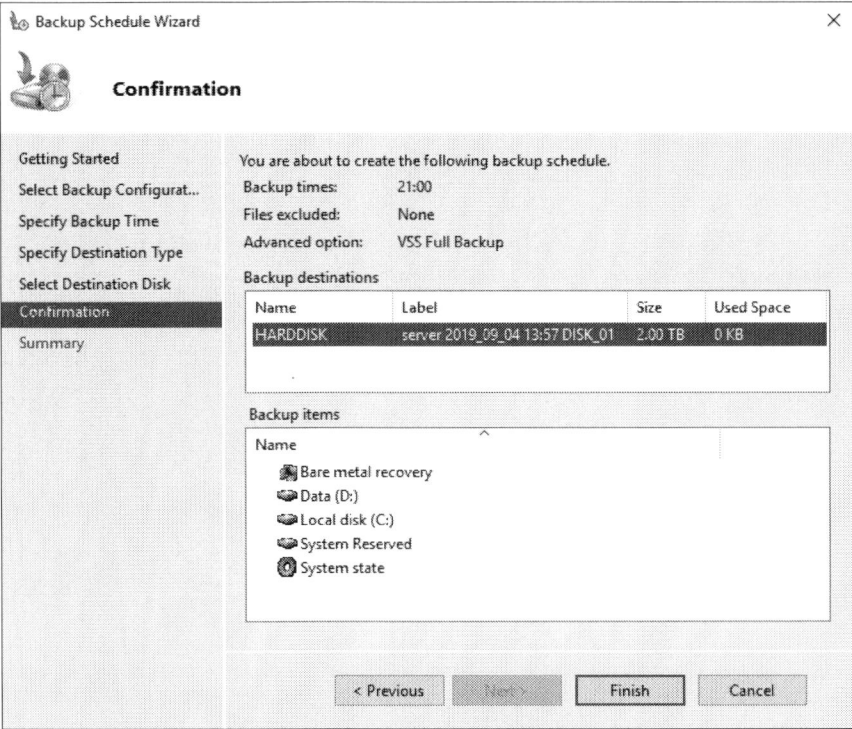

Figure 91: Confirmation of settings

After a short while a Summary screen is displayed:

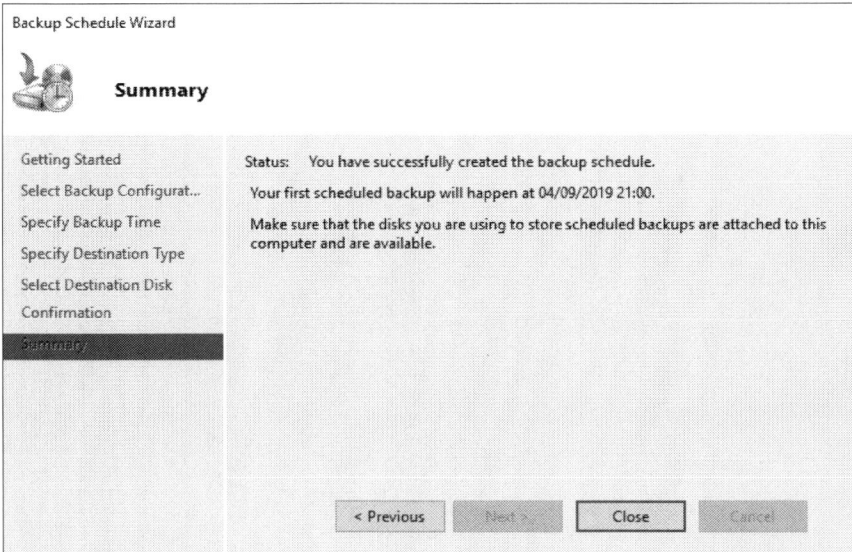

Figure 92: Summary screen from the Backup Schedule Wizard

Using the main *Windows Server Backup* screen, the backup job can be checked each day to make sure that it has completed successfully.

Having created a backup, you may wish to run it immediately to test that it is working, rather than wait for the scheduled time. From the main backup screen, click **Backup Once** in the *Actions* column. On the *Backup Options* screen that appears, choose **Scheduled backup options** and click **Next**. The next screen is the *Confirmation* screen – click **Backup** and the backup will run immediately. When it has completed, click **Close**. The regular scheduled job will not be affected in any way.

7.3 Restoring Files to the Server

In the event of data loss or there being a need to recover (restore) deleted or older versions of files, the *Recovery Wizard* can be used. Launch Windows Server Backup (**Server Manager > Tools > Windows Server Backup)**. On the left-hand panel, click **Local Backup** and on the right-hand of the screen, listed under **Actions**, click **Recover,** which will cause the *Recovery Wizard* to run. Make sure **This server (SERVER)** is selected and click **Next**:

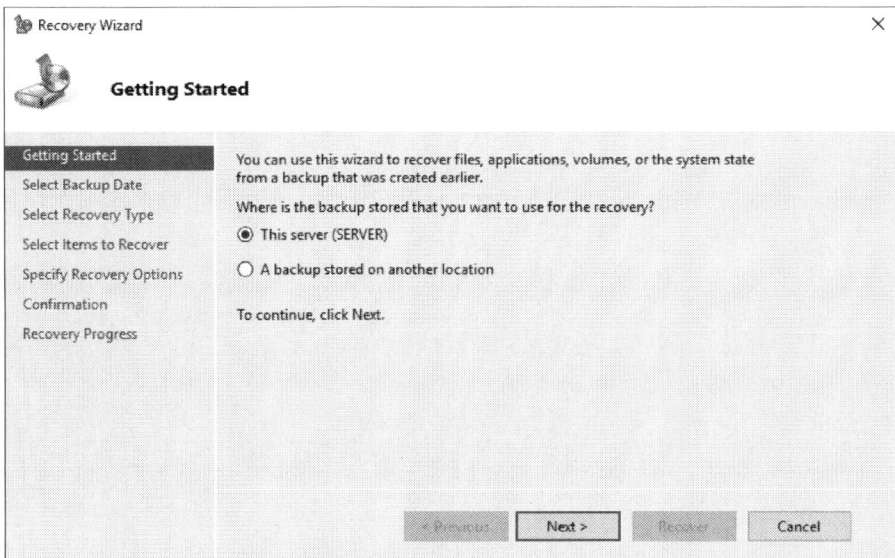

Figure 93: Recovery Wizard Getting Started screen

On the next screen, select a backup to be restored using the calendar and time fields – days for which backups are available are highlighted in bold - then click **Next**:

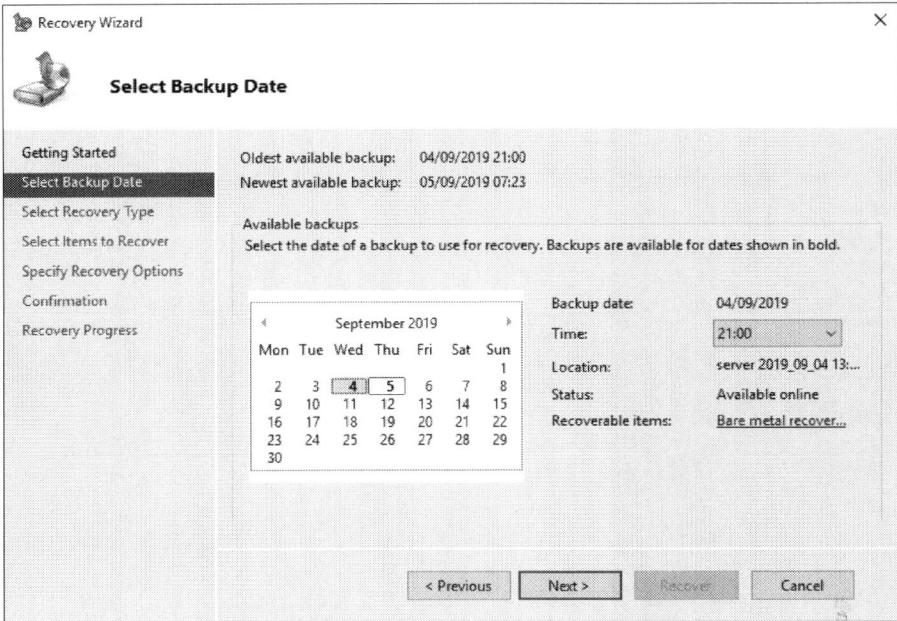

Figure 94: Choose a backup to recover from

The subsequent screen is for specifying what needs to be recovered. Most commonly, you would be recovering files and folders:

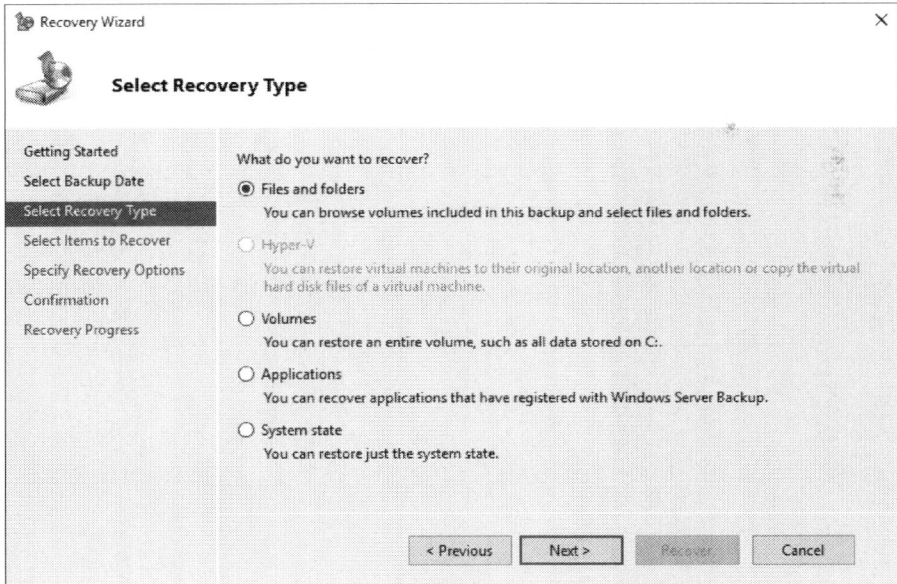

Figure 95: Select the recovery type

This is followed by a screen where the actual folders and files to be recovered are specified. Drill-down through the file structure in the left-hand panel and highlight the resultant items in the right-hand one. Then click **Next**:

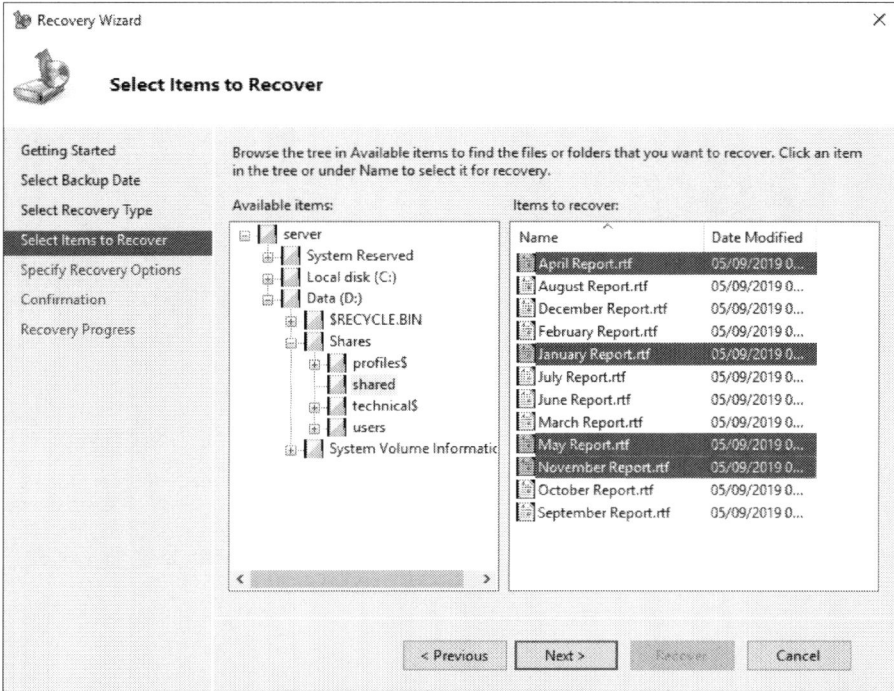

Figure 96: Select the items to recover

The next screen is for specifying options when recovering files. Specifically, should they be recovered to the original location or to another location and what to do when duplicates are found? Make a decision, leave the *Security settings* box ticked and click **Next**:

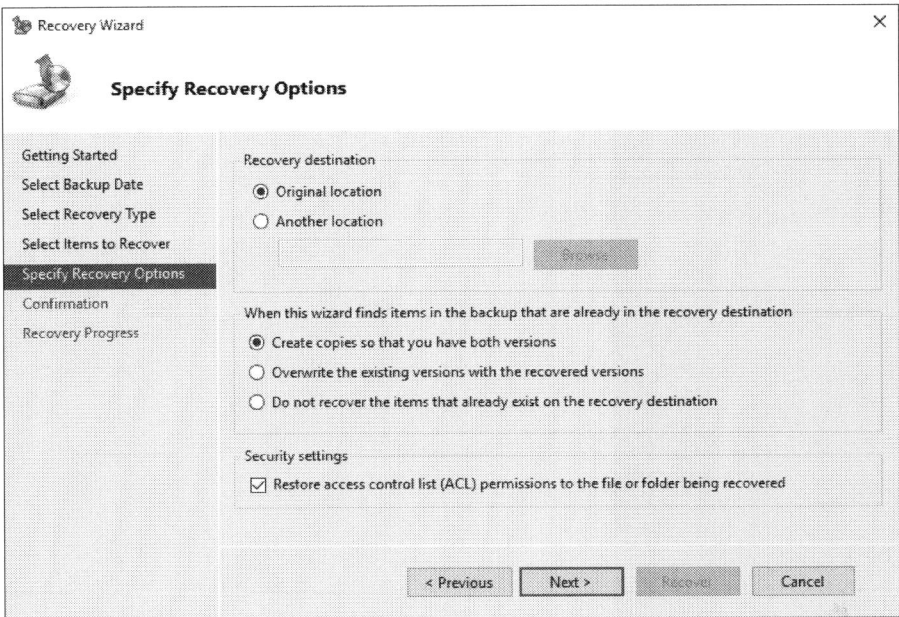

Figure 97: Specify recovery options

After clicking **Next**, a Confirmation screen is displayed. Click the **Recover** button to begin restoring the folders and files, during which time a status screen is shown. When complete, click **Close**.

7.4 Backing up the Server to a NAS Drive

One potential downside of using an USB drive for the backups is that it must be physically located close to the server. In the event of a disaster – for instance, fire, flood or theft – not only might the server be lost but the backup drive might be as well. One way to mitigate against this is to use a networked drive for backups, such as a NAS (Network Attached Storage) device. This gives a lot more flexibility as to where it is located, such as in a totally different part of the building. The network drive can be in addition to or in place of the USB drive; a further advantage of using NAS drives is that they are available in higher capacities that regular USB drives.

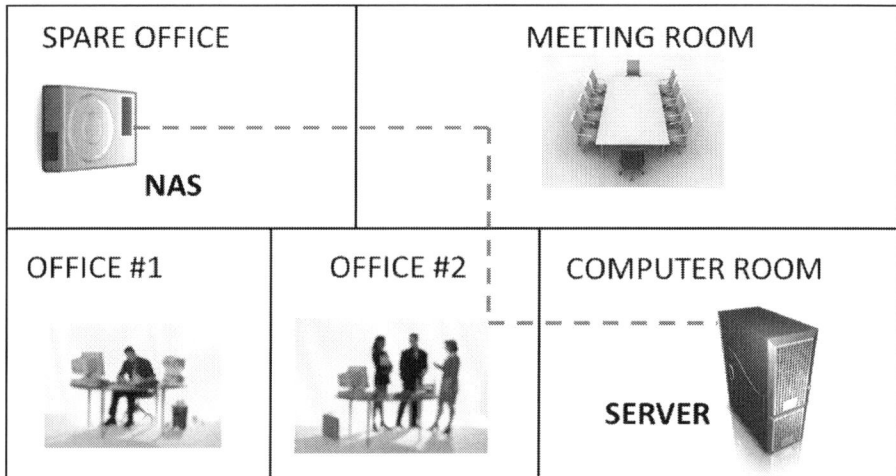

Figure 98: Locate the NAS drive in a separate part of the premises

As there are many different brands of NAS to choose from (e.g. Synology, QNAP, Netgear, TerraMaster and so on), the specifics of setting up a particular brand will not be covered and the manufacturer's documentation should be referred to. However, the basic principle is that a dedicated shared folder for backups with read/write access should be created on the NAS, along with a dedicated user backup account which will typically have administrative rights.

On the server run *Windows Server Backup*, click **Local Backup** followed by **Backup Once…** to create a new backup job. On the screen that appears choose **Different options** and click **Next**:

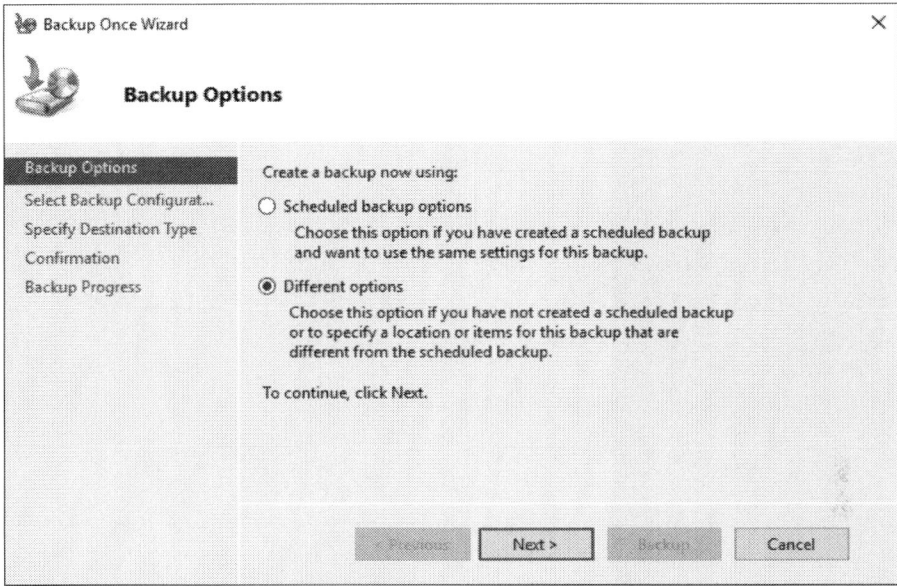

Figure 99: Choose a backup option

The subsequent screen gives a choice between a *Full server (recommended)* or *Custom* backup. Although the former might seem a better choice, choose **Custom** as the Full server backup will not work correctly with a networked backup drive. Click **Next**. On the following screen click **Add Items** and choose the items to be backed up. This would normally be just the disk volume containing the data, in our example the D: drive. Click **OK**.

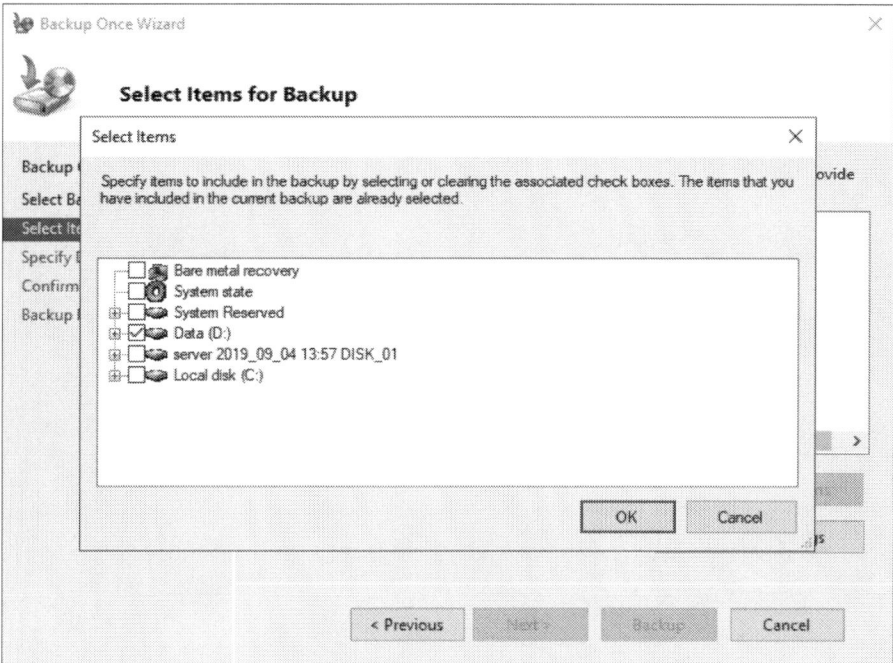

Figure 100: Select items to backup

You will be returned to the previous screen, where you should click **Next**. On the following screen the backup destination type has to be chosen – click **Remote shared folder** followed by **Next**. On the subsequent screen, enter the location of the NAS folder in the form *NAS_name**folder_name*. In this example, the NAS is called *nas-server* and the backup folder is called *netbackup*, hence *nas-server**netbackup*. Choose the **Do not inherit** option to enhance security and click **Next**:

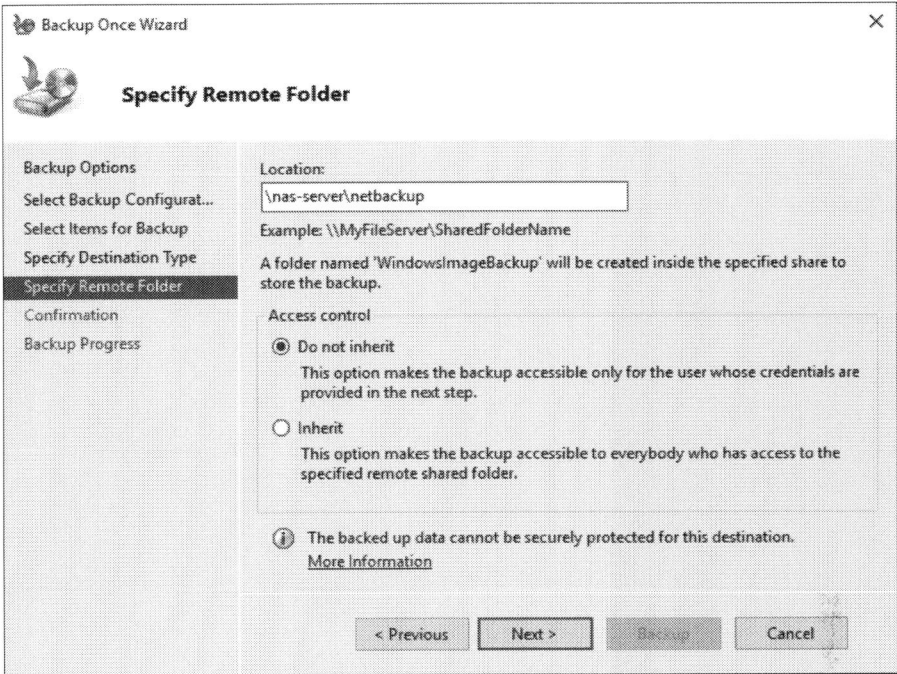

Figure 101: Specify the remote location

After a few seconds, there will be a prompt to enter a user name and password for the backup: this is for an account that has been defined on the NAS box, not one on the file server. Continue, and a confirmation screen will be shown. Click the **Backup** button to run the backup:

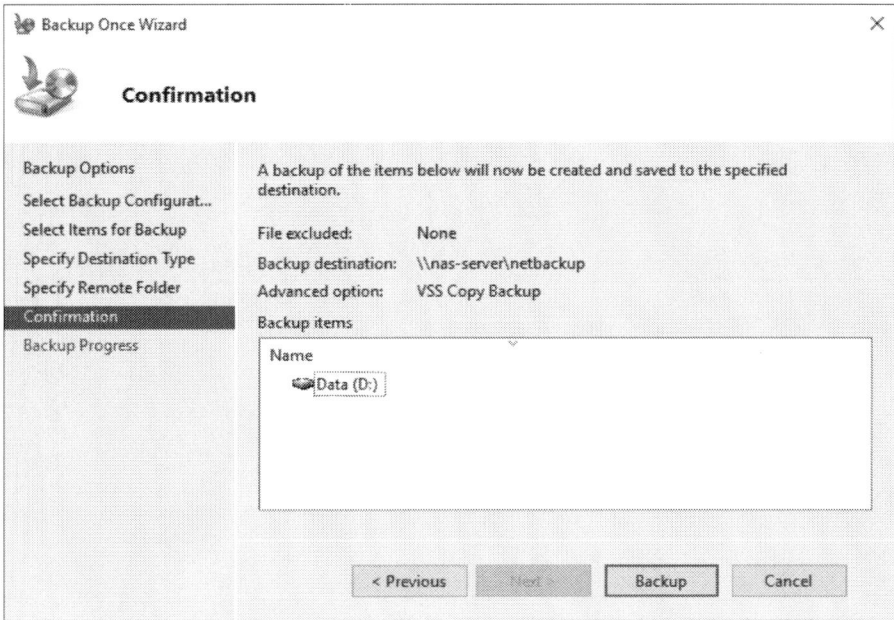

Figure 102: Backup confirmation screen

In this example, the backup to NAS has been run manually and in a way that does not interfere with the scheduled backup to USB. However, if backing up to NAS is to be the main backup, it can instead be scheduled as a regular job.

An additional advantage of using NAS devices is that they can be of higher storage capacities than USB drives. For instance, suppose the server had, say, 20 TB of data. At the time of writing it is not possible to buy USB drives of this capacity, whereas this amount of storage is readily achievable with a NAS. However, a disadvantage of using a NAS is that whereas an USB drive can hold multiple backups, when used with Windows Server Backup a network drive can only hold a single backup i.e. the most recent one. So, in the event of problems, it is only possible to revert to the last backup rather than a selection of older ones. Consequently, NAS might be more appropriate as a secondary or archive backup solution.

7.5 Backup Performance Settings

As mentioned previously, the backup process can be quite intensive in terms of impacting the performance of the server and for this reason it is possible to 'fine tune' it to some degree. From the main backup screen click **Configure Performance Settings...** on the right-hand side to display the following panel:

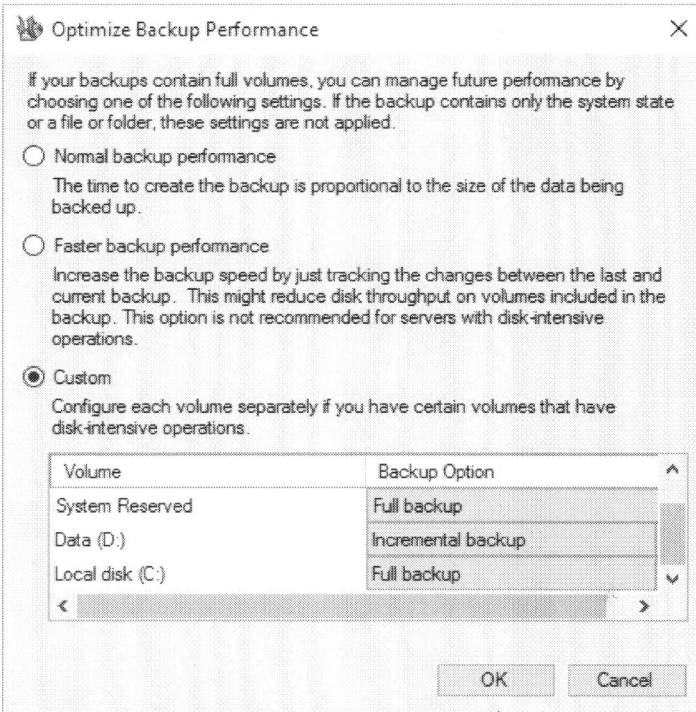

Figure 103: Optimize Backup Performance

There are three options:

Normal backup performance – the default – results in a full backup in which everything on the volume is backed up

Faster backup performance – only items which have changed since the last backup are backed up. Also known as an incremental backup

Custom – allows different volumes to be treated differently. For instance, you could choose to always do a full backup of the C: drive containing Windows, but incremental backups of the data drive(s) as shown above

Having made any changes click **OK**.

7.6 Backing up Computers to the Server

If users store data on their computers rather than on the network, then there is probably a requirement to be able to backup that data; consider, for example, laptop users who take their computers offsite. This can be done using the built-in backup programs in Windows Professional clients, with the backups stored on the server. As the server itself is being backed up, this will ensure multiple copies of the data, hopefully enough to cope with any eventuality. It is assumed that the user has a mapped home drive on the server, as described in section **5.10 Home Folders, User Profiles and Logon Scripts**.

Backing up Windows 10 Computers

Click **Start** > **Settings** > **Update & Security** > **Backup**. Click **Add a drive** and after a few seconds the list of mapped drives will be displayed – click on the user's home drive:

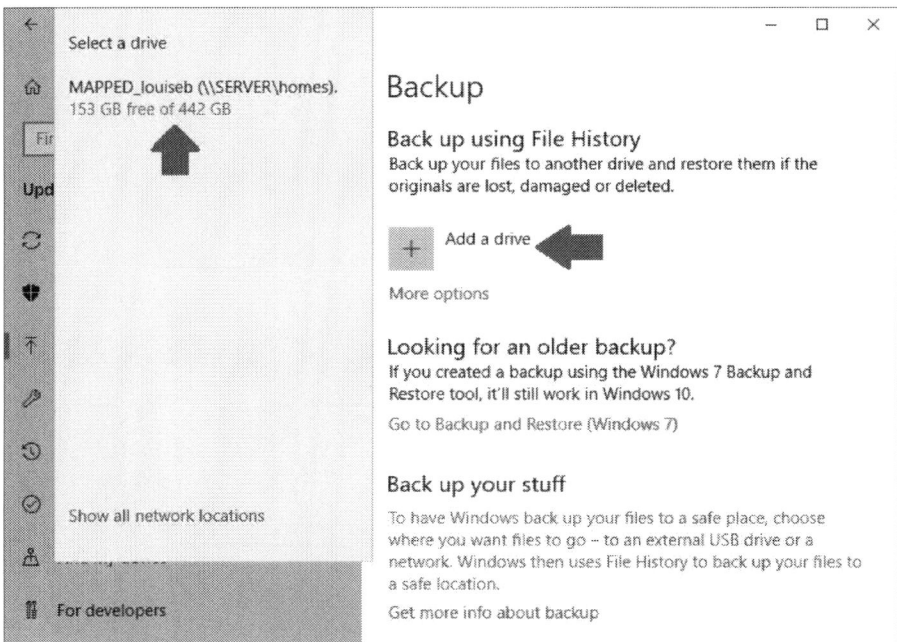

Figure 104: Specify the user's home folder as the backup drive

Having done so you will be returned to the main Backup panel, where an option to *Automatically back up my files will have appeared* and been set to **On**. That's it – a backup will now run on an hourly basis, copying the user's files from the computer to their home drive on the server.

For greater control over the process, such as controlling the frequency at which the backup runs, click M**ore options**. From here you can: review the backup status; make the backup run immediately; change the backup frequency (anything from every 10 minutes through to 1 day); change the retention period for the backed-up data:

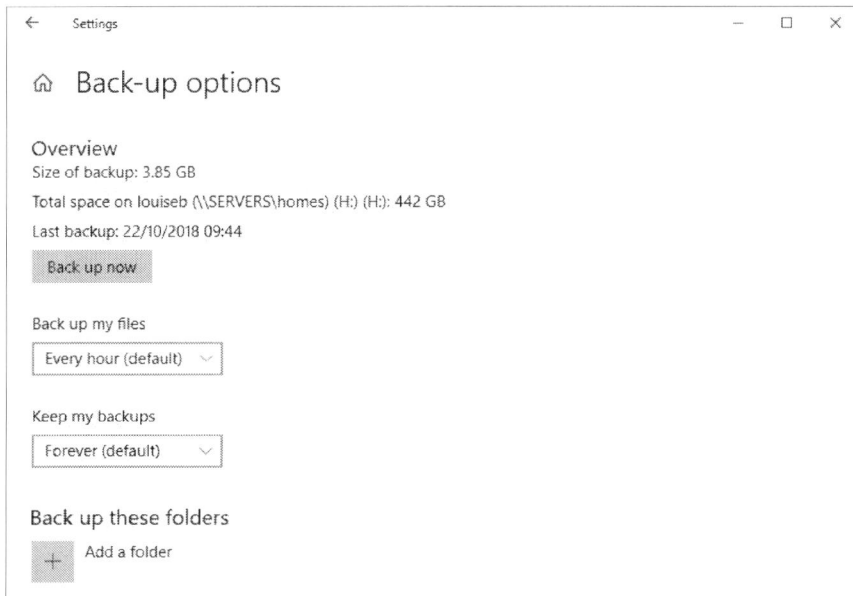

Figure 105: Additional backup options

Backing up Windows 7 Computers

Click **Start**, followed by **All Programs**, **Maintenance** then **Backup and Restore**. Click **Set up Backup** and then the **Save on a network** button. On the next panel, enter the **Network Location**. Specify the user's home folder, using the format *server**homes**username* (or click the **Browse** button to navigate to it).

You may be prompted to login - enter the user name and password as defined on the server and click **OK**:

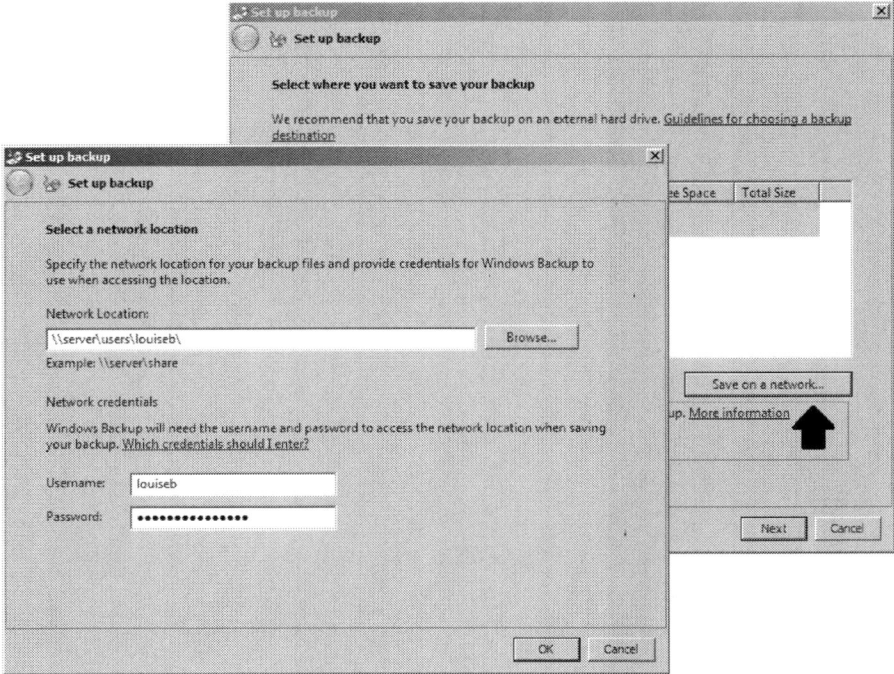

Figure 106: Enter network details

The subsequent screen is for choosing which data files are backed up. The default option of **Let Windows choose (recommended)** is fine in most cases, so just click **Next**. The follow-on screen is a summary of settings: click **Save settings and run backup**. The backup will then run for the first time, during which the status is displayed. By default, Windows has defined a schedule to subsequently run backups automatically on a regular basis (in this case, every Sunday at 7:00pm). If this setting is not suitable it can be changed by clicking **Change settings**.

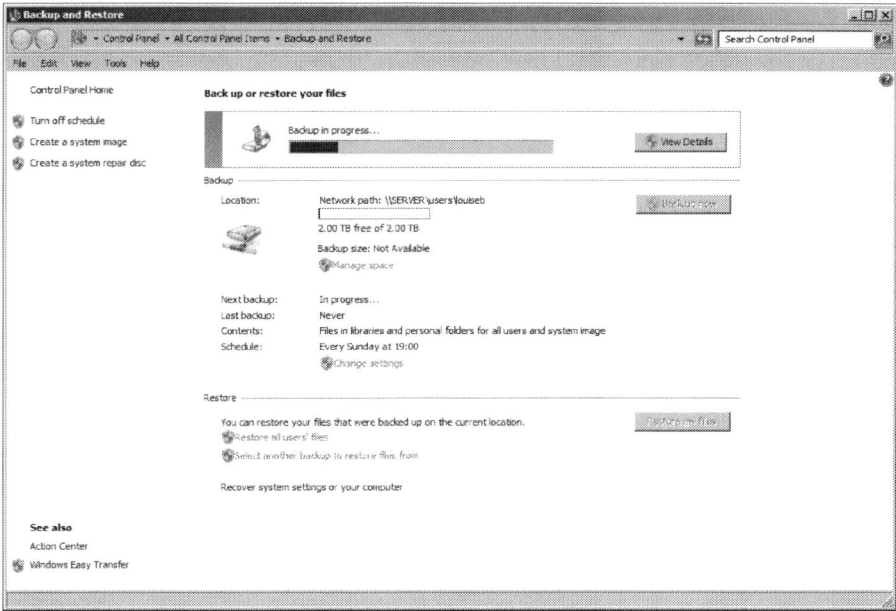

Figure 107: Backup in progress

8

PRINTING

8.1 Overview

An advantage of networking is that it allows printers to be shared, thus potentially saving money as well as physical space. There are several different techniques for setting up printers in a networked environment and two of them are discussed in this chapter. Each of them has benefits and disadvantages and there is probably no such thing as 'the best' solution; however, some explanation is given as to when you might take a particular approach.

Before beginning, identify the client operating systems that are in use and download all the appropriate printer drivers from the printer manufacturer's website. Generally speaking, modern printers have universal drivers that will work with all modern versions of Windows, but sometimes there are separate drivers for 32-bit versions (usually referred to as x86 or x32) and 64-bit versions (usually referred to as x64). Some manufacturers offer an additional choice of drivers, for instance a basic one as well as a full-featured one. Use the basic one – the 'full feature' ones sometimes have superfluous features designed to capture marketing information and try to sell you more consumables. Be aware that with some multifunction devices (combined printers/copiers/scanners), not all functions may be available in a networked environment, or may require additional software from the manufacturer to fully utilize them.

Next, physically setup the printer and give it a static IP address consistent with the IP addressing scheme used in the network. This can be done on the printer itself, or via an IP reservation on the router or other source of DHCP. Check that the printer is working correctly before beginning the installations on the clients. You may well find that upon setting up the printer and powering it on, Windows Server may detect it automatically.

Suggestion: a good location to store the printer drivers is the *technical* share, accessible as *server**technical$* by administrative users.

8.2 Independent Networked Printer

Most printers, other than very low cost and old models, have built-in network adaptors, either wired and/or wireless. This means that they can operate independently of the file server, with the computers talking to them directly. This is the simplest and most effective method for setting up a printer in a small business network and will suit many organizations. This approach also works very well in a scenario where many different operating systems are in use.

The printer(s) should be physically setup and connected to the network **before** the computers are added to the domain. Then:

- Visit each individual computer and login as a local user with administrative rights. Or, if developing a master disk image that will subsequently be cloned - also referred to as *Ghosting* - work on that image.
- Install the printer through the standard Windows methods; with Windows 10, **Start > Settings > Devices > Printers & scanners > Add a printer or scanner**; with previous versions of Windows, **Control Panel > Devices and Printers > Add Printer**. Or, by using the manufacturer's provided installation program.
- Specify the printer as being on a TCP/IP port. Provide the static IP address of the printer.
- Set the printer as the default printer.
- Change any defaults if necessary e.g. paper size, print quality and so on.
- Remove any superfluous 'virtual' printers if they are not going to be used (e.g. OneNote, fax, XPS)
- Print a test page to verify correct operation

The computers can then be added to the domain. The printer will appear in the list of printers for each user, although they may have to explicitly choose it and assign it as their default printer.

8.3 Shared Printer via Active Directory

With this method, the printer(s) are installed initially on the server and defined as shared resources; users can then choose to connect to them from their computers if they so wish. This approach has value where there are multiple printers in use and the users are technically literate. Also, it allows new printers to be installed retrospectively after the network has already been setup, in contrast with the previous method where the printer(s) are installed before the computers are connected to the domain. However, with this approach the users need to have some administrative rights on the domain; one way of doing this is described in **13.3 Setup Alternative Administrator Account(s)**. Alternatively the printer can be installed by the administrator.

Sometimes, the act of powering up a new printer will cause Windows Server to recognize it and automatically install it for the server. If this has happened, you can skip the next few paragraphs and jump to the 'Sharing Settings' section below.

Install Printer

From **Server Manager**, click **Tools > Print Management**. Expand the left-hand panel and highlight *Printers*, then right-click it and choose **Add Printer** (alternatively, on the right-hand *Actions* panel, click **More Actions > Add Printer**). This will cause the server to look for the printer.

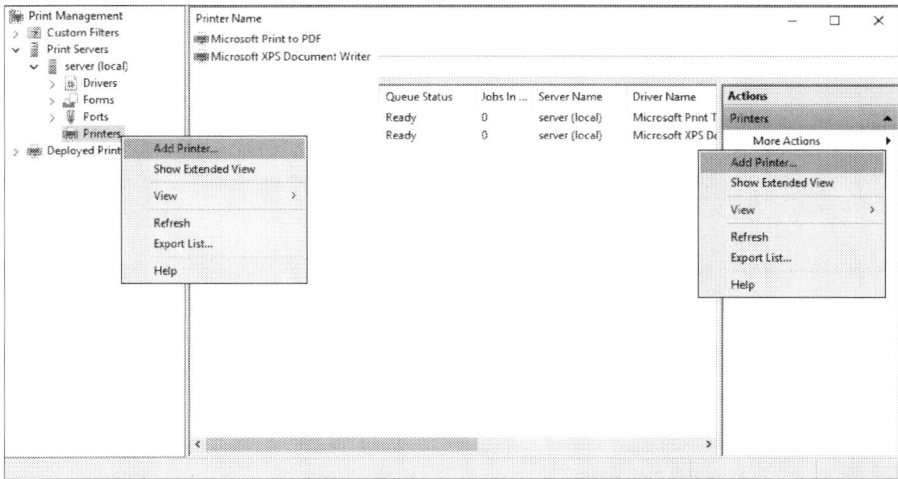

Figure 108: Adding a printer

If the printer is not found during the search phase: click **Back**; choose **Add a TCP/IP or Web Services printer by IP address or hostname**; click **Next**. Specify the *Device type* as **TCP/IP Device,** enter the printer's IP address and click **Next**. There may be a delay of several minutes whilst the port and printer type are identified. Work through each page in turn and install the printer driver, which can be a matter of choosing it from the list, clicking **Windows Update** or clicking **Have Disk** as appropriate.

On the *Printer Name and Sharing Settings* panel, tick the **Share this printer** box. Give it a meaningful **Share name** and use the **Location** and **Comment** fields to provide helpful information, then click **Next**:

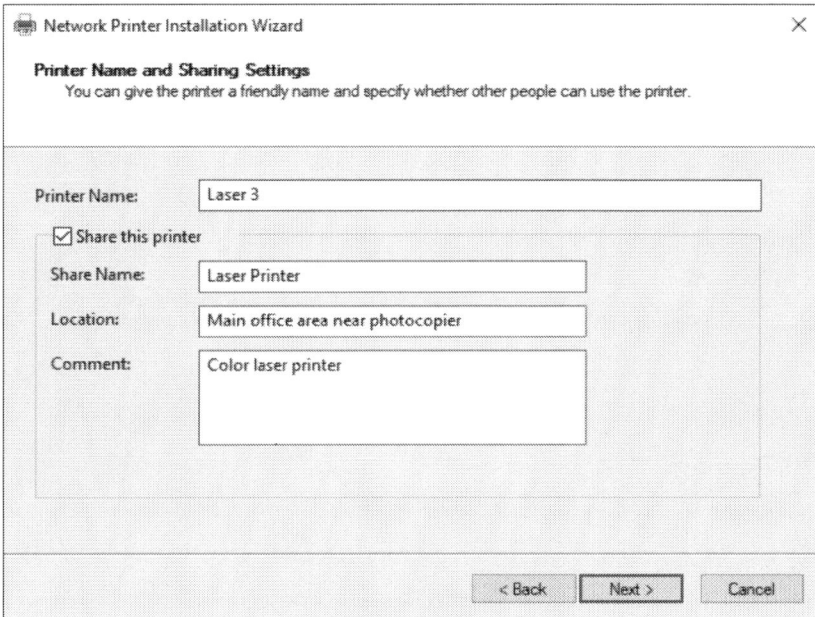

Figure 109: Printer Sharing

Complete the installation and check that it is working by printing a test page.

Sharing Settings

The printer should be listed within the main Print Management screen. Right-click it and choose **Properties**. Click the **Sharing** tab. Make sure that the **Share this printer, Render print jobs on client computers** and **List in the directory** boxes are ticked:

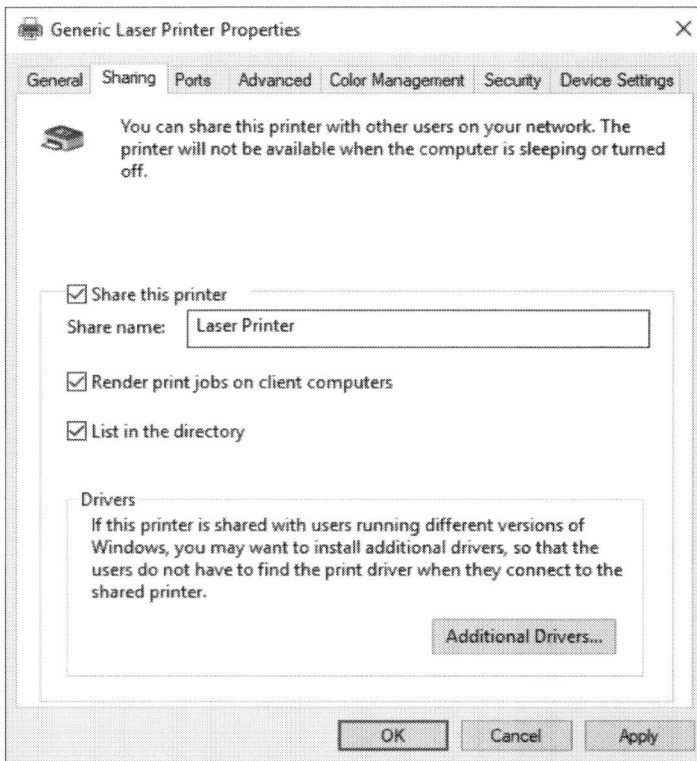

Figure 110: Properties for shared printer

If all the client computers are using 64-bit versions of Windows, then we are complete on the server side, so click **Apply** and **OK**. However, if any client computers are using 32-bit versions of Windows or ARM-based versions, then click the **Additional Drivers** button. On the next panel, tick the appropriate box(es) and click **OK**. This reflects a not uncommon scenario with printers, referred to by Microsoft as *Type 3* printers. With some printers – usually more recent models referred to by Microsoft as *Type 4* printers – this step is not needed as the drivers will work with all modern versions of Windows regardless of whether they are 32-bit or 64-bit:

Figure 111: Additional printer drivers

Having clicked **OK**, you will then be prompted to enter the location of the x86 ("32-bit") driver and/or ARM driver. Follow the screens through then click **Apply** followed by **OK**.

The printer can now be installed on the client computers. To do this, a user must have administrative rights or, when prompted, enter the account details of an administrative user. This procedure varies slightly, depending upon the version of Windows - this example uses Windows 10. Click **Start > Settings > Devices > Printers & scanners**. Click **Add a printer or scanner**. The computer will search for printers and list the one(s) provided by the server. Highlight the desired printer and click **Add device**. The printer will be installed, picking up the appropriate driver from the server, and after a short delay will appear in the list of Printers & scanners. It is now available for normal use:

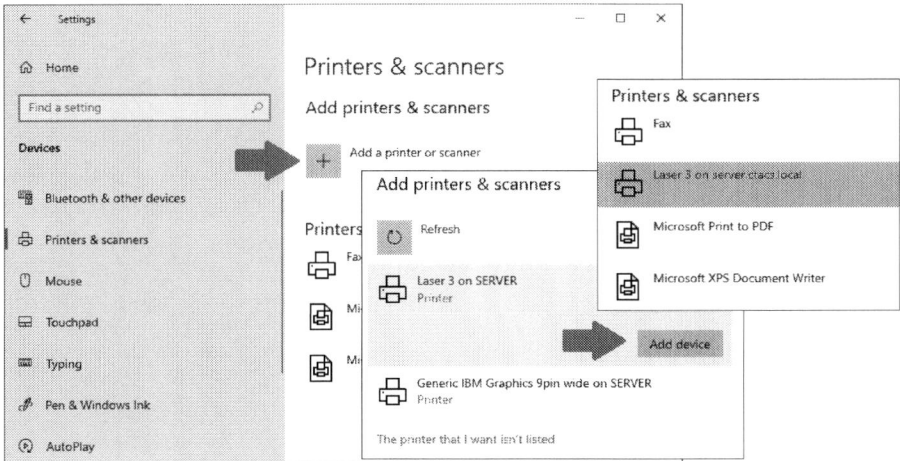

Figure 112: Adding a printer

9

REMOTE ACCESS:
VPN & CLOUD SERVICES

9.1 Overview

Note 1: some governments block VPN access, particularly to computer systems located outside of their territory.

Note 2: VPN services are also used to provide anonymous access to the internet, for instance to avoid censorship and geographical restrictions. That is a very different use of the term and Windows-based VPNs do not provide this capability.

The purpose of a *Virtual Private Network* or VPN is to securely extend a network to users who are offsite, such as home workers or those in a remote office. Think of it as the equivalent of having a very long network cable that reaches out from the office for 10, 100, 1000 miles/km or more. However, instead of an actual cable the connection goes over the internet, with powerful encryption and other techniques used to maintain security. One advantage of a VPN is that it allows full access to files and folders for editing, just as in the office. One big disadvantage: VPNs can be notoriously difficult to setup, configure and diagnose. For many users, virtual private networks are an advanced topic and because of this, some small business users may wish to look at simpler alternatives for remote access, for example a cloud-based service such as Dropbox (see **9.7 Using Dropbox with Windows Server**).

To use a VPN, you will need a *domain name* or *host name*. You may recall that you have an *internal domain name*, for example *ctacs.local*, but this cannot be accessed from over the internet and you therefore also require an *external domain name*, which can be accessed. Examples of external domain names would be *www.ctacs.co.uk, www.google.com, www.microsoft.com* and so on. They can be obtained from domain registration companies such as *GoDaddy, Register.Com, Name.Com* and others. Your internet service provider (ISP) may also be able to provide a domain name.

An alternative is to use a *Dynamic Domain Naming Service* or *DDNS*. Rather than registering your own domain name, you use an off-the-shelf name from a DDNS provider, some of which operate on a commercial basis, whilst others are totally free. The name is programmed into your router; if the IP address provided by your ISP changes - as it may do when the router is restarted for instance - then the router advises the DDNS provider and their records are instantly updated. Do not be discouraged by the use of the term 'programmed' – this feature is supported in most routers and it is just a matter of typing in the name of the domain, although not all DDNS providers are supported by all routers. Free DDNS providers include *No-IP*, *DNSdynamic.org*, *zonedit* and others.

VPNs come in a variety of 'flavors', based around different protocols. The most popular one is called *L2TP/IPSec*; it has good security and is supported natively by modern versions of Windows and other platforms. In this walkthrough we will concentrate on connecting Windows 10 and Windows 7 clients, as these are the most common environments.

There are four stages to setting up a VPN: first, install the appropriate role on the server; second, configure the router; thirdly, enable remote access for users; finally, configure the client computers.

9.2 Installing & Configuring Remote Access

Begin by installing the *Remote Access* role to the server. From Server Manager, click **Manage > Add Roles and Features**. Choose **Role-based or feature-based installation** and click **Next**. Select the server on the following screen and click **Next**. From the list of server roles, tick **Remote Access** and click **Next**:

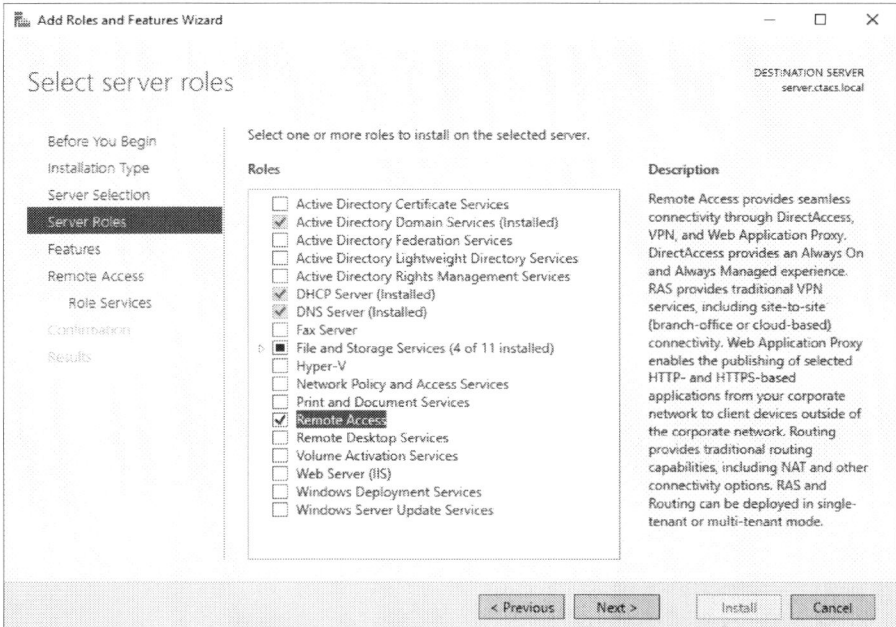

Figure 113: Select Remote Access role

Click **Next** on the following two screens then, on the *Role Services* screen, tick **Direct Access and VPN (RAS)**. Immediately, another panel will appear about adding features that are required. Click **Add Features** and then **Next** when returned to the previous screen:

155

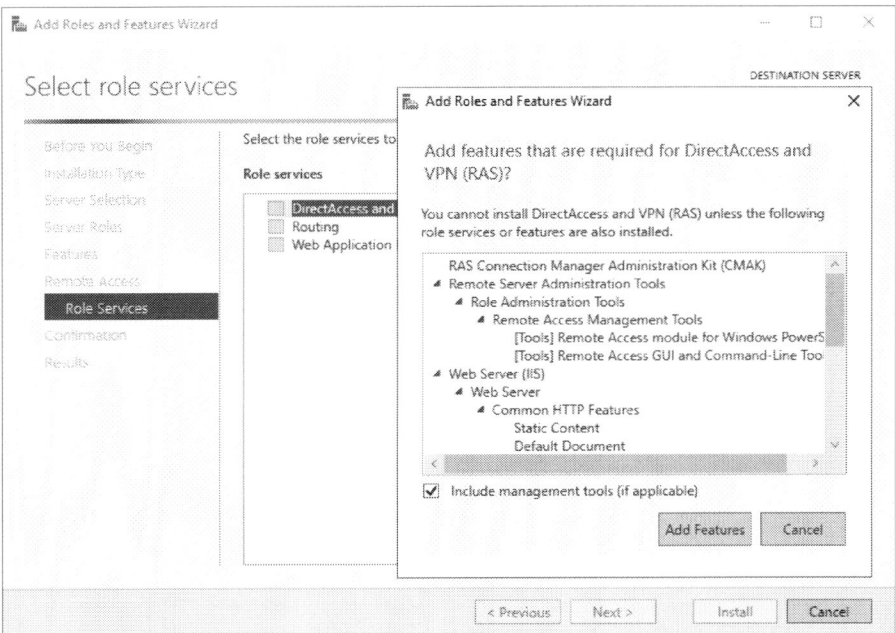

Figure 114: Add additional features

A screen about installing the *Web Server Role (IIS)* is displayed
– click **Next** and then **Next** again on the subsequent screen
about 'Selecting role services':

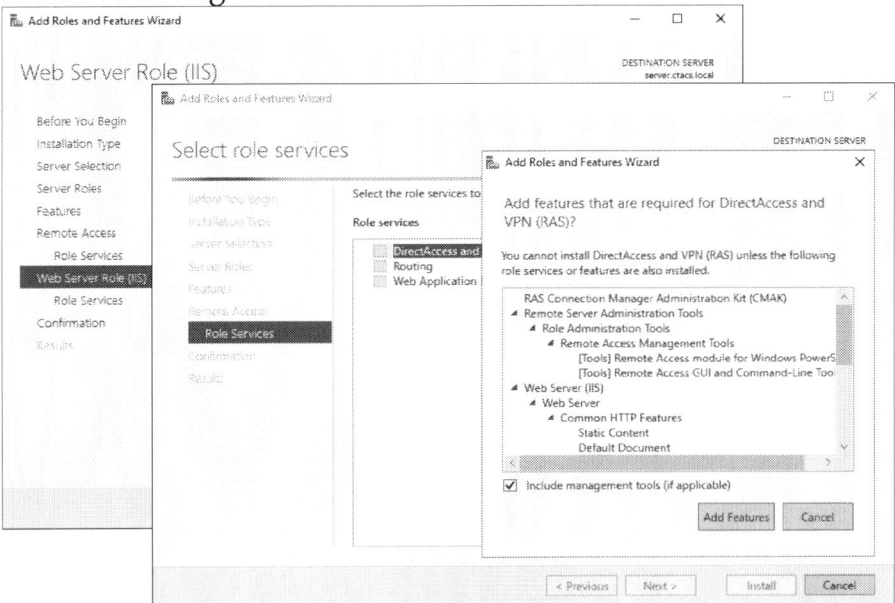

Figure 115: Server Roles

On the *Confirm installation selections* screen, tick the **Restart the destination server automatically if required box**, followed by **Install** button. When the installation has completed, which will take a couple of minutes, click **Close**.

Within the main Server Manager screen, click the newly added *Remote Access* option on the left-hand side. There is a message towards the top of the screen, advising *'Configuration required for DirectAccess and VPN(RAS)'* - click where it reads **More:**

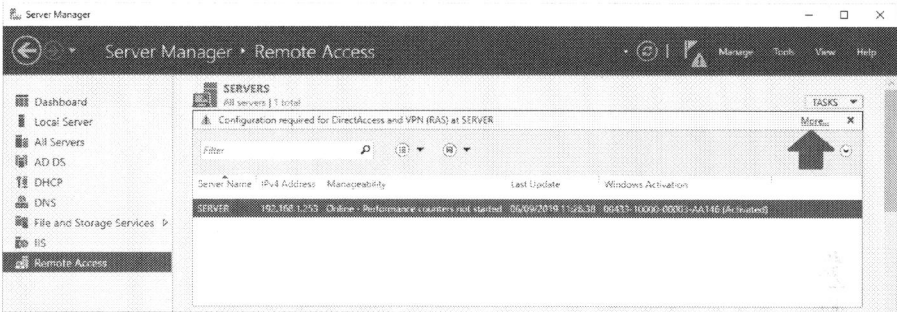

Figure 116: Configuration required message

On the resultant panel, click **Open the Getting Started Wizard** to display the following. Click **Deploy VPN only**:

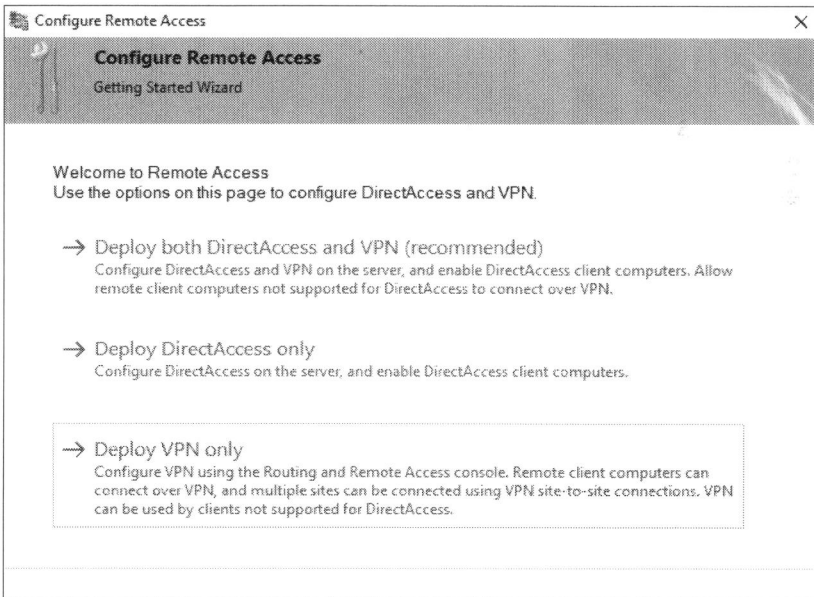

Figure 117: Configure Remote Access Wizard

The *Routing and Remote Access Management Console* is displayed; right-click the server and choose **Configure and Enable Routing and Remote Access** from the pop-up menu:

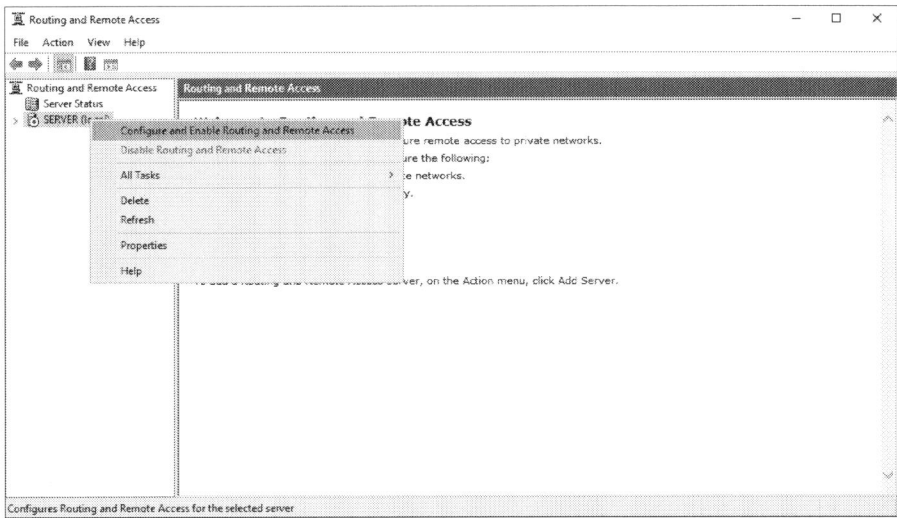

Figure 118: Routing and Remote Access Management Console

The *Routing and Remote Access Server Setup Wizard* will run. Click **Next** on the first panel. On the second one, choose **Custom configuration**, click **Next**, followed by **VPN access** and **Next** on the subsequent one:

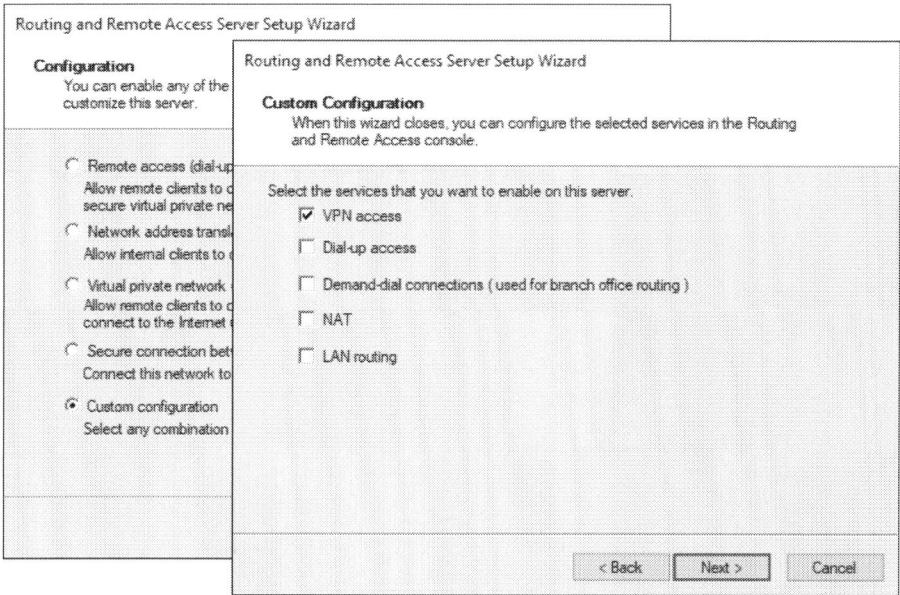

Figure 119: Choose Custom Configuration

A confirmation message is then displayed; click **Finish**, followed by **Start Service**:

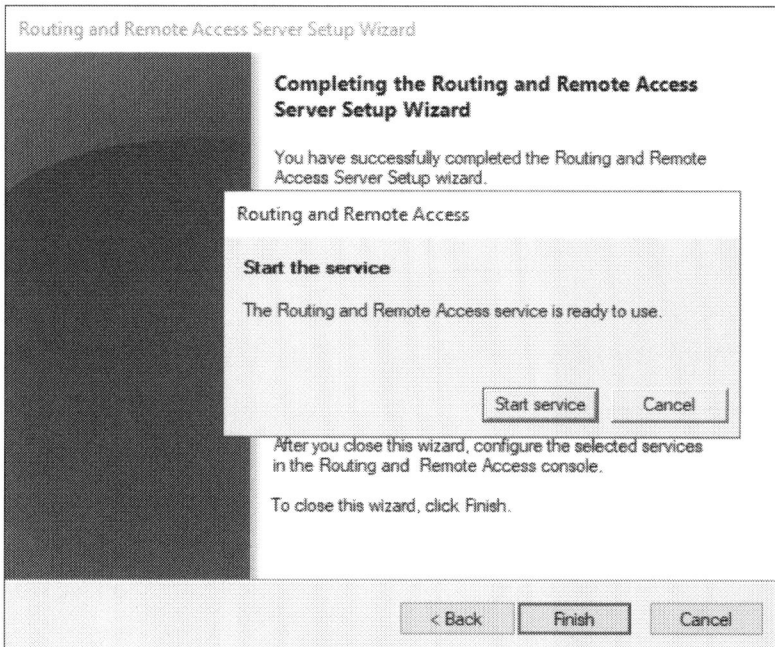

Figure 120: Start the Routing and Remote Access service

It was mentioned previously that VPNs are available in several varieties and we will be using L2TP/IPSec flavor. Within the Routing and Remote Access console, right-click the server, click **Properties** on the pop-up menu, then click the **Security** tab on the resultant panel. Tick the **Allow custom Ipsec policy for L2TP/IKEv2 connection** box and specify a **Preshared Key**, which can be considered as a type of system-wide password. It is best to choose something non-obvious, such as a random mix of upper- and lower-case letters, numbers and symbols:

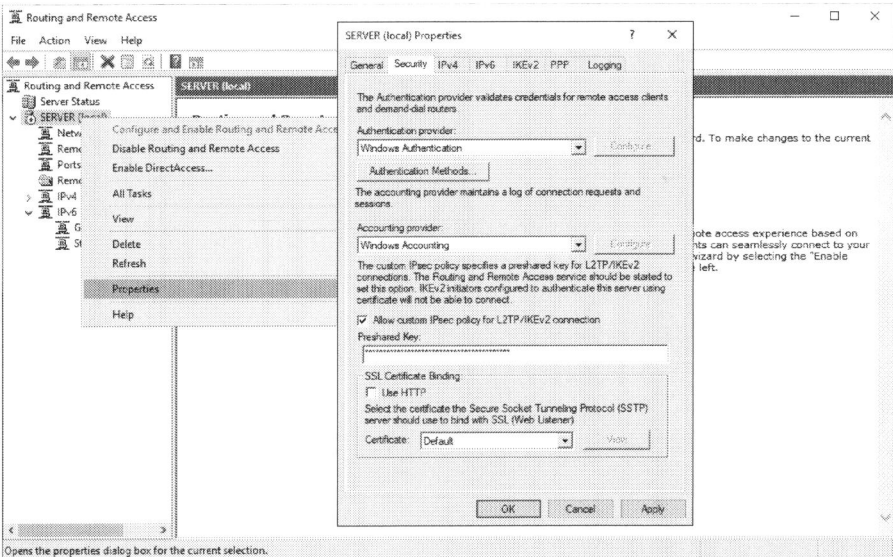

Figure 121: Specify the Preshared Key

Click **OK**. A message is displayed, advising that Routing and Remote Access needs to be restarted. Click **OK** to return to the main screen and on it right-click the server and choose **All Tasks > Restart**.

9.3 Configure the Router

For remote access to work, the appropriate ports on the router need to be forwarded to the internal IP address of the server. Specifically:

- For PPTP, port 1723 TCP should be forwarded to the server
- For L2TP/IPSEC, ports 1701 TCP and 500 UDP need to be forwarded to the server
- For SSTP, port 443 TCP needs to be forwarded to the server

Windows Server cannot setup the port forwarding by itself; rather, it is necessary to login to the router and configure it. As there are thousands of different routers available, it is not appropriate to give a worked example here. However, instructions for doing so for most popular routers can be found at the *www.portforward.com* website.

If you are working in an environment with a separate firewall appliance, this should also be configured to allow network traffic through the appropriate ports reference above.

9.4 Enabling Remote Access for Users

Users do not receive remote access capabilities by default and have to be specifically enabled. From the Server Manager Dashboard, choose **Tools > Active Directory Administrative Centre**. Locate the user and double-click their name or right-click the name and choose **Properties**. Scroll down to the *Extensions* section and click the archaically-named **Dial-in** tab. In the *Network Access Permission section*, click **Allow access**, followed by **OK**:

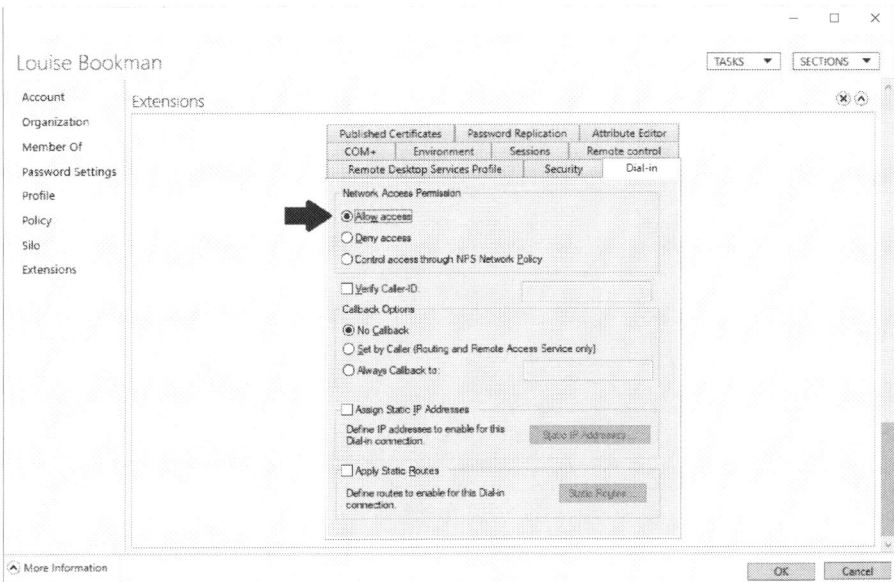

Figure 122: Enable remote access for a user

9.5 Connecting Client Computers

VPN support is built-in on most versions of Windows and client software is readily available for other platforms. This section covers installation on two popular platforms: Windows 10 and Windows 7. There may be some minor variations depending on what type of VPN you are using plus any security options you may have chosen (here we are using L2TP/IPSec).

Windows 10 Clients

Click **Start > Settings > Network & Internet > VPN > Add a VPN connection** to display the following panel:

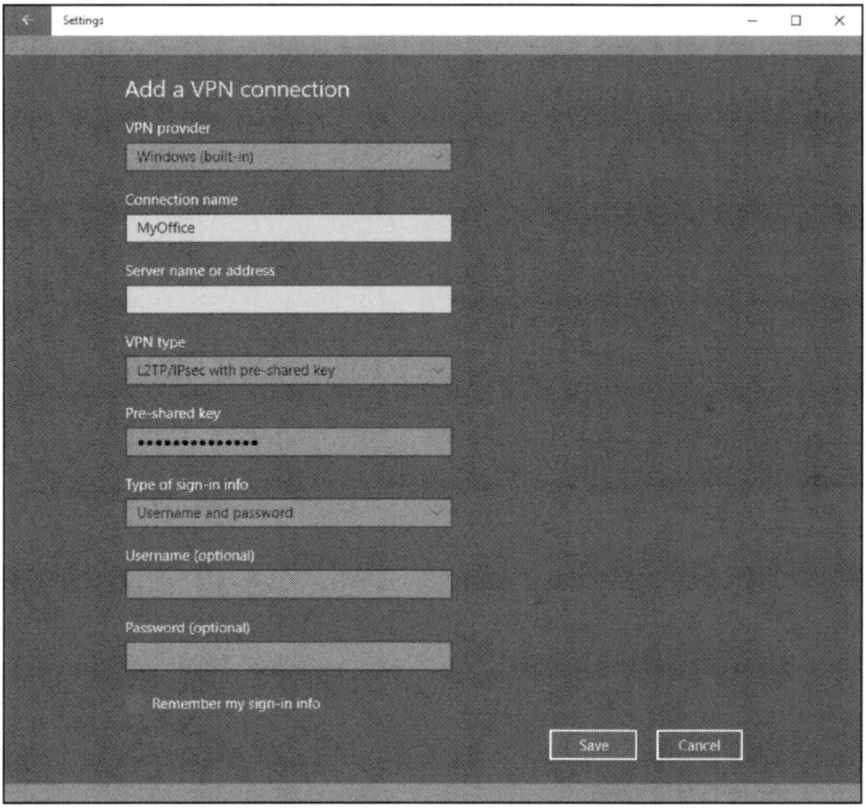

Figure 123: Adding a new VPN connection

Click **VPN provider** and choose *Windows (built-in)*, which will normally be the only option available. Specify a **Connection name** e.g. *MyOffice*. For the **Server name or address** enter the external domain name or IP address of the server. Set the **VPN type** to **L2TP/Ipsec with pre-shared key** and enter the pre-shared key you specified when configuring Routing and Remote Access on the server. The **Type of sign-in info** should be *Username and password*. For security reasons it is suggested that you do not specify what the **Username** and **Password** are and do not tick the **Remember my sign-in info** box. Click **Save**.

The newly defined connection will now be listed on the VPN section within *Settings*. Click it and then click the **Connect** button. You will be prompted to Sign in – enter your **Username** and **Password** as defined on the server and click **OK**. After a short while, the status will change to *Connected*.

You can now access resources on the server as though you were in the office. For instance, press the **Windows key** and the **R key** simultaneously and in the run box type \ \ *server* \ *shared* to display and access the shared folder.

When you have finished using the VPN, click the **Disconnect** button.

Windows 7 Clients
Go into the **Control Panel** and choose **Network and Sharing Centre**, then click **Setup a new connection or network**. On the panel that pops up choose **Connect to a workplace** followed by **Next**; on the subsequent screen click **Use my Internet connection (VPN)**:

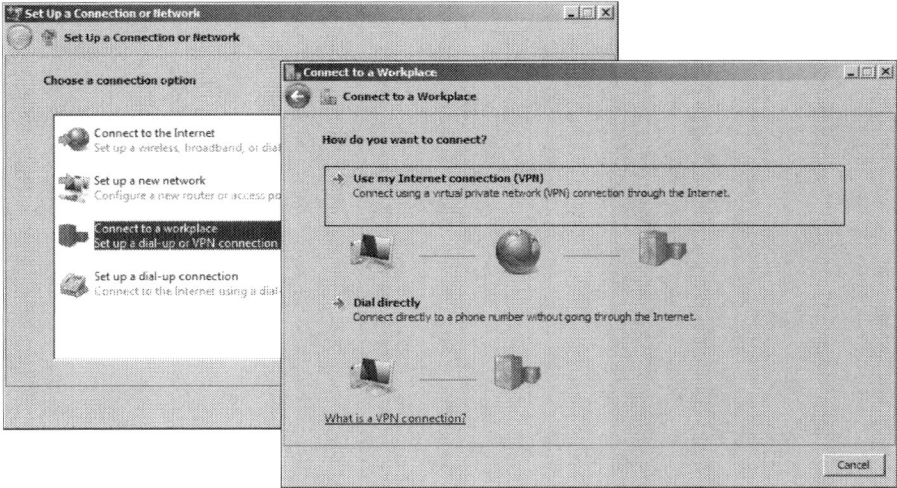

Figure 124: Setup a new connection in Windows 7

On the next panel, specify the external domain name or IP address of the server. Specify a **Destination name**, such as *MyOffice*. Tick the **Don't connect now** box and click **Next**:

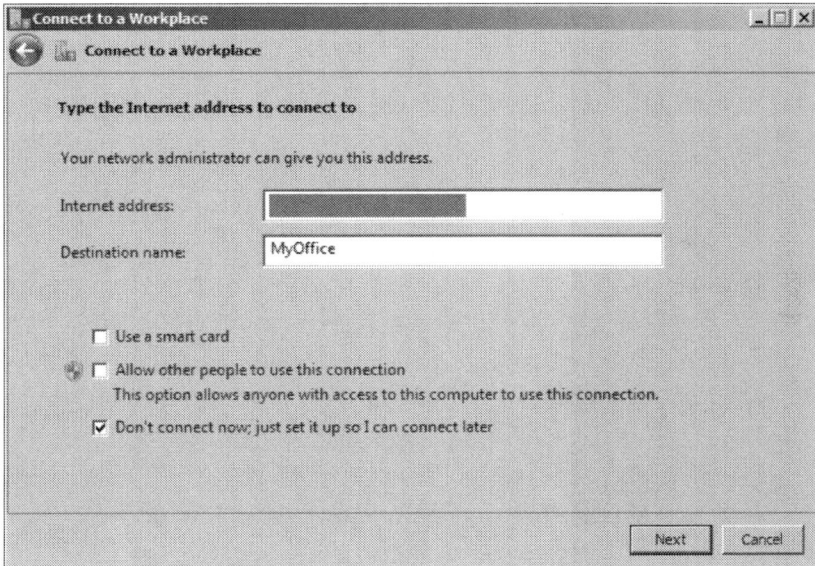

Figure 125: Specify the internet address of the server

On the following screen enter the user name and password (it is not necessary to enter the Domain name):

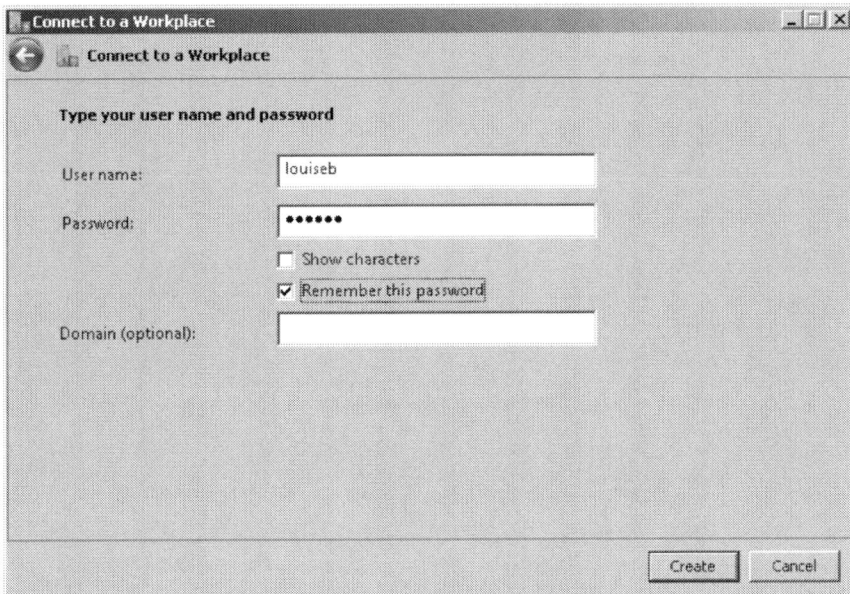

Figure 126: Enter user name and password

Assuming all is well, a few seconds later a confirmation screen will be shown. Click **Close**.

Return to the **Control Panel** and choose **Network and Sharing Center**. Click **Change adapter settings**; the newly created VPN connection will be listed alongside the computer's normal network connection(s). Right-click it and choose **Properties**. Click the **Security** tab. Change the *Type of VPN* to **Layer 2 Tunneling Protocol with IPSec (L2TP/IPSec)** and change *Data Encryption* to read **Optional encryption (connect even if no encryption).** Click the **Allow these protocols** option. Click the **Advanced settings** button and enter the *Pre-shared key for authentication* which you specified when configuring Routing and Remote Access on the server. Click **OK**. The panel should now appear as follows; click **OK**:

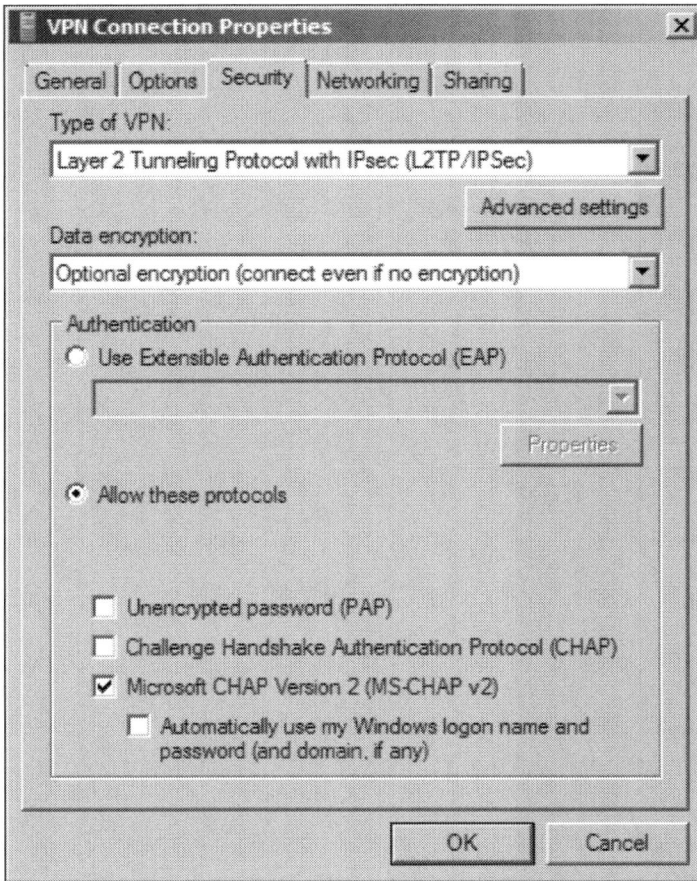

Figure 127: VPN connection properties

At this point the connection should be tested from outside the premises. Click the network icon on the Taskbar to display a list of available network connections, then click the VPN Connection (*MyOffice* in our example) and the **Connect** button that subsequently appears. A logon panel is shown; enter the user name and password (there is no Domain name) and click **Connect**:

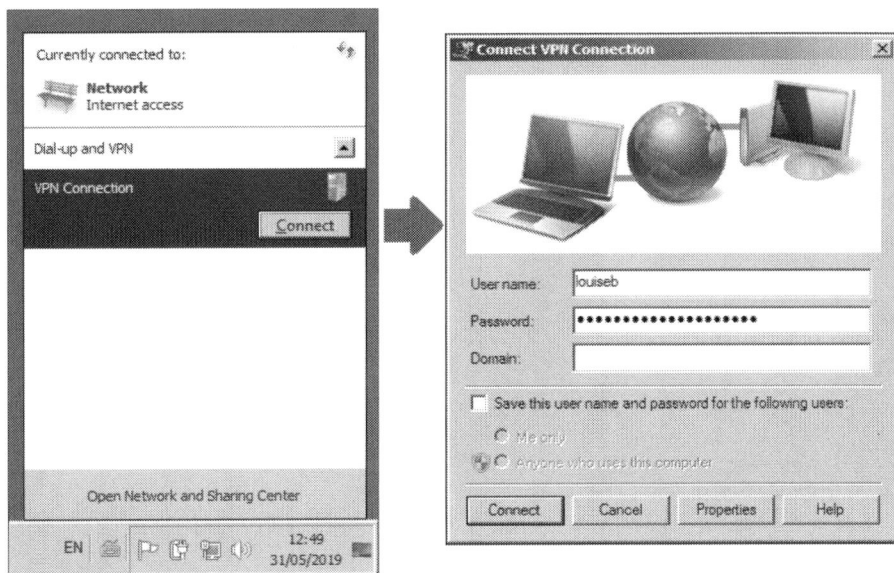

Figure 128: Connecting to the VPN

A few seconds later you should be connected. The first time you connect you may receive a prompt asking you to choose the network location; a choice of *Home, Work* and *Public* is given, if so choose **Home** or **Work** (they are effectively the same thing). You can now access resources on the server as though you were in the office. For instance, press the **Windows key** and the **R key** simultaneously and in the run box type \ *server\shared* to display and access the shared folder.

When you have finished, click the network icon on the Taskbar to again display the list of network connections on the right-hand side of the screen. This time click the VPN Connection (*'MyOffice'*) followed by the **Disconnect** button.

9.6 Checking and Monitoring Remote Users

To manage remote users, go into Server Manager and choose **Tool**s > **Remote Access Management**. On the resultant screen that appears – the *Remote Access Dashboard* – click **Remote Client Status** on the left-hand side and the list of connected users will be displayed.

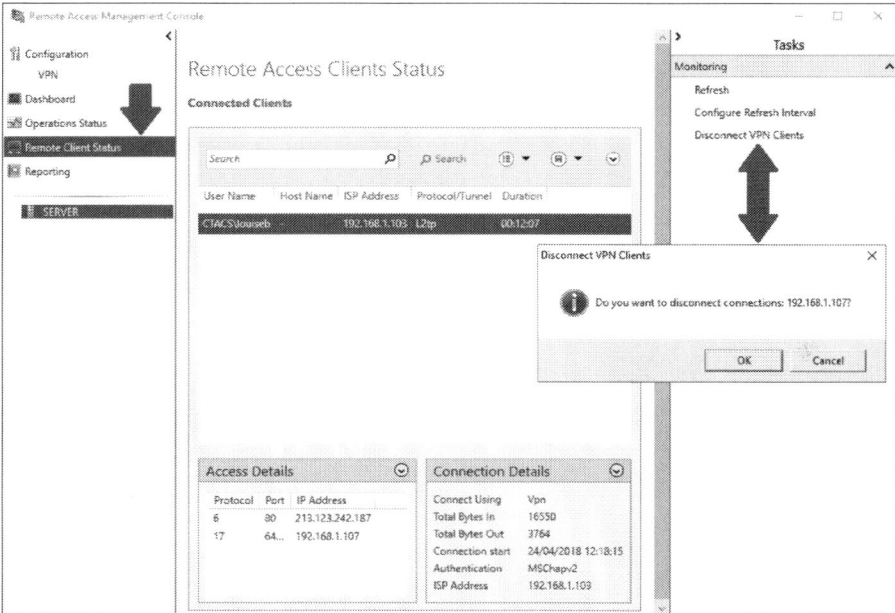

Figure 129: Remote Access Clients Status

To disconnect clients, click **Disconnect VPN Clients** from the right-hand side of the screen. A confirmation message is displayed, which has to be acknowledged.

9.7 Using Dropbox with Windows Server

Whilst a VPN can provide a comprehensive solution for remote working, it can be complicated to setup and operate. However, a simple and popular method to indirectly provide remote access to a selection of data is by using a Cloud-based file sync service, such as *Dropbox*. Dropbox can provide remote access to data in an easier fashion, with less effort and on a wider range of devices, plus it can provide controlled access to selected files for third parties via emailed links. It can also or alternatively be used as a way of backing up data from the server, providing offsite storage to complement the internal backup. Microsoft have a direct competitor to Dropbox in the form of *OneDrive*, although this is not installed as part of Windows Server in the way that it is with Windows 10, possibly because Microsoft would rather you use their more comprehensive and lucrative *Azure* offering (and there are some technical challenges in getting it to work properly, in case you are tempted). Other cloud-based file sync services are available, but in practice Dropbox just seems to work very well.

There are several considerations when using Dropbox with Windows Server:

1. A single Dropbox account is used for everyone
2. The account should have sufficient storage space. Dropbox offer different accounts with varying amounts of storage in the form of *Dropbox Basic, Dropbox Plus* and *Dropbox Business*, with some targeted at individuals and others at teams. Dropbox Basic is free but has only 2GB of space, although it is possible to gain additional space through referrals. This is unlikely to be enough so consider a paid account, such as a Dropbox Business account that can provide terabytes of space for a relatively low monthly charge, along with some other benefits.

3. Some versions only permit a limited number of users/devices e.g. Dropbox Basic is restricted to three computers.
4. Decide whether it will be used for additional backups or as a means of providing remote access to data from outside of the office
5. Who has access to it? If used for backups only, then only the server administrator needs access.
6. Who will be responsible for managing it (usually the person who controls the server administrator account)?
7. What happens when individuals leave the organization?

If you are uncertain as to whether Dropbox is suitable for your organization, then consider using a free or trial version to first assess it. Begin by installing the Dropbox client on the server; this is best done by downloading it directly from the Dropbox home page. Note: this will be easier if you first disable the Internet Explorer Enhanced Security feature using the instructions in **13.4 Accessing the Internet from the Server**. As soon as the installation is complete, click **Advanced settings** as this allows you to specify the Dropbox location. For the location, choose the top-level shared folders location i.e. *D:\Shares* (although it may be on a different drive on your system). Note that Dropbox automatically installs itself as what is called a *service*, meaning it will start-up automatically each time the server starts.

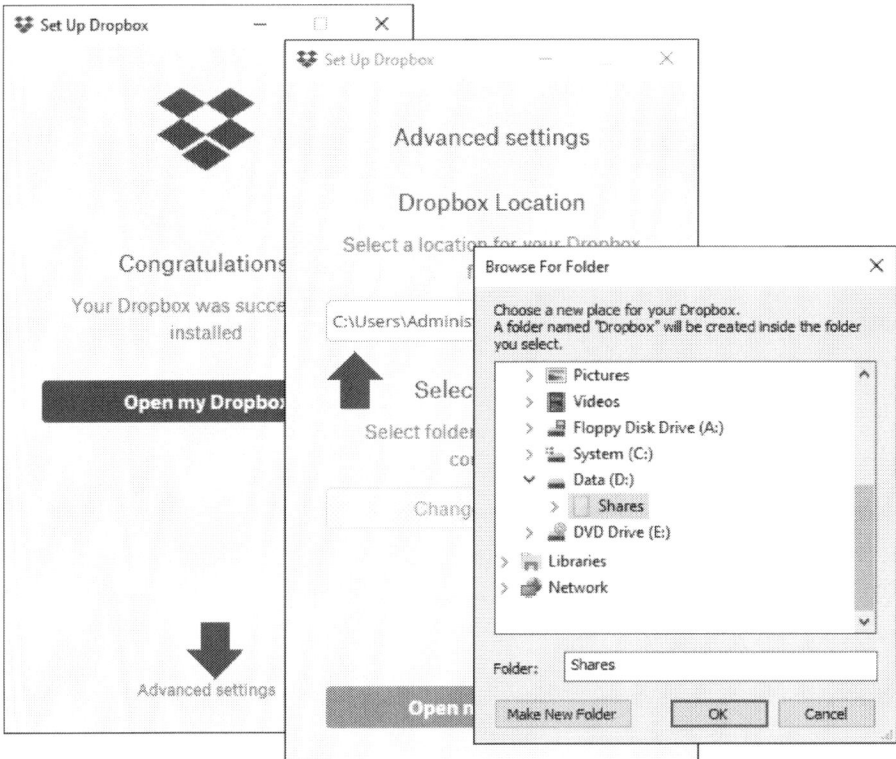

Figure 130: Choose a location for the Dropbox folder

Remote Access Usage

It is now necessary to specify who has access to the Dropbox folder. This can be done using File Explorer. Navigate to where the *Dropbox* folder is located; right-click it and select **Give access to > Specific people**. On the resultant panel, type in the user's name and click **Add** so they appear in the box underneath. Click on the *Permission Level* for the user; the choices are choices are *Read/Write* (i.e. full access), *Read Only* (i.e. retrieve things from Dropbox but not be able to add things) or *Remove* (i.e. remove access for an existing user of the folder). Click **Share** and acknowledge the messages. Suggestion: if you want all users to have access, choose the built-in *Everyone* group.

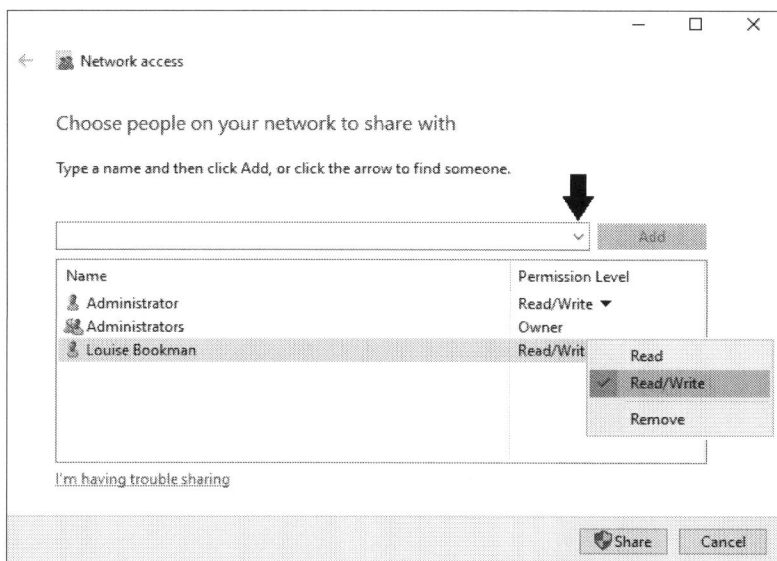

Figure 131: Specify which users have access

To gain access, the permitted users should now have the Dropbox client installed on the devices they use outside of the office, downloadable from *www.dropbox.com*. It is suggested that the users are not given the password and allowed to install it themselves, so as to reduce the risk of errors or abuse. At the time of writing, Dropbox is available for: Windows, macOS, iOS, Android, Windows Phone and selected Linux distributions.

To make files available outside of the office, they simply have to be placed in the *Shares\Dropbox* folder on the server.

One thing to consider is what happens when people leave the organization, as if they have Dropbox installed on a home computer they will continue to have access to whatever is stored on the server's Dropbox folder. In such circumstances it will be necessary for the administrator to change the password of the Dropbox account and advise remaining staff of the new password. Dropbox Business has the extremely useful capability to 'remote wipe' devices and this can be used to remove the organization's data from the former user's computer.

Use as a Backup Tool

If Dropbox is being used for backups, then only the Administrator needs access and there is no requirement to install client software on any other computers. At the simplest level, a backup is simply a matter of copying a selection of files and/or folders from the server into the Dropbox folder; be sure to copy them rather than drag them into the folder, otherwise they will no longer be available from their normal location.

To facilitate matters, a simple script file can be created. In this example, data from the shared communal folder on the server is copied to the Dropbox folder, from where it is then synced to the cloud. The various switches used with the XCOPY command are to ensure that only files and folders which have changed are backed up:

@Echo Off
Xcopy d:\shares\shared d:\shares\dropbox /m /e /c /k /o /y

The script file can be placed on the Desktop and manually run as required. Clearly this is not a very sophisticated approach and it may be useful to schedule it to run automatically using the Windows Task Scheduler or a third-party program.

10

GROUP POLICY

10.1 Overview

This chapter is concerned with making the network more capable, easier to use and more manageable using *Group Policy*. Computers and user accounts have many hundreds of settings that control their behavior, such as how often passwords need to be changed, what items appear on the Desktop, the default home page within Internet Explorer and much more. Building upon Active Directory, Group Policy enables such things to be defined and then enforced across groups of computers and users, thereby creating a more consistent and controlled environment. This chapter is not intended as an in-depth tutorial about Group Policy, rather the focus is on some simple practical examples of using it.

10.2 Group Policy Management Console

Group policies are created and controlled using the *Group Policy Management* console. It is one of the Administrative Tools and can be accessed in a variety of ways:

- Click **Start > Server Manager > Tools > Group Policy Management** or
- Click **Start > Windows Administrative Tools > Group Policy Management** or
- Press **Windows key + R**. Type **gpmc.msc** in the box and press **Enter**

Fully expand the tree in the left-hand panel to display the overall structure of the domain. The structure can be added to but to keep things simple we will leave things as they are. Notice an entry called *Default Domain Policy*; as the name might imply, this covers default settings for the entire network. Any changes to this will therefore apply to all computers or users in the system and our examples will focus on this:

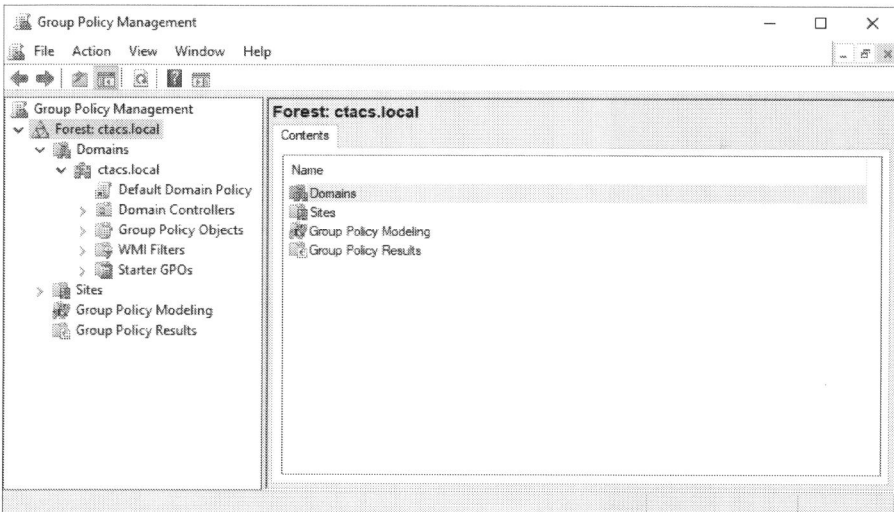

Figure 132: Group Policy Management console

Making a change involves right-clicking an item – such as *Default Domain Policy* – and choosing **Edit**. Sometimes when doing so you will receive the following warning and you may wish to tick the **Do not show this message again** box so as to avoid it on future occasions:

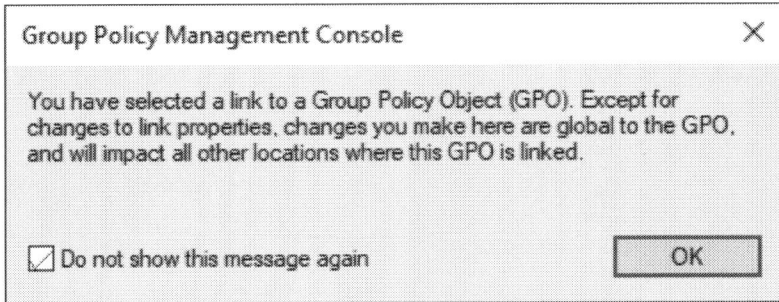

Figure 133: Group Policy Management console warning message

Policies are created or modified for the *Computer Configuration* or *User Configuration*, the former affecting all computers and the latter affecting all users. There is no method to explicitly save changes, as it is implicit when making modifications. The policies and preferences do not immediately propagate, rather they are applied the next time a client logs in to the network or when a computer starts up. However, it is sometimes possible to expedite matters by bringing up a command prompt ("DOS prompt") on a workstation and typing the command *gpupdate /force*.

One thing to note is that some Group Policy settings are operating system dependent. For instance, some may only be applicable to, say, Windows 10 and not relevant to, say, Windows 7 at all. However, the majority are applicable to most versions of Windows.

10.3 Specifying the Home Page

Some organizations require that all users have a standard home page within Internet Explorer, for example the company's website or an email system such as *Office365* or *Google Mail*. Group Policy can be used to achieve this.

Launch the **Group Policy Management Console**. Expand the tree in the left-hand panel, right-click the entry for *Default Domain Policy* and choose **Edit**. In the new window, expand the tree and drill down to **User Configuration** > **Preferences** > **Control Panel Settings**. Right-click the entry for **Internet Settings** and choose **New**. A pop-up listing various versions of Internet Explorer is shown; note that most of these are now long obsolete and should no longer be in general use, also that the most recent version from 2013, Internet Explorer 11, is not listed (although it will in fact use the Internet Explorer 10 settings), nor is the Edge browser:

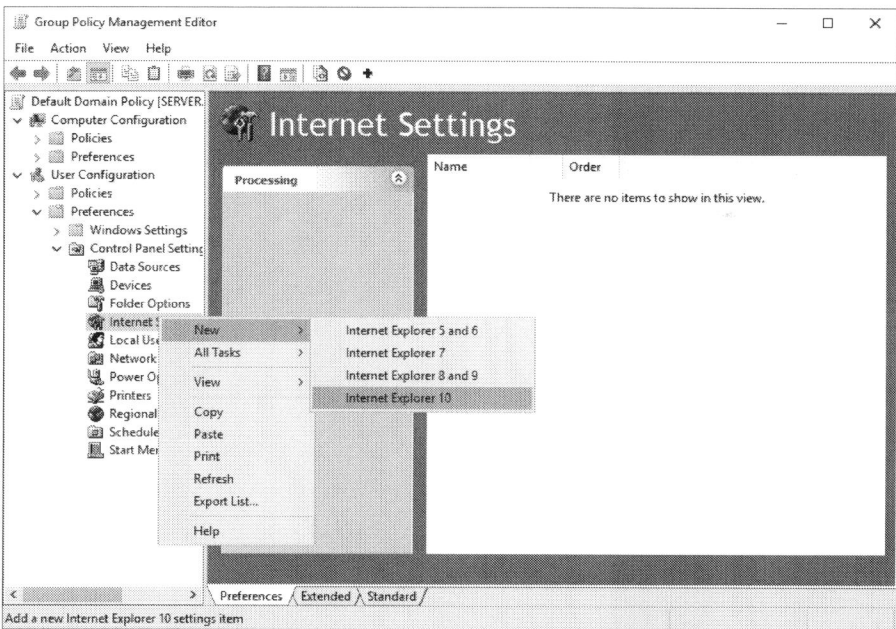

Figure 134: Choose the version of Internet Explorer

On the assumption that the organization is indeed using IE11 or IE10, click **Internet Explorer 10** and the properties box is displayed. Type in the details for the desired standard home page:

Figure 135: Specify the home page settings

In the *Home page* section there is a red dotted line – press the **F6** key and it will change to a solid green line. This step is very important and unless this is done the setting will not apply. Also, click the **Start with home page** option. There are some optional settings; for instance, you can choose to have the browsing history deleted when the user exits Internet Explorer.

Click **Apply** and **OK**. Close down the Group Policy Management Console.

The effect of this is that all users will now have the specified page as their home page within Internet Explorer.

Other browsers, such as Microsoft Edge, Mozilla Firefox and Google Chrome, are not supported out of the box. They can be managed using *ADMX* files, which are extension files that are imported into Active Directory; for example, Google provide their own ADMX files that allow over 200 settings in Chrome to be managed. As this is a more advanced and specialized use of Group Policy it is not appropriate to cover it in this guide.

10.4 Windows Logon Behavior

By default, Windows 7 clients and later display the name of the last person to use the computer. This can be confusing in an environment in which people share computers, as it necessary for the next person using it to explicitly specify 'Logon as other user', which is inconvenient for some people. However, this behavior can be changed, such that a blank user name and password are always presented to users and this is done through Group Policy.

On the server, launch the Group Policy Management Console. Right-click the *Default Domain Policy* and click **Edit**. Drill down to **Computer Configuration** > **Policies** > **Windows Settings** > **Security Settings** > **Local Policies** > **Security Options**. Find *Interactive login: Don't display last signed-in..* Double-click it then click **Define this policy setting** and **Enabled**, followed by **OK**.

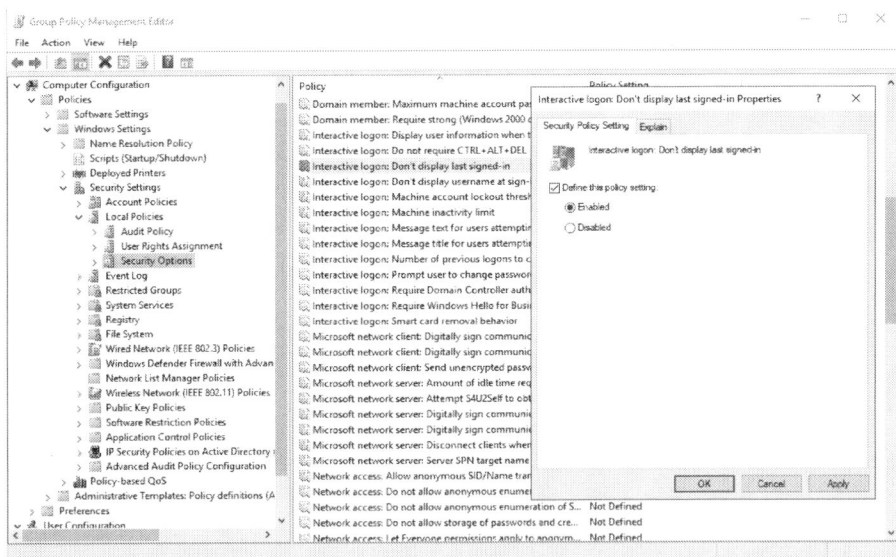

Figure 136: Interactive logon settings

10.5 Logon Warning/Security Message

Group Policy can be used to specify a message that appears at the logon screen. For instance, the message could state the name of the organization ("ACME Inc.") along with an advisory or warning message ("Do not attempt to use this computer system unless you have been authorized to do so"). There are two entries that need to be set: one for the title and one for the message itself.

On the server, open the Group Policy Management Console. Right-click the *Default Domain Policy* and choose **Edit**. Drill down to **Computer Configuration > Policies > Windows Settings > Security Settings > Local Policies > Security Options**. Find *Interactive login: Message title for users attempting to logon*. Tick the *Define this policy setting* box, enter the name of the organization and click OK. Then repeat for *Interactive login: Message text for users attempting to log on* and specify the detailed warning or greeting message. Click **OK**.

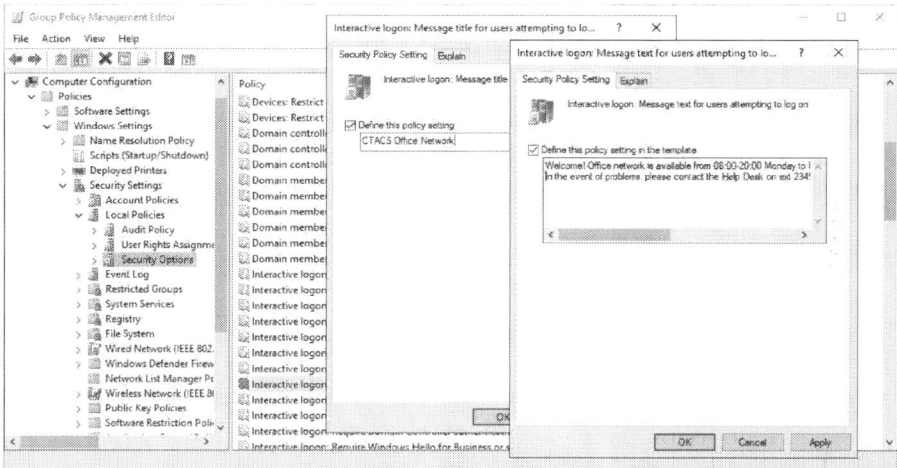

Figure 137: Logon messages

10.6 Changing the Password Policy

By default, Windows Server has a password policy of *complex passwords*, which means that passwords must comprise a mixture of letters, numbers and special characters. By using complex passwords, security is enhanced. For instance, it is very unlikely that an unauthorized user or hacker would be able to guess a password such as *!!40#mgzjeu23!398ab*. However, in some scenarios such passwords are too complicated - for example, in a school or in a work environment with many casual users - in which case the policy can be adjusted accordingly.

To do so, go into **Group Policy Management;** expand the tree to display the *Default Domain Policy*, right-click it and choose **Edit**. Drill down to: **Computer Configuration** > **Policies** > **Windows Settings** > **Security Settings** > **Account Policies** > **Password Policy**:

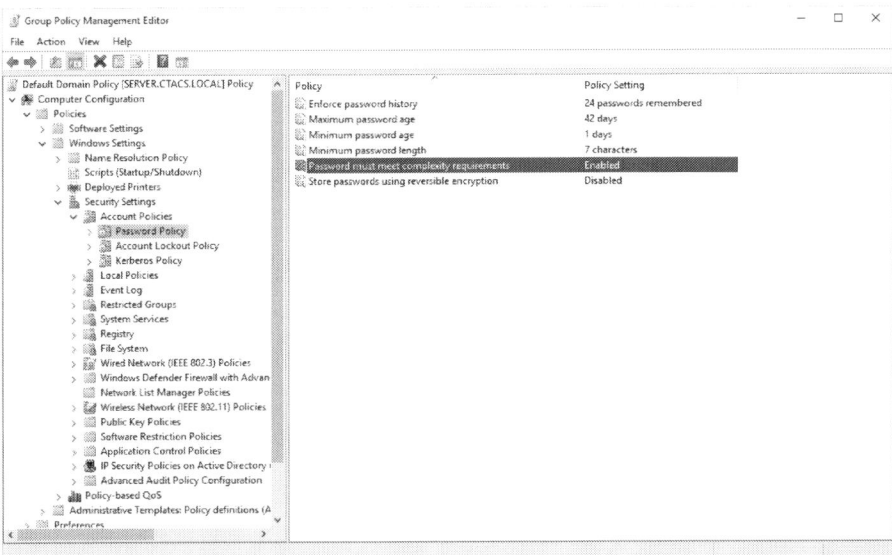

Figure 138: Specifying the Password Policy

To remove the requirement for complex passwords, change **Password must meet complexity requirements** to **Disabled**.

To prevent users being forced to change their passwords on a regular basis, change **Maximum password age** to 0 and **Minimum password age** to 0.

To remove the requirement for passwords to be of a minimum length, change **Minimum password length** to 0.

The defaults provided by Microsoft are sensible and designed to support a secure environment. You are free to change them as described above, but best practice is not to have them too weak.

10.7 Account Lockout Policy

Windows Server can be configured to temporarily lock a user account if there are too many unsuccessful login attempts. This can improve security, as multiple failed logins may indicate that an unauthorized user is guessing passwords in order to gain access.

To configure this, go into **Group Policy Management;** expand the tree to display the *Default Domain Policy*, right-click it and choose **Edit**. Drill down to: **Computer Configuration > Policies > Windows Settings > Security Settings > Account Policies > Account Lockout Policy**:

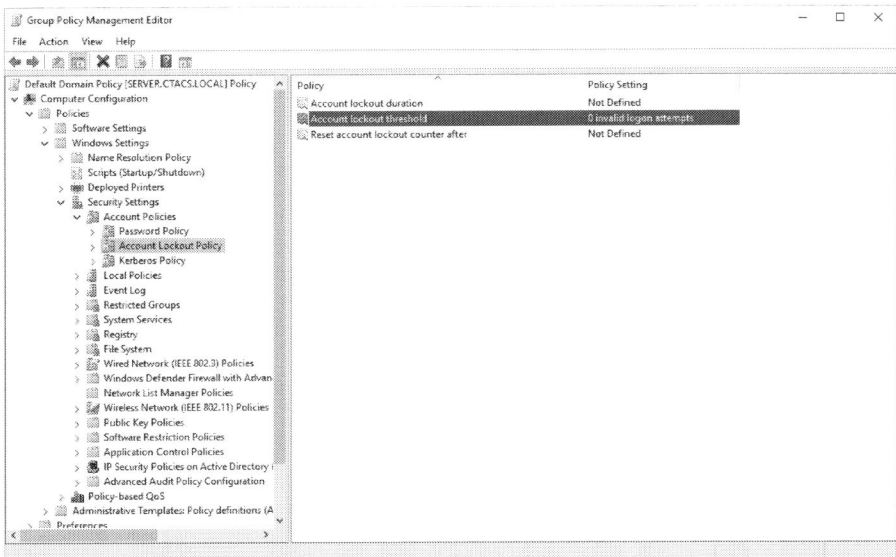

Figure 139: Account Lockout Policy

To enable account lockout: double-click **Account lockout threshold**; tick the **Define this policy setting** box; specify the number of invalid logon attempts (typically, a value of 3 is used); click **OK**. A message is displayed with suggested values of 30 minutes for the two other items, which define the duration of an account lock and how long must pass before the account lockout counter is reset. If these values are acceptable, click **OK**.

If they are not, they can be altered using the **Account lockout duration** and **Reset account lockout counter after** properties.

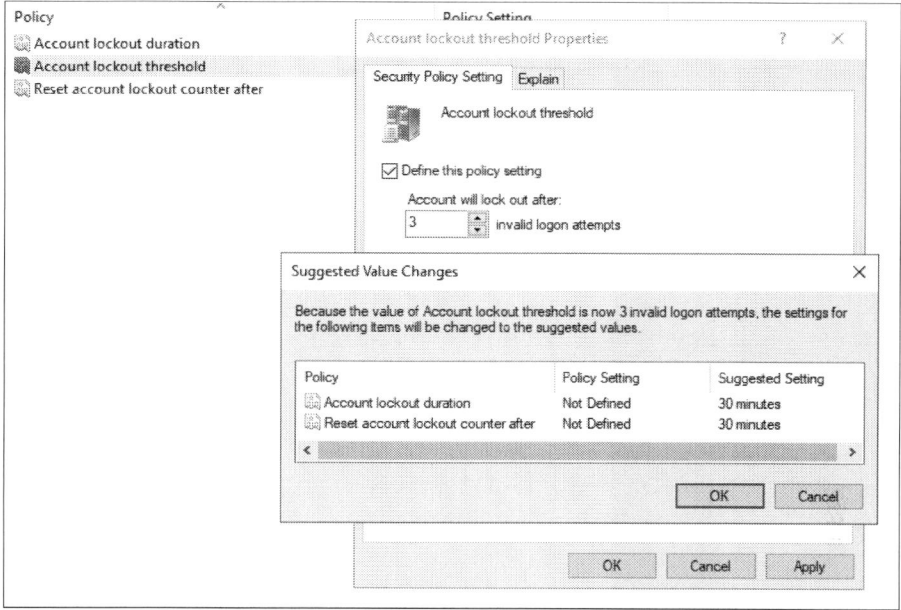

Figure 140: Suggested account lockout policies

10.8 Redirect the User's Documents Folder

The purpose of this is to redirect the user's *Documents* folder (also sometimes known as *My Documents*) from their computer to their home drive on the network. By doing so, any files the user creates will automatically be stored on the network and hence be available to them from any computer on the network, without the user having specifically to remember to store them on their networked home drive. An advantage of redirecting the home folder is that a feature called *offline folders* is also enabled; users who have laptops will still have their home folder documents available when working offsite and any changes made will be automatically synced when they come back into the office.

To configure this, launch **Group Policy Management** and expand the console tree. Right-click the *Default Domain Policy* and choose **Edit**. Expand the tree to **User Configuration > Policies > Windows Settings > Folder Redirection > Documents**. Right-click **Documents** and choose **Properties**.

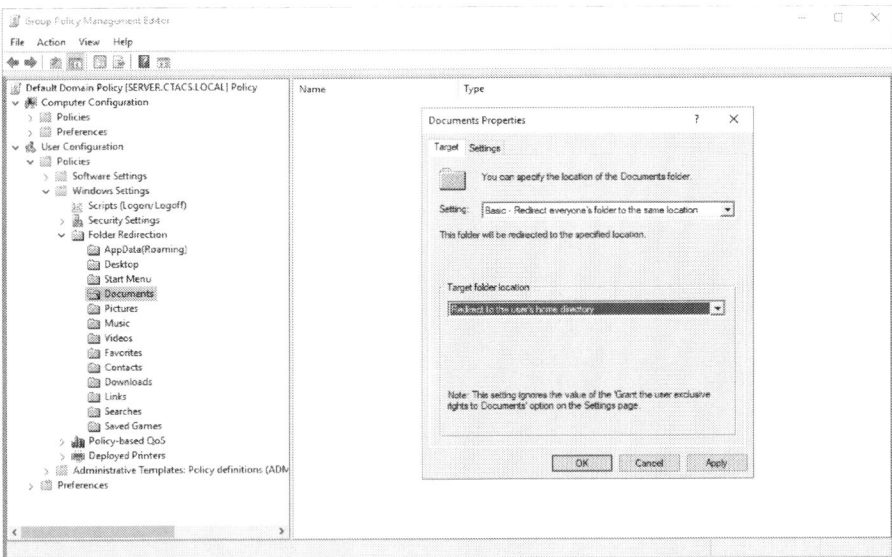

Figure 141: Specify location of the Documents folder

On the **Target** tab, change the **Setting** to **Basic - redirect everyone's folder to the same location** and the **Target folder location** to **Redirect to the user's home directory**. Click **Apply** and click **Yes** to the warning message.

Click the **Settings** tab and make sure it looks as shown below. If very old versions of Windows are in use at the site – hopefully not - ensure the box for Windows XP and other earlier operating systems is ticked. Click **OK**. A warning message may be displayed, which can safely be ignored by clicking **Yes**.

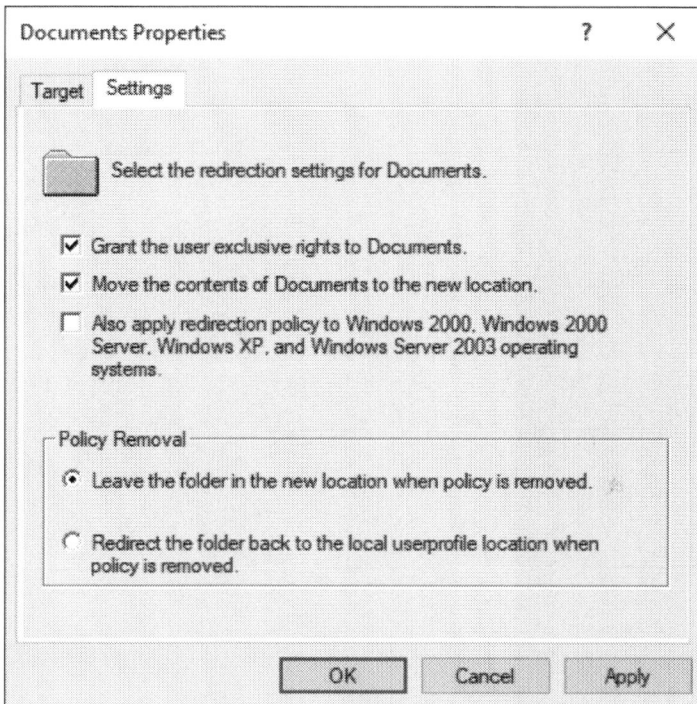

Figure 142: Redirection settings

An additional step is then needed:

From within **Group Policy Management** view the settings for the *Default Domain Policy*. Expand to **Computer Configuration > Policies > Administrative Templates > Network > Offline Files**.

The setting in the right-hand panel for **Allow or Disallow use of the Offline Files feature** should be set to **Enabled**. The setting for **Subfolders always available offline** should be set to **Enabled** if very old versions of Windows are in use.

Troubleshooting: Unfortunately, it is not uncommon to experience problems with the Offline files facility, particularly with older versions of Windows. If it is not working, try this additional change to Group Policy. For the *Default Domain Policy*, go to **Computer Configuration > Policies > Administrative Templates > System > Logon**. Enable the **Always wait for the network at computer startup and logon** option.

10.9 Configure Wireless Settings

Group Policy can be used to push out wireless settings to users within the organization. This makes it easier to deploy wi-fi as it is not necessary to visit each computer; once the policy has been pushed out, all the user has to do is enter the password.

Launch the **Group Policy Management Console**. Expand the tree in the left-hand panel, right-click the entry for *Default Domain Policy* and choose **Edit**. In the new window, expand the tree and drill down to **Computer Configuration > Policies > Windows Settings > Security Setings > Wireless Network (IEEE 802.11) Policies**. Right-click the empty section in the right-hand panel and select **Create a New Wireless Policy for Windows Vista and Later Releases**:

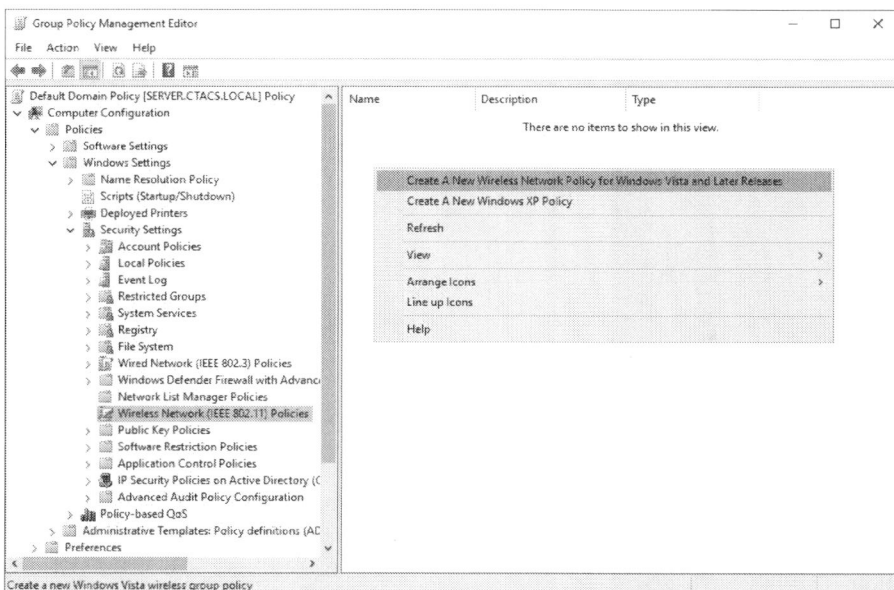

Figure 143: Create a new wireless policy

Give the new policy a name and an optional description. Click the **Add** button and select **Infrastructure**:

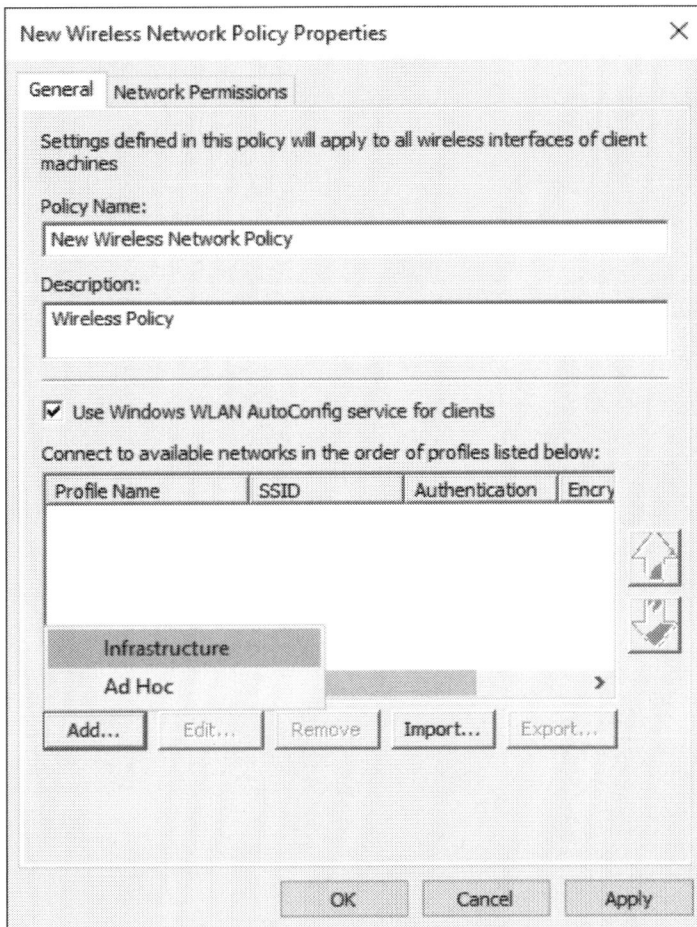

Figure 144: Select Infrastructure

On the next panel, specify a **Profile Name** and type in the **Network Name (SSID)**. The **Connect automatically when this network is in range** and **Connect to a more preferred network if available** options should be ticked. If you are using a hidden SSID, tick the **Connect even if the network is not broadcasting** option. Click **Add**. On the **Security** tab, select the **Authentication** and **Encryption** standards that are used then click **OK** and **OK** again:

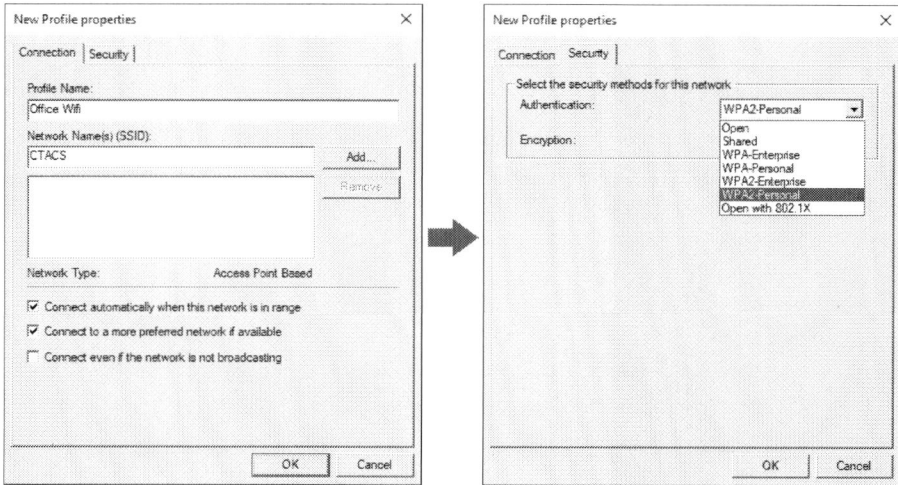

Figure 145: Specify wireless network details

In this example, we have defined the policy for all computers in the domain. However, in practice it is often useful to define organizational units (OUs) and apply as required e.g. create an OU for laptop users. Another example might be, say, a business where each floor has its own wireless access point and you wish to associate the users on that floor only with it.

11

HOUSEKEEPING

11.1 Overview

Servers need to be checked on a regular basis to ensure that there are no problems and that they are in good health. Clearly some type of problems will be immediately apparent, for example if the server is powered down for whatever reason then nobody will be able to use it. But there are plenty of other things that need to be monitored; for instance: Has the backup completed successfully? Is the server running out of storage space? Additionally, there are some housekeeping tasks that need to be carried out on an occasional basis. This section also includes some ideas for making the server more convenient to work with for the administrator.

11.2 Shutting Down & Restarting the Server

The server is usually left running continuously but there will be occasions when it needs to be restarted e.g. following major updates or shutdown altogether e.g. to add hardware. To do so, click **Start** followed by **Power**; you will be given a choice of **Shut down** or **Restart**. You will be prompted to enter a reason for shutting down the server – choose one from the drop-down menu and click **Continue**.

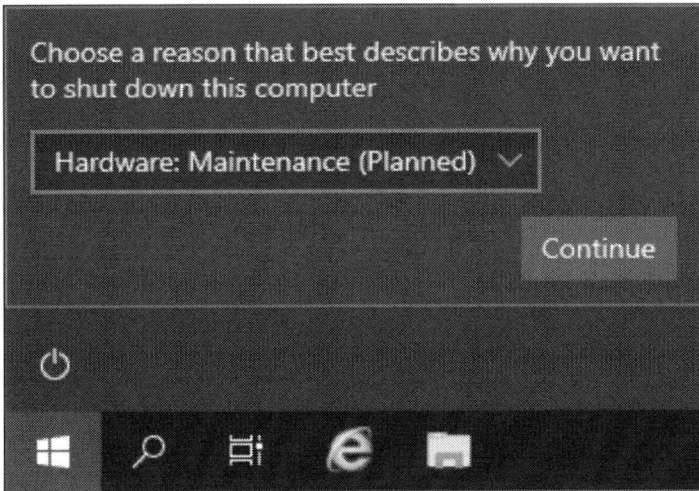

Figure 146: Shutting down dialog

You can also shut down the server from within Server Manager. From the Local Server *Properties* page, click **Tasks** and choose **Shut Down Local Server**. You will be prompted to provide a reason for doing so:

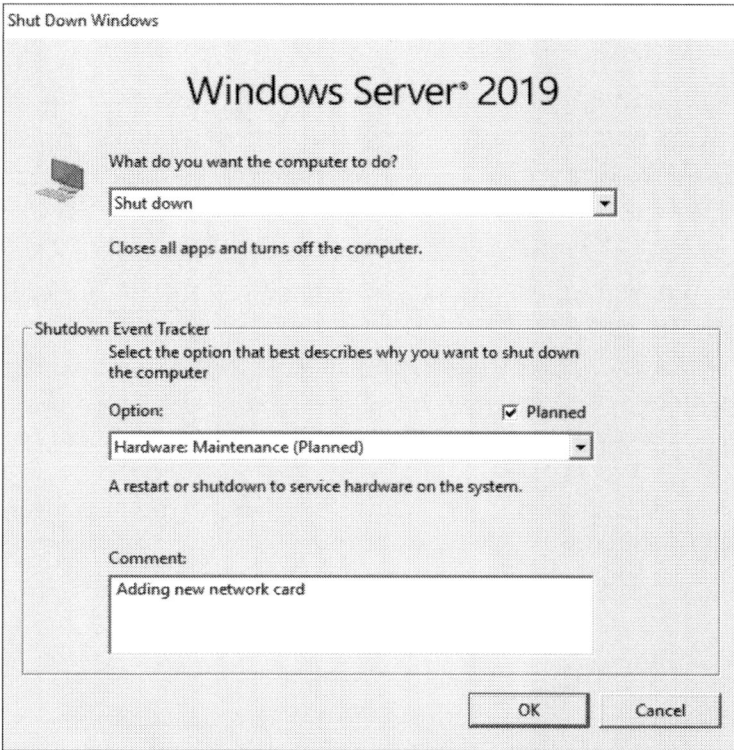

Figure 147: Shutting down dialog from Server Manager

11.3 Windows Updates

Microsoft provides updates to Windows Server on a regular basis. Such updates may provide improved or additional functionality, but more typically address security issues that could compromise the system. In previous versions of Windows Server, there was considerable latitude as to when updates were applied, such that it was even possible to switch them off altogether, thereby incurring security risks. In current versions, things have been greatly tightened up and updates are largely applied automatically; however, there are some parameters that can usefully be adjusted.

Go into **Settings** and click **Update & Security** and make sure you are in the *Windows Update* section:

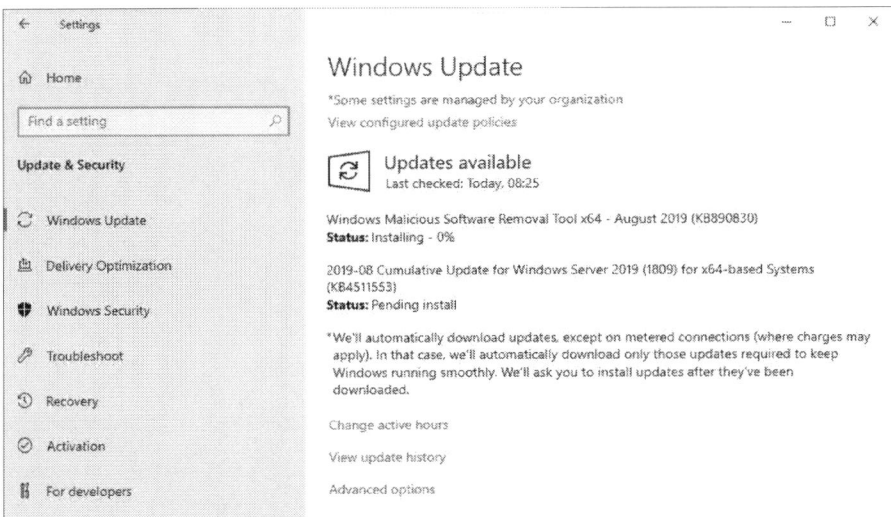

Figure 148: Windows Update settings

Any available updates will be listed, along with an option to **Install now**. Invariably, there will be a *Definition Update for Windows Defender Antivirus*, as it is updated every day or two. The next section provides control over the update process and there are three options: *Change active hours*; *View update history*; *Advanced options*.

Change active hours – this controls when the server can restart after applying updates. Clearly the server should not suddenly restart during the working day, as this could be highly disruptive, so you can define the active hours when the server is normally in use and hence, by implication, when it is not and therefore available for restarts. Click **Change active hours** to display the following panel, change the *Start time* and *End time* as required and click **Save**. Somewhat oddly, the maximum time that the server can be defined as 'active' is only 18 hours:

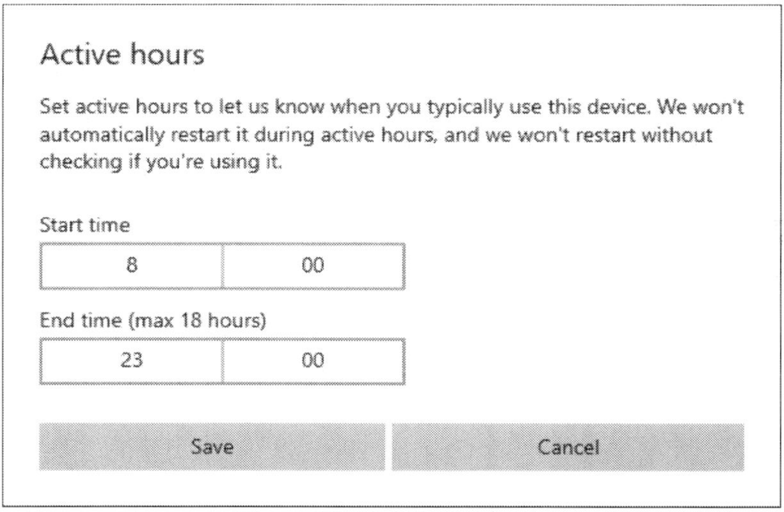

Active hours

Set active hours to let us know when you typically use this device. We won't automatically restart it during active hours, and we won't restart without checking if you're using it.

Start time

8	00

End time (max 18 hours)

23	00

Save	Cancel

Figure 149: Set Active hours

View update history - *View Update history* shows which updates have recently been applied. There is also an option to *Uninstall Updates*, should that ever be necessary for some reason. The *Recovery options* are used to help recover the server when there are startup problems.

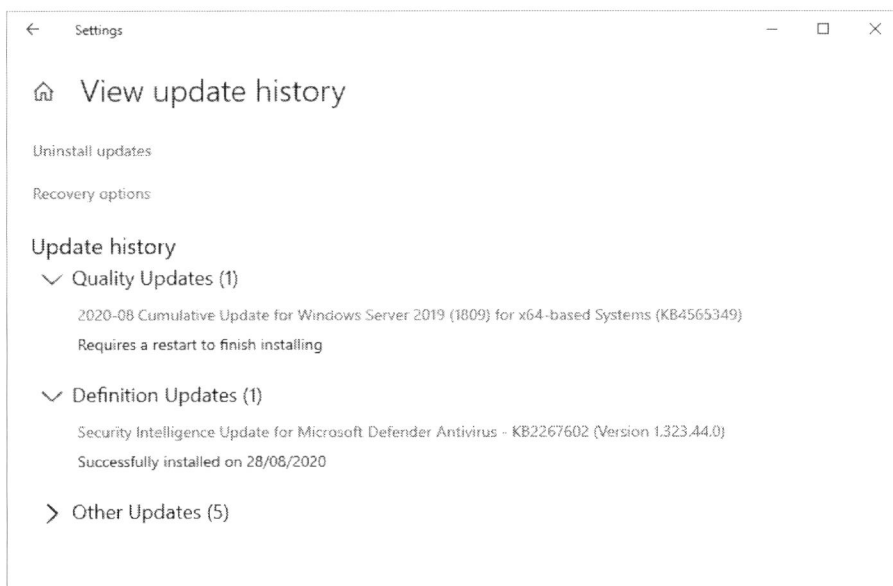

Figure 150: View update history

Advanced options – this contains several options for fine-tuning the updating process, some of which you may wish to change. Firstly, slide the restart reminder in *Update notifications* to the 'On' position, so you will be advised when the server needs to restart following an update:

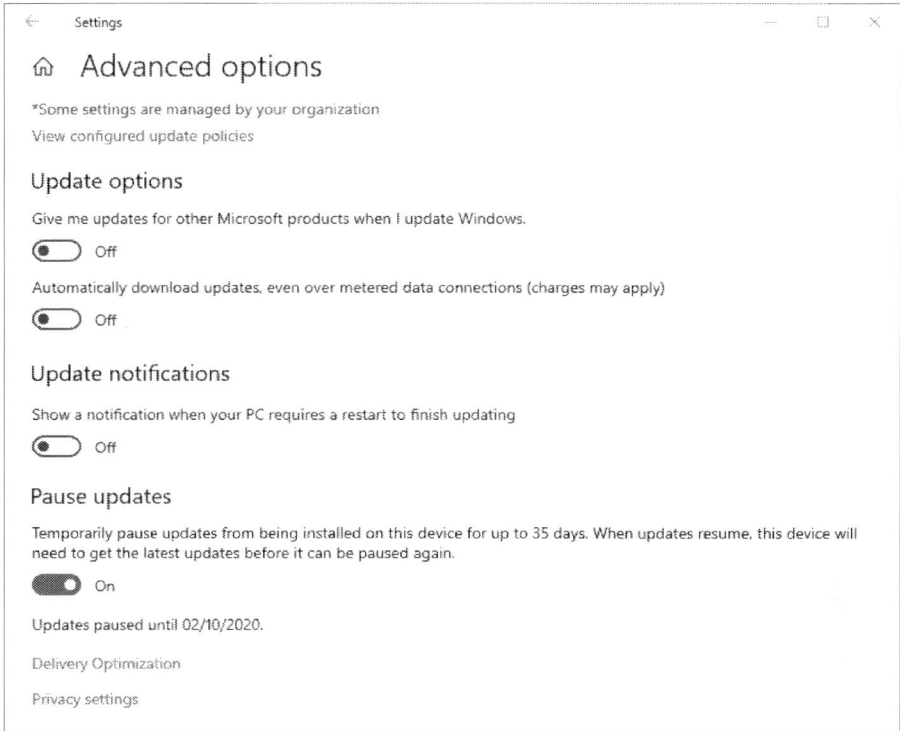

Figure 151: Windows Update Advanced options

Secondly, it is possible to *Pause updates* altogether for 35 days, by sliding the switch to the 'On' position. This can be useful to avoid the risk of disruption during a critical period, for instance, year end processing in a company.

Finally, control can be exercised over what Microsoft calls *Delivery Optimization*. The principle here is that instead of each individual computer in the network downloading its own set of updates, they can share the task and update each other, thereby saving bandwidth i.e. if one already has an update it can pass it on to the other machines in the network. Best practice with a server is to set this facility to **Off.**

Note about Release Channels

Note: this section is mainly for users of Windows Server Standard.

Microsoft operate what they call two *primary release channels* with regards to Windows Server. The *Long-Term Servicing Channel* or LTSC is the traditional method for updating Windows Server, with a major new version released every few years e.g. Windows 2016, Windows 2019. This provides long term stability and is most suitable for most business customers. Although regular security and bug fixes are provided, the functionality of Windows Server remains constant, such that this guide will be equally applicable until the next major release.

The second channel is the *Semi-Annual Channel* or SAC. As the name implies, Windows Server is updated twice a year, in order to provide early access to new features and technologies for customers who want them. Eventually, some of these features will make their way into the next LTSC release. SAC is available to volume-licensed customers who have signed up for Microsoft's Software Assurance plan and is generally not appropriate to most small business users.

11.4 Event Viewer

Windows Server maintains comprehensive records of the myriad events that take place during the operation of the server. Some of these are simply records of normal usage (user logs on, user logs off, etc.), whereas others are generated in response to error conditions and can be used to help diagnose problems. The events are categorized into several main types and recorded in log files, which should be specifically checked in the event of problems and otherwise on an occasional basis.

To access the Event Logs, right-click the **Start** button and choose **Event Viewer**. Click **Windows Logs** in the left-hand panel and a screen along the following lines is displayed (it may take several seconds to fully populate):

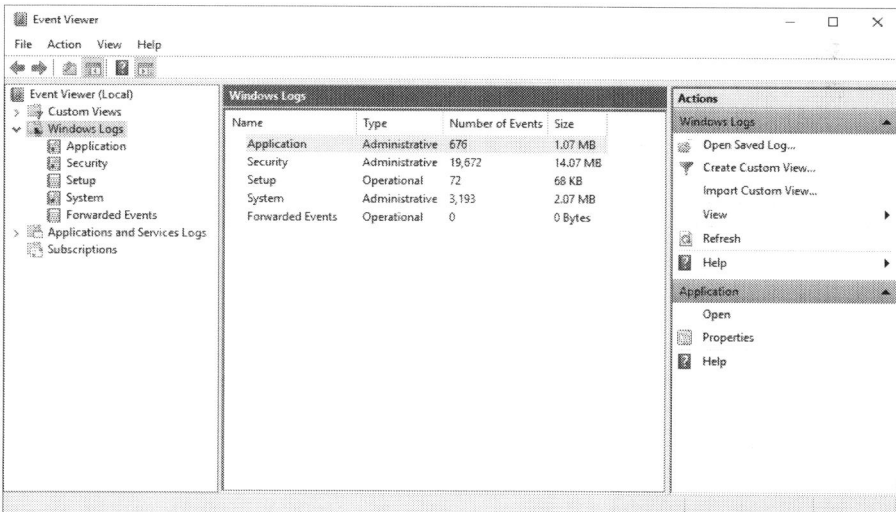

Figure 152: The Event Viewer

Some of the event logs are more useful than others. In the left-hand panel, expand the tree to display the **Windows Logs** section and reveal five main logs: *Application, Security, Setup, System* and *Forwarded Events*. To view a particular log, click it. Each event is categorized as *Error, Warning* or *Information,* along with a timestamp plus a short description, with a longer description provided at the bottom of the screen. The listing can be sorted by clicking on the heading for a column:

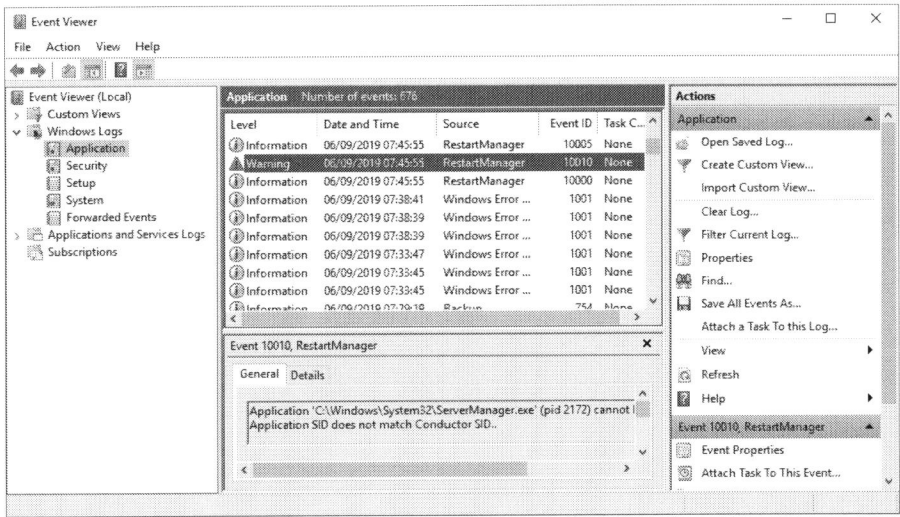

Figure 153: Example of an Event log

For practical purposes, the System and Application logs contain the most relevant information. If a server crashes or freezes – which is a very rare occurrence, if at all – there may well be clues as to the cause in the System log. If there are suspected security violations, then the Security log may contain details. However, note that the Security log is very "noisy" and typically generates thousands of events every hour.

The Event logs will start to overwrite when they are full. If required, they can be archived as permanent records or to preserve evidence. To do so, right-click an Event Log and from the pop-up menu choose **Clear Log**. A message is displayed offering three choices – click the **Save and Clear** button. In the resultant dialog box specify a name for the file: a good choice is its name plus the date e.g. *setup-12092019*.

11.5 Windows Security

Servers are susceptible to viruses and malware in the same way that regular desktop and laptops are and for this reason need to be protected. Microsoft have a free product called *Windows Security*, which is an integral part of the Windows Server package and is installed automatically by default.

To check the status of Windows Security, click **Start > Settings > Update & Security > Windows Security** to display the following overview screen.

Figure 154: Windows Security

Windows Security covers four areas: *Virus & threat protection*; *Firewall & network protection*; *App & browser control*; *Device security*. A healthy status is indicated by the presence of a green and white tick against each topic; if this is present then no action is needed, otherwise click the appropriate icon.

11.6 Virus & threat protection

One aspect of particular importance is the anti-virus component; click the first icon – **Virus & threat protection** – to show this screen:

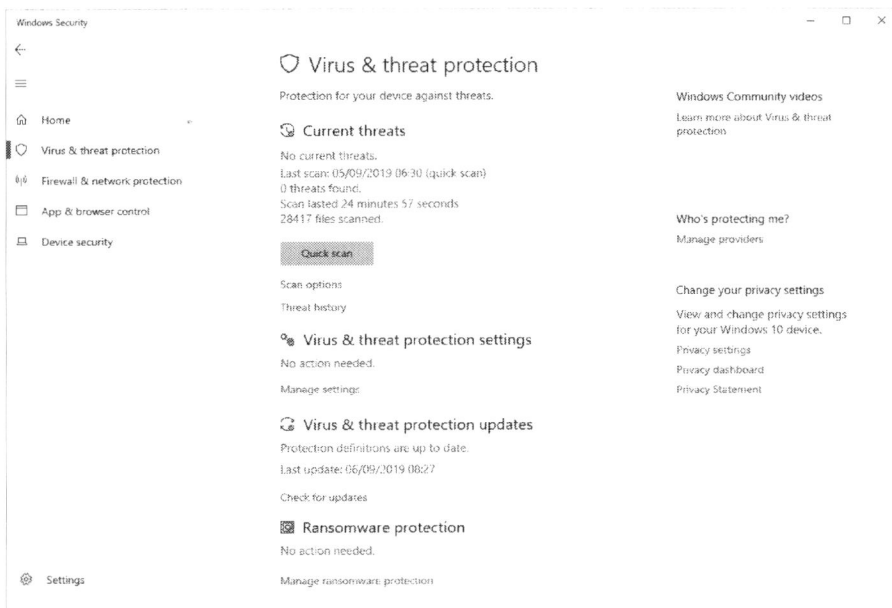

Figure 155: Virus & threat protection

Windows Security provides real-time protection against threats and runs a Quick scan on a regular basis; alternatively, click the **Quick scan** button to run a check at any point. For a more systematic scan, click **Scan options** and choose **Full scan** or **Custom scan** and click the **Scan now** button (it is worthwhile doing a Full scan on a regular basis e.g. weekly).

Within the Virus & threat protection screen, various controls are available to available to set options and fine-tune the protection mechanisms. These are accessible under the different sections; there is also a settings cogwheel in the bottom left-hand corner of the screen.

Commercial alternatives to Windows Security are available from vendors such as Symantec, McAfee, Sophos and Malwarebytes and others.

11.7 Firewall & network protection

Within a private local area network, the connected computers can be considered as being *trusted*. However, the server is also connected to the outside world through the internet, but as the internet is not under your control it cannot be considered trusted. For instance, you may wish to browse websites but you do not want external hackers and miscreants able to access the server. The purpose of a *Firewall* is to help protect a network by controlling incoming and outgoing network traffic, based upon a set of predetermined rules. Firewalls can be hardware-based, in the form of dedicated appliances that sit between the internal network and the outside world (commonly built-in to the router in a small network), or software-based and running on a computer.

Windows Server features built-in firewall software. It does not assume particular technical knowledge and largely operates silently behind the scenes. It features sensible built-in default values and configures itself appropriately to permit correct operation of the server; for instance, the ports necessary to use remote access are opened automatically. As such, it is not usually necessary to have any dealings with the firewall, but there are some scenarios in which you might need to. For instance, you may have installed a specialist application on the server that needs to communicate with an external service or organization but is unable to do so, or there may be a suspected security violation of the server that requires investigation. The purpose of this section is simply to introduce the firewall, rather than describe in detail how to configure it. As configuring firewalls is a specialized task, you may wish to seek external expertise if it is not something with which you are familiar.

To access the firewall, click **Start** > **Settings** > **Update & Security** > **Firewall & network protection** to display this panel.

The three options listed – *Domain network*, *Private network* and *Public network* – are each clickable, although commonly there is no requirement to make changes at this level.

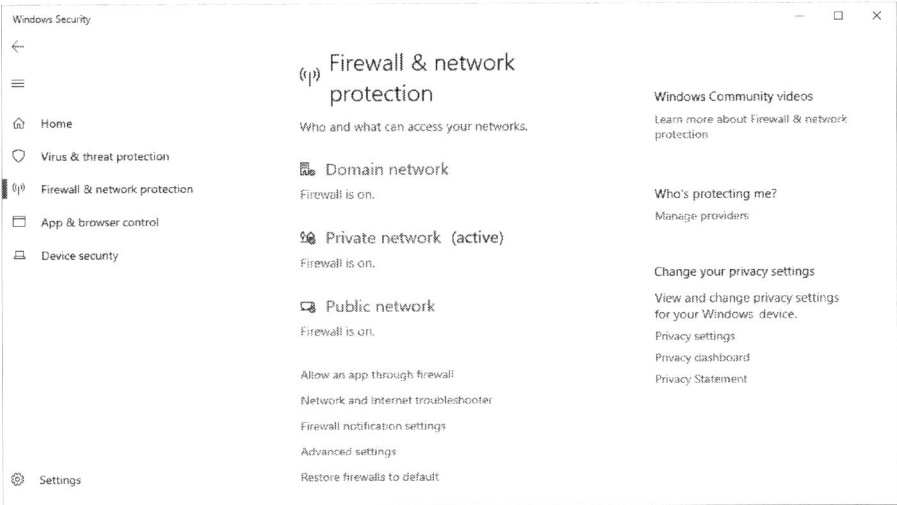

Figure 156: Firewall & network protection

To control which applications can pass through or are blocked by the firewall, click **Allow an app through firewall**. The standard apps and services required by Windows Server are listed; to add a new app, click **Allow another app**:

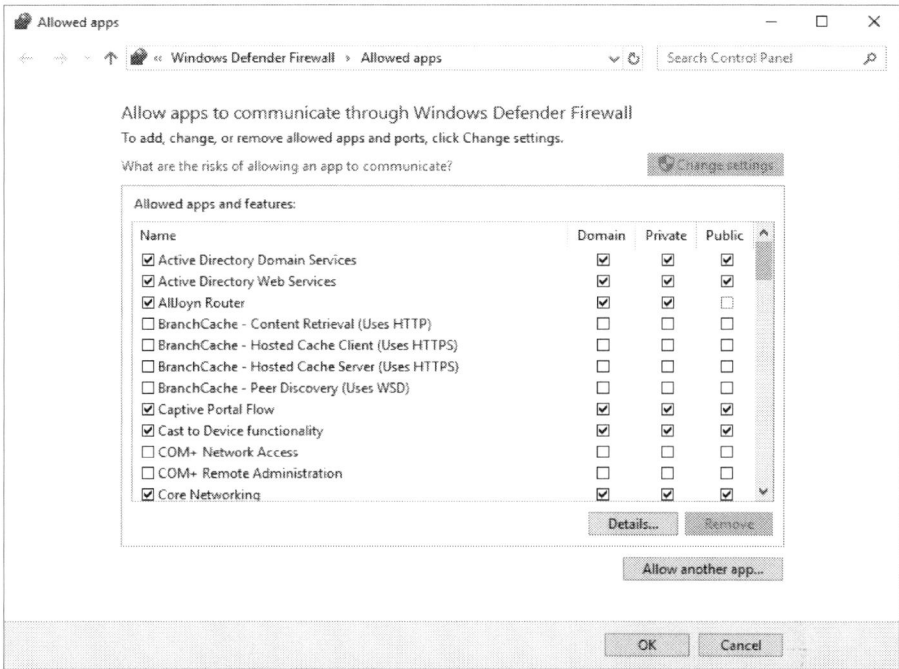

Figure 157: Controlling apps through the Firewall

The above screen presents a greatly simplified view of matters. Selecting or deselecting an app causes one or more corresponding rules to be activated or deactivated behind the scenes. To view and work with these rules directly, click **Advanced settings** from the initial Firewall & network panel, or click **Start > Windows Administrative Tools > Windows Defender Firewall with Advanced Security**, which will display the following screen:

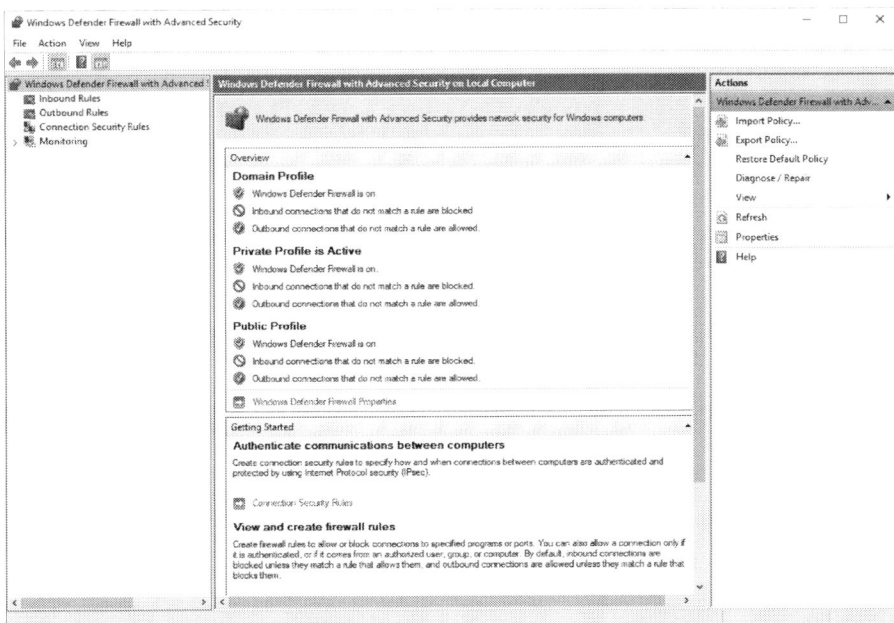

Figure 158: Windows Firewall console

The layout matches that of the other Microsoft console screens, with key categories listed in the left-hand panel, detail in the middle and a context-sensitive list of actions in the right-hand panel. Concentrating on the middle column, there are two main sections: *Overview* and *Getting Started*. The *Overview* provides a summary and relates to the network profiles on the server; they can be adjusted by clicking where it reads **Windows Firewall Properties**. *Getting Started* allows the individual rules to be viewed, modified and added to by clicking on **Inbound Rules** or **Outbound Rules**. If you do so, you will see that there are several hundred individual rules. Clicking **Monitoring** allows a logfile of firewall activity and violations to be established.

Tip: as stated above, adjusting the firewall is a relatively specialized task. In the event of problems, it is possible to revert it to the default settings. To do so, click **Restore firewalls to default** on the initial *Firewall & network protection* panel shown at the beginning of this section.

11.8 Checking Disk Space

The amount of free space on the storage drive(s) should be checked on a regular basis and there are three easy ways of doing this. One method is by going into File Explorer, clicking on *This PC* and looking at the drive(s). The second method is to right-click **Start** and go into **Disk Management**. The third method is: click **Start** > **Settings** > **System** > **Storage** to show the following. The individual storage locations (drives) on the right-hand side can be clicked to expand them and show more information:

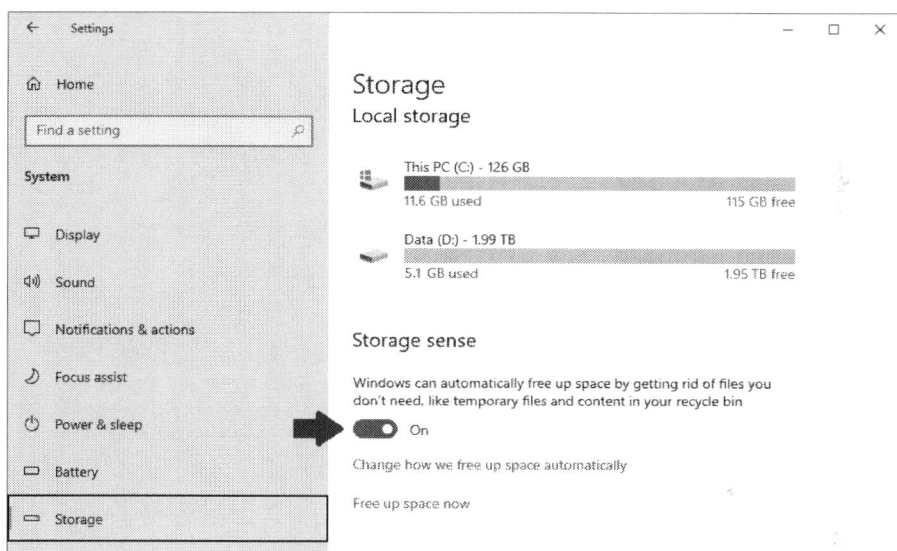

Figure 159: Checking disk space

During the normal daily operation of a computer, a variety of temporary and other files are generated. If *Storage sense* is enabled, Windows can automatically free up space by deleting these files on a regular basis; for greater control over the process, click **Change how we free up space automatically**. To manually free up space at any stage, click **Free up space now**. If the panel is scrolled, there are additional options towards the bottom; however, these are more applicable to personal Windows 10 computers than Windows Server.

11.9 Optimizing the Hard Drives

The hard drives on the server should be optimized (defragmented) on a regular basis to reduce file fragmentation and maximize performance. As with all modern versions of Windows, this can be scheduled to take place automatically.

Click **Start** and choose **File Explorer** (or launch it from the Taskbar). Expand *This PC*; right-click one of the disk drives (it does not matter which one if you have several to choose from); click **Properties**; click the **Tools** tab and then the **Optimize** button to show the following panel:

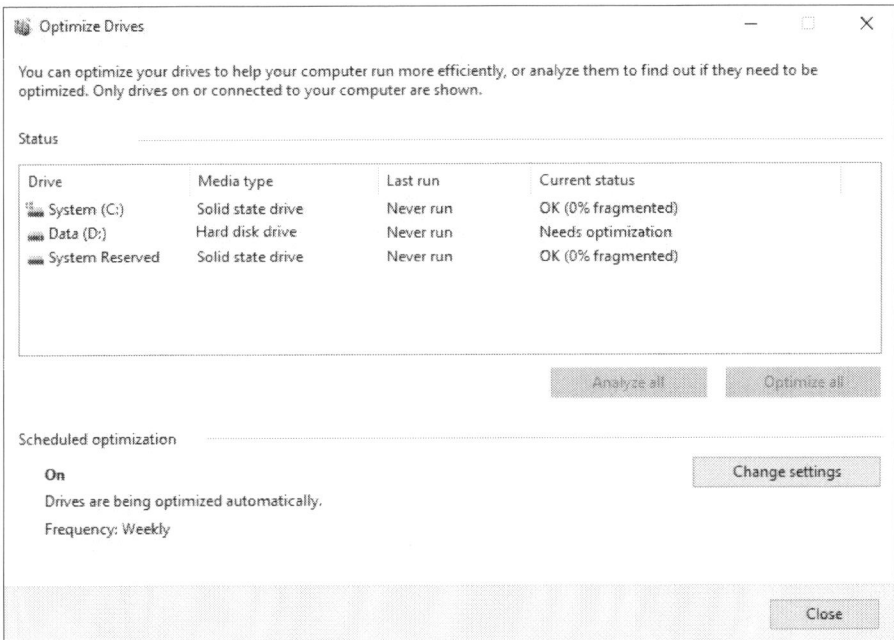

Figure 160: Optimize the hard drives

Towards the bottom left-hand corner it should read that Scheduled optimization is 'On' and that the drives are being optimized automatically on a weekly frequency. If this is not the case, click the **Change settings** button and adjust the settings accordingly.

If you have used earlier versions of Windows, you may be aware that you are not supposed to defragment Solid State Drives (SSDs) as it is not necessary and will shorten their lifespan. However, it is no longer necessary to worry about this, as the Optimize process simply runs the TRIM command and does not attempt to defragment SSDs.

11.10 Task Manager and Resource Monitor

Task Manager and *Resource Monitor* are built-in tools that can be used to help identify bottlenecks on servers that have performance problems, such as running slowly. Whilst the diagnosis and resolution of problems is a specialist topic that goes outside of the remit of this guide, they do provide useful information that most system administrators will find helpful. For instance, if a bottleneck with the network adapter was identified then it might be an option to add a second adapter and 'team' it as described in **13.10 Multiple Network Adapters (NIC Teaming)**.

Many users will be familiar with the Task Manager as it is common to all versions of Windows. To start it, right-click the **Taskbar** and choose **Task Manager** from the pop-up menu. Initially it will appear as a blank panel: click the **More details** button in the bottom left-hand corner to display the following screen:

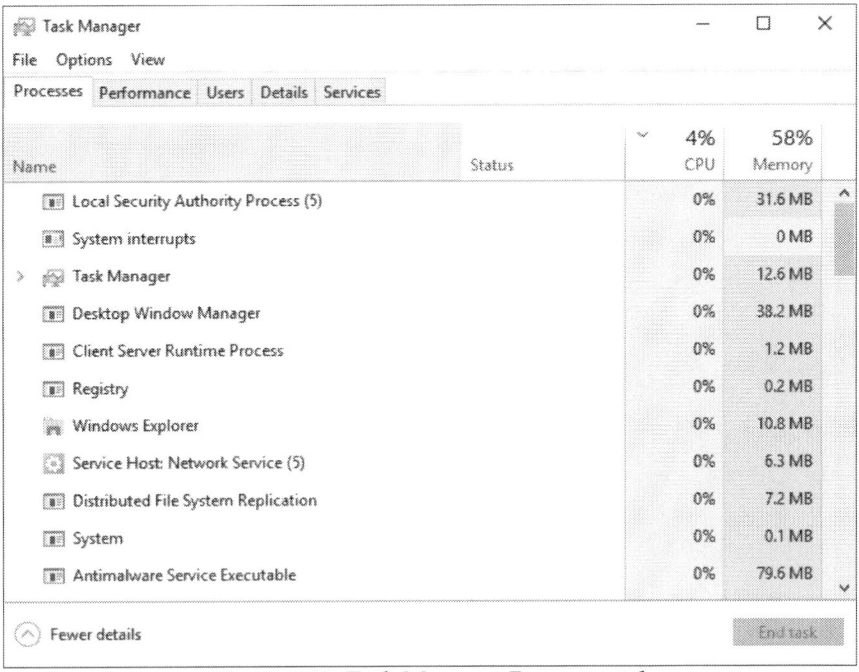

Figure 161: Task Manager Processes tab

On this *Processes* tab, Task Manager provides useful information about how busy the server is and how much memory is being used. For instance, if a process is hogging the CPU or memory it can be identified and, if appropriate, terminated.

Clicking on the **Performance** tab provides information in a graphical format for CPU, Memory and Ethernet (i.e. the network connection), and is useful for monitoring what is happening with the server:

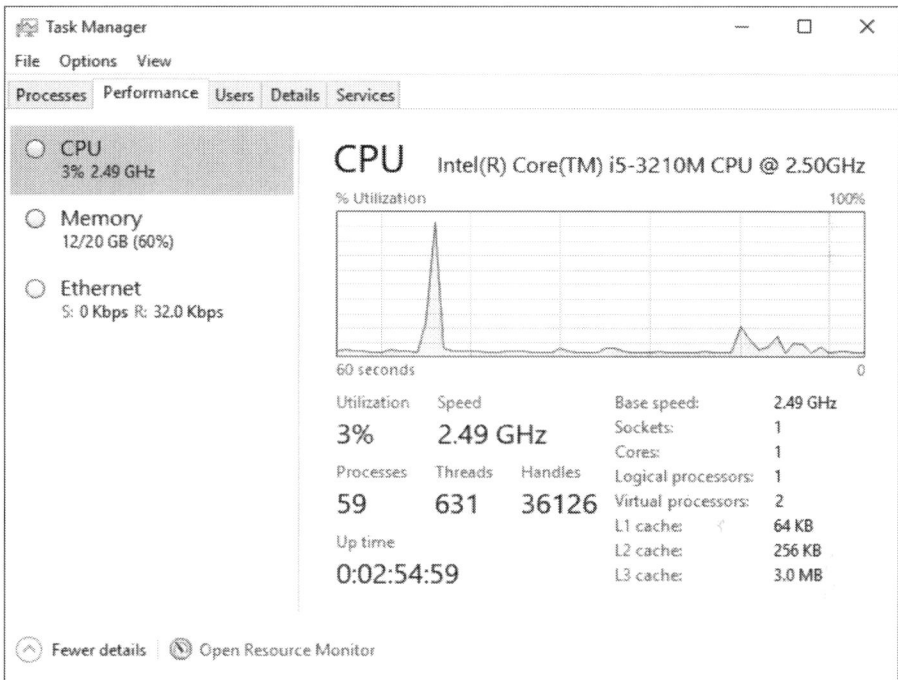

Figure 162: Task Manager Performance tab

More detailed information can be obtained by clicking **Open Resource Monitor** in the bottom left-hand corner of the Performance tab screen. This displays the following screen, which can be thought of as 'Task Manager on steroids'. Resource Monitor can be invoked from Windows Administrative Tools.

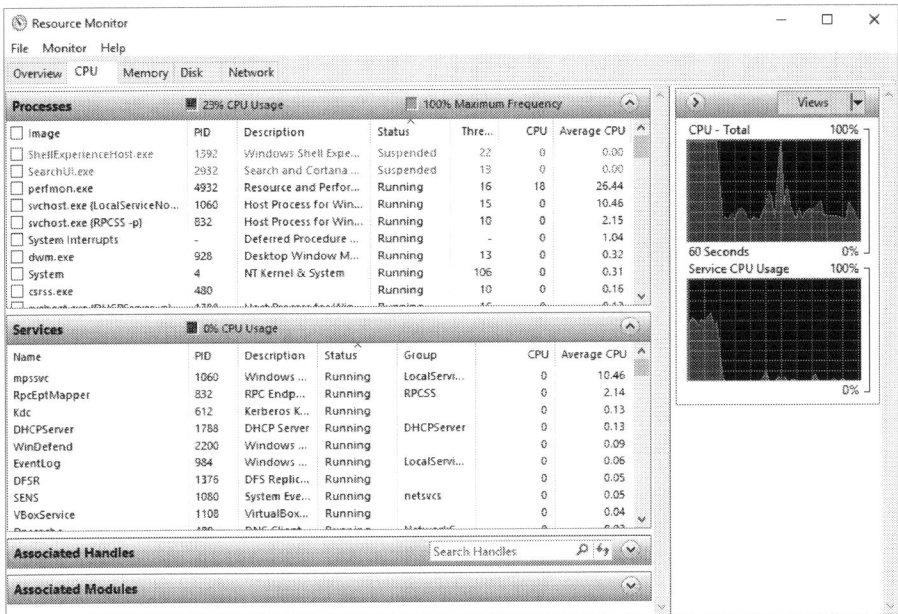

Figure 163: Resource Monitor screen

11.11 Headless Operation using Remote Desktop

When installing Windows Server, it is necessary to use a standard monitor, keyboard and mouse (usually, although some manufacturers have workarounds). However, once the server is up and running these can be dispensed with and it can be run in so-called *headless* mode. To access it for support purposes, the *Remote Desktop* capability is used. This has several advantages: firstly, the server can be accessed using any computer on the network and it is not necessary to have physical access to the server, which may be a consideration if it is situated in a secure, locked or otherwise inaccessible location. Secondly, dispensing with a physical screen, keyboard and mouse saves space and possibly a small amount of electrical power. Thirdly, in some small organizations the server may have to be physically located in a general-purpose office and not having a keyboard and screen will reduce the temptation for staff to treat it as just another computer.

Go into **Settings** and click **System** followed by **Remote Desktop**. Slide the *Enable Remote Desktop* switch to the **On** position:

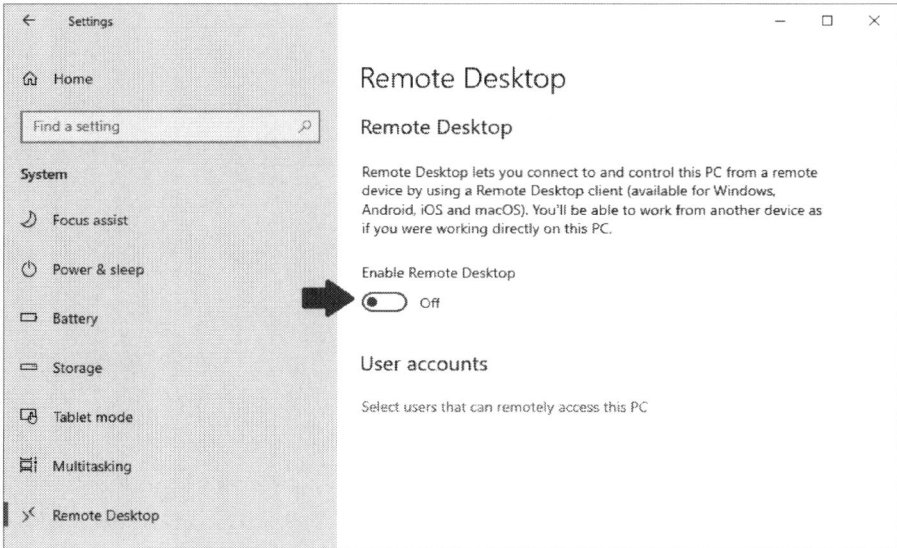

Figure 164: Enabling Remote Desktop on the server

All members of the Administrators group have access to the Remote Desktop by default, so it is not necessary to use the **Select users that can remotely access this PC** option. Click **OK**.

Test the facility by going to a computer on the network and launching the *Remote Desktop Connection* program. This program is a standard part of Windows and can be located at **Start > All Programs > Accessories** in Windows 7, from the Start Screen in Windows 8/8.1 and at **Start > Windows Accessories in Windows 10**. Enter the name of the server or its IP address. Provide logon credentials i.e. the name of an Administrative account and its password. Note that when the remote session is established, the current user on the physical server, if there is one, will be logged out.

Remote Desktop programs are also available for macOS and Linux, plus Microsoft have their own Remote Desktop app for Android and iOS devices, available from the respective App stores.

12

WINDOWS ADMIN CENTER
(WAC)

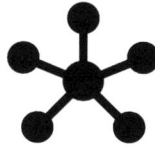

12.1 Overview

There are several methods for accessing the server in order to manage it. The simplest method is by logging into it directly, which is what we have done throughout this guide. Another method is by using Remote Desktop, as described in section **11.11 Headless Operation using Remote Desktop**. Microsoft offer several other tools, some of which are targeted at enterprise users, but *Windows Admin Center* or *WAC*, is a browser-based app for managing both servers as well as Windows 10 PCs and may eventually become a universal solution.. It does not have to be installed on the server itself, nor does it require anything to be installed on the server. Rather, it is typically installed on a computer running the 64-bit version of Windows 10. Some sources within Microsoft have suggested that WAC is the best method of managing Essentials, describing it as a replacement for the *Dashboard* – a greatly simplified version of Server Manager - that was in earlier versions of Essentials. This is somewhat optimistic, as many features are not available in the single-server environment that Essentials provides. However, WAC is particularly useful if the network environment consists exclusively of Windows 10 PCs, as everything can be managed from one place.

12.2 Installation

When launching Server Manager, you may have seen a small advertisement for WAC. Following the link will take you a webpage that gives more information and a download link, but as WAC will not run on a domain controller you need to switch to a regular PC at this point; as stated above, this must be running a 64-bit version of Windows 10. This computer will be referred to as the *Gateway*.

Download WAC from Microsoft – locate it by Googling 'Windows Admin Center'. You may be taken to their evaluation software website; however, the software is free, fully functional, without any restrictions and will not expire. During installation, it will default to using port 443 and a self-signed SSL certificate and it is suggested that you leave the settings as they are and do change them. The address for connecting to the Gateway from another PC will be displayed, which is of the form *https://computer:443*, where *computer* is the name of the computer that you have just installed WAC upon. In this example we have installed it on a PC called *win10-pc2*, so the address of the Gateway would be *https://win10-pc2:443*

Entering the address for the WAC Gateway in a browser will display the following screen (any messages about the site not being secure can be ignored). Initially, only the Gateway itself will be listed under *All Connections* i.e. the list of computers that can be managed. In this example, we have installed it on a regular computer called WIN10-PC2. To add the server PC, click where it read **+Add** on the left-hand side of the screen. On the panel that appears, click the **Windows Server** box:

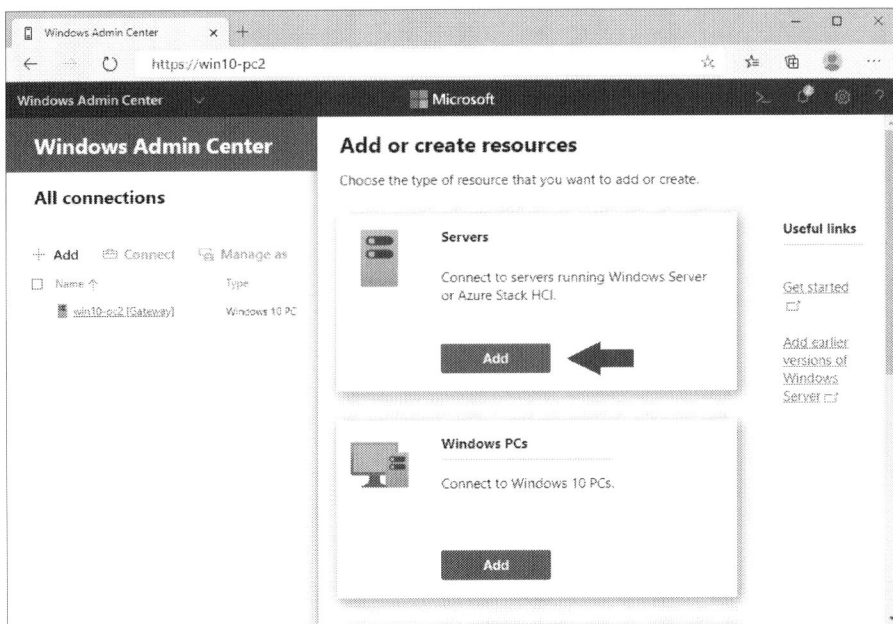

Figure 165: WAC – Adding a new connection

On the next panel, enter the name of the server to be managed, which in our example is *SERVER*. It is also possible to search Active Directory, which is particularly useful when connecting other PCs. It is necessary to specify login credentials; the best option is to choose **Use another account for this connection** and enter the administrator account and password of the server. Click **Add With Credentials**:

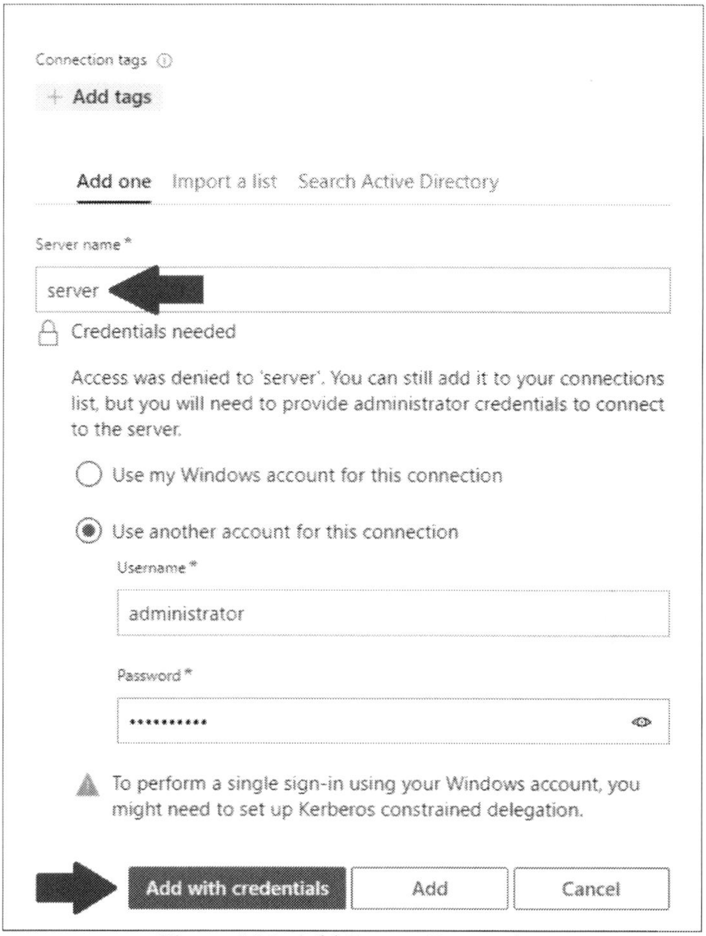

Figure 166: Add Server Connection

After a few seconds, the server will be added to the list of available connections; click it and you will be connected. After a short delay, an overview screen for the server will be displayed:

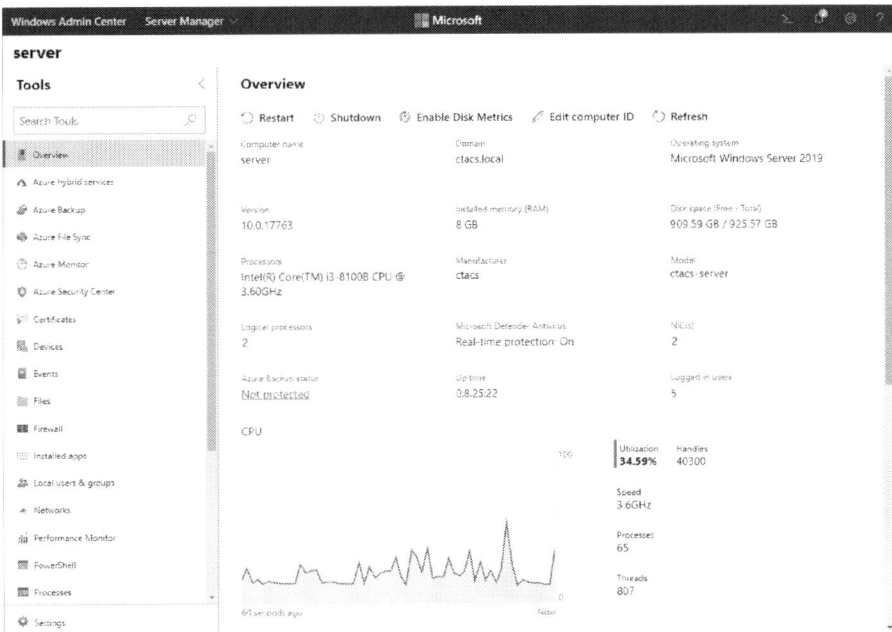

Figure 167: Overview of Server in WAC

Down the left-hand side of the screen are a selection of *Tools*, which enable many aspects of the server to be configured and managed. The selection of tools and the contents of the Overview screen will vary, depending on whether you are managing a server or a workstation PC. For instance, if a server then there will be additional focus on Microsoft's Azure offerings. The tools are outlined in the next section.

Note: WAC is under constant development, so available functionality and features may vary depending upon what version you are using

12.3 Tools within Windows Admin Center

Overview: Provides an 'at a glance' summary of the server. The top half of the screen is similar to the Local Server Properties page within Server Manager, and with server performance information displayed in the bottom half. The server can be restarted and shutdown from here.

Azure: The first sections comprises a number of options for managing Azure cloud-based services. Azure is not covered in this manual.

Certificates: Certificates are a method of ensuring that a website or service is what it purports to be, rather than a hoax or compromised one. The basic principle is that certificates are provided by recognised issuing authorities – known as CAs or Certificate Authorities – and may be provided on a commercial or free basis (albeit sometimes with restrictions). Certificates may also be self-certified, and Windows Server makes extensive use of these and ones issued by Microsoft.

Devices: This refers to the hardware components inside the server, enabling technical information to be obtained and driver updates to be applied. It is analogous to right-clicking the **Start** button and choosing **Device Manager**.

Events: An alternative method of viewing the event logs (as opposed to the method described in **11.4 Event Viewer**).

Files: This useful facility provides access to the folders and files on the server, analogous to using File Explorer. Files can be copied, deleted, renamed, uploaded and downloaded etc.

Firewall: For managing the firewall on the server (the firewall is discussed in **11.7 Firewall & network protection**).

Installed Apps: Provides a list of applications installed on the server. Applications can be removed if required. Analogous to **Settings > Apps**.

Local Users & Groups: For managing users on connected Windows 10 PCs (cannot be used on servers).

Network: Used for managing network adapters (alternative to right-click **Start** > **Network Connections**).

Performance Monitor: Provides a method for monitoring, comparing and recording the performance of Windows, Apps and Devices.

PowerShell: Runs a PowerShell session on the server.

Processes: Lists all the processes running on the server and enables them to be managed (comparable to using Task Manager).

Registry: Enables the registry information on the server to be modified (use with caution!).

Remote Desktop: Provides remote desktop access to the server, as discussed in **11.11 Headless Operation using Remote Desktop**. Requires the use of Windows 10 Professional or better on the client PC and that Remote Desktop has been enabled.

Roles & Features: For viewing, adding and removing roles and features on the server. An alternative to the use of Server Manager.

Scheduled Tasks: Behind the scenes, the server runs numerous tasks on a scheduled basis as part of its normal operation. This tool provides access to those tasks.

Services: For management of the services running on the server. Conventionally these would be accessed by right-click the **Start** button, choosing **Computer Management** and drilling down to **Services**.

Storage: Provides information about storage and disk usage on the server, plus enables shared folders to be managed.

Storage Replica: Enables volumes to be replicated across multiple servers for resilience and disaster recovery.

Updates: For controlling Windows Updates (similar to **11.3 Windows Updates**).

Settings: Controls a limited number of settings, such as whether Remote Desktop can be used.

13

MISCELLANEOUS & ADVANCED TOPICS

13.1 Overview

This chapter contains a selection of miscellaneous topics which do not fit elsewhere or of a more advanced or less frequently required nature.

13.2 Windows Activation

Depending on the license and type of installation you have, you may need to activate Windows Server. If this is the case, you will receive warning messages until you do so and may find that some functions do not work properly. To check and activate if necessary, click **Start > Settings > Update & Security > Activation**. If it states Windows is not activated, click **Change product key** and enter a valid product key. The key is 25-digits long and is located on the Windows Server packaging or disk, as a sticker on the server, in an email if it was purchased online, or online from the Microsoft account website.

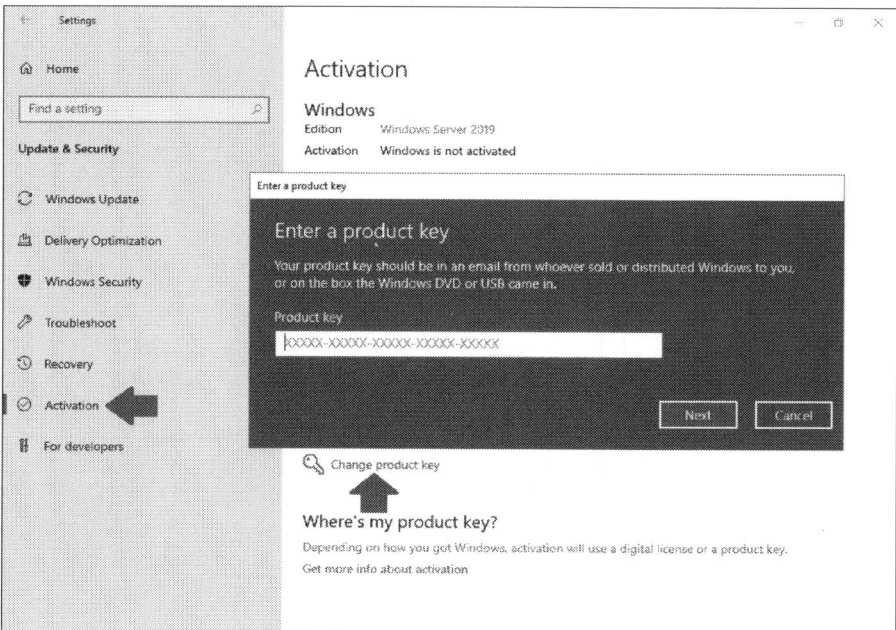

Figure 168: Activating Windows

13.3 Setup Alternative Administrator Account(s)

For a variety of reasons, it is not good practice to use the main Administrator account any more than is strictly necessary. Firstly, in case the account accidentally gets locked or disabled. Secondly, it can be confusing when using Windows 7 clients, which have a built-in local account of the same name. Instead, an alternative administrative account should be setup and, once the server has gone live, this is the one that should be normally used. This could be called *systemadmin*, for instance. To create it:

- Go into **Administrative Tools** and choose **Active Directory Users and Computers**.
- Find *Administrator* in the *Users* section.
- Right-click on *Administrator* and choose **Copy**.
- Complete the dialogue box and create a new user called *systemadmin*. You could set the password to the same as that of the *Administrator*.
- Having created the user, go into **Properties** and specify any drives, scripts, settings as used by the regular Administrator account.

Suggestion: in order to install some software and printers on client's PCs, administrative rights may be required. If you wish users to be able to do these things themselves, setup another administrative account, perhaps called *userinstaller*. Do not use the same password as the main Administrator/Systemadmin accounts and do not specify any of the profile information. The details of this account can then be passed to trusted users.

13.4 Accessing the Internet from the Server

There are several reasons why general internet browsing is not a good idea on a server – such as the risk of picking up malware from an infected website - but not being able to access the internet freely can make things difficult, particularly in a small network. Internet Explorer 11 is the preferred browser in Windows Server and the Edge browser of Windows 10 is not provided. However, by default it has limited internet connectivity due to a feature called *Internet Explorer Enhanced Security* being enabled. To change this:

Go into **Server Manager** and click **Local Server** to display the Properties for the server. On the right-hand side of the first panel is an entry for *IE Enhanced Security Configuration*; click where it reads **On** and the following dialog box will be displayed:

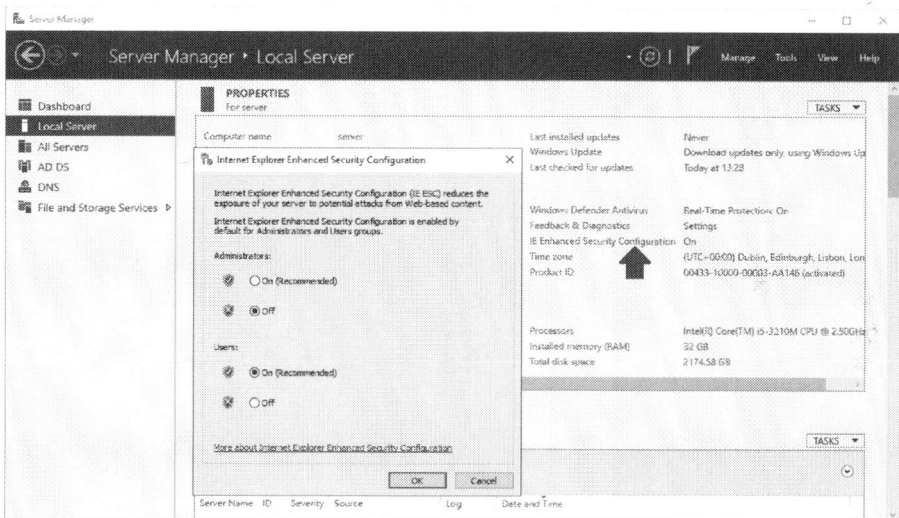

Figure 169: Internet Explorer Enhanced Security Configuration

Change the entry for Administrators to **Off** and click **OK**. It is not necessary to change the entry for Users and nobody other than an Administrator should ever have direct access to the server.

13.5 Controlling User Logon Times

It is possible to control the times when a particular user can logon to the system. Many organizations will probably not bother with this facility, but there are some situations when it can be useful. For instance, a school or college may not wish for students to be able to use the system outside of normal hours. Or, a business may have an important application which is updated overnight and whilst this is taking place they do not want users to access it.

Go into *Active Directory Administrative Center* and drill down to find the user. Double-click on the user's name to bring up the main form that summarizes their details. Click where it reads **Log on hours...** in the *Accounts* section. Click on the segments – you can select more than one at a time by holding down the mouse button – and click **Logon Permitted** or **Logon Denied** as required. When finished click **OK**.

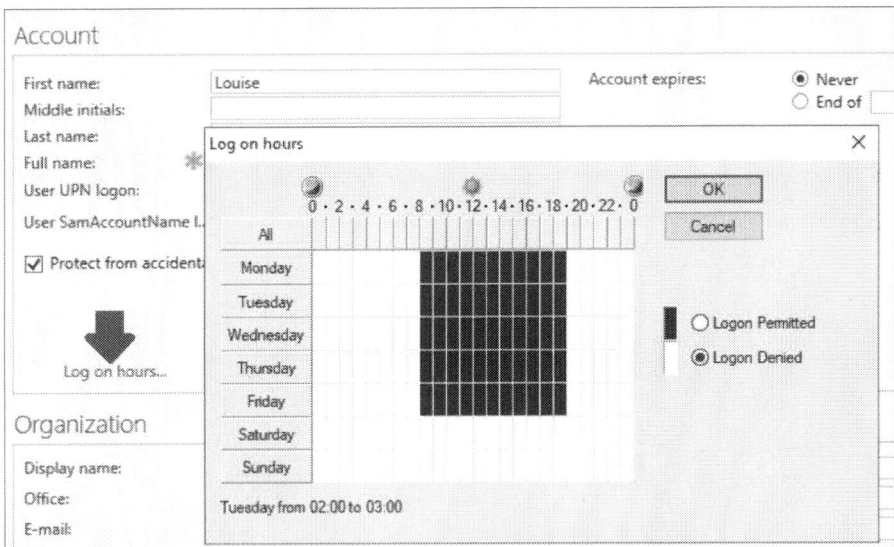

Figure 170: Controlling logon hours for a user

13.6 Controlling Server Manager Startup

On Essentials, Server Manager does not startup automatically when the administrator logs into the server; however, on Windows Server Standard it does so. Many people will find this useful, but if you do not then it can be disabled so you are taken straight to the Desktop, as with Essentials. From within Server Manager, click **Manage > Server Manager Properties**. On the resultant panel, place a tick against **Do not start Server Manager automatically at logon** followed by **OK**. It is also possible to change the data refresh period for Server Manager, although the default value of 10 minutes is fine for most purposes.

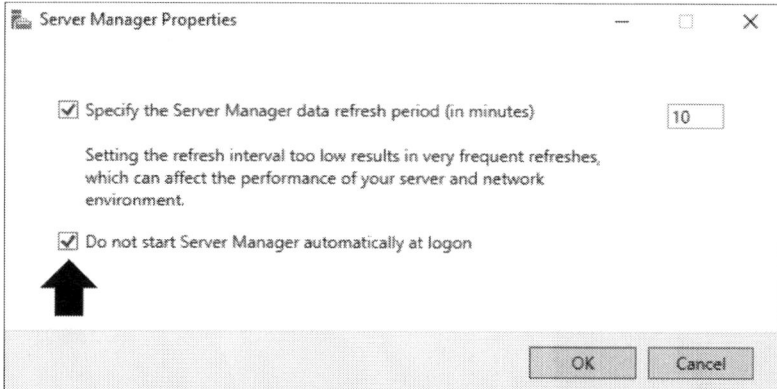

Figure 171: Server Manager logon behavior

13.7 Diagnostics & feedback

Windows operating systems automatically send diagnostic data back to Microsoft as part of their normal operation. According to Microsoft: *'Diagnostic data is used to help keep Windows secure and up to date, troubleshoot problems, and make product improvement'*. This data can include information on websites that are visited, plus which applications and features are used and how they are used. Some people refer to this collection of information as 'data slurping' or 'spying'. An alternative technical name is *telemetry*.

It is not possible to turn off these diagnostics, but you can control the amount of information that is sent. Go into **Settings > Privacy > Diagnostics & feedback** and choose the **Basic** option. Scrolling down the screen, there is an option to *Delete diagnostic data* that has been sent to Microsoft. There is also an option to control the *Feedback frequency*, which can be set to **Never**.

13.8 Ease of Access

There are a number of features to improve usage of the server for people with hearing, visual and other impairments. These are not specific to Windows Server or Essentials, but rather are the features provided by Windows. They can be located through **Start > Settings > Ease of Access** and include:

Narrator – a screen reader that reads all the elements on the screen, such as the text, dialog boxes and buttons. There are different voices to choose from, plus the speed and pitch can be adjusted

Magnifier – increases the size of screen elements

High Contrast – provides a choice of themes to improve screen contrast

Keyboard – provides an On-Screen keyboard if required plus controls audio feedback and the behavior of keyboard shortcuts

Mouse – control over the mouse and mouse pointer

13.9 Installing DHCP

Windows Server assumes that IP addresses are being provided by an all-in-one internet router or hub or other source, as will often be the case in a small business setting; accordingly, it does not run a DHCP service by default and it has to be manually installed if such a router is not being used. This is done using the instructions below.

Click **Start** and launch *Server Manager*. Click **Manage** and choose **Add roles and features**. Click **Next** on the *Add Roles and Features Wizard* and on the resultant screen choose **Role-based or feature-based installation** followed by **Next**. On the subsequent screen make sure the server is highlighted and click **Next**. On the list of roles click **DHCP Server**. A message will appear asking if additional required features should be added; check the **Include management tools (if applicable)** box is ticked and click the **Add Features** button:

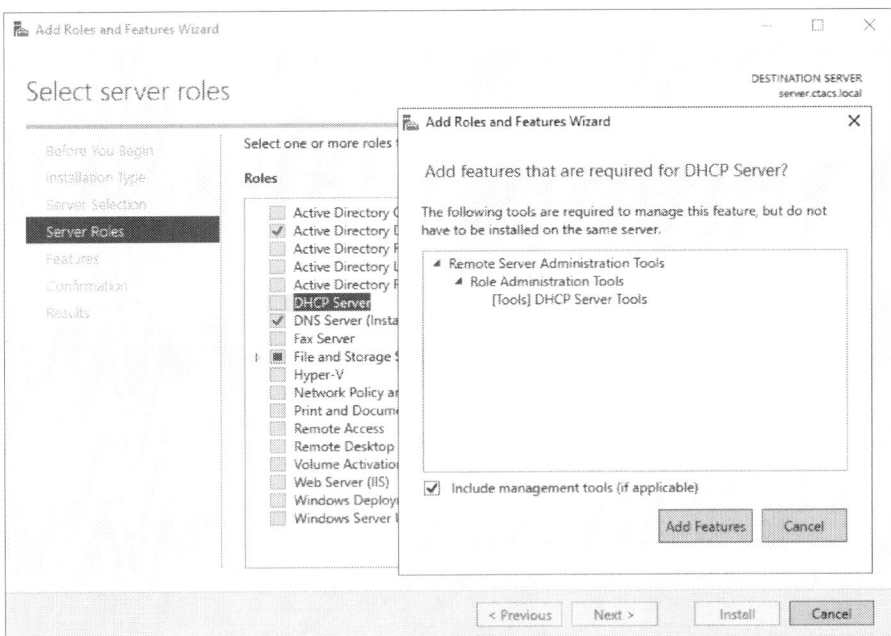

Figure 172: Choose DHCP Server

Continue clicking **Next** on each of the subsequent screens. Eventually a *Confirm installation selections* screen is displayed; tick the **Restart the destination server automatically if required** box followed by **Yes** to the message that pops up. Finally, click the **Install** button. Whilst the process is running, which will take several minutes, a progress screen is shown; when complete, click **Close**.

There will now be an entry for DHCP in the left-hand panel of Server Manager - click it. At the top of the resultant screen is a message that reads *'Configuration required for DHCP Server'* - click where it says **More...** to display the following panel, then click the **Complete DHCP configuration** link:

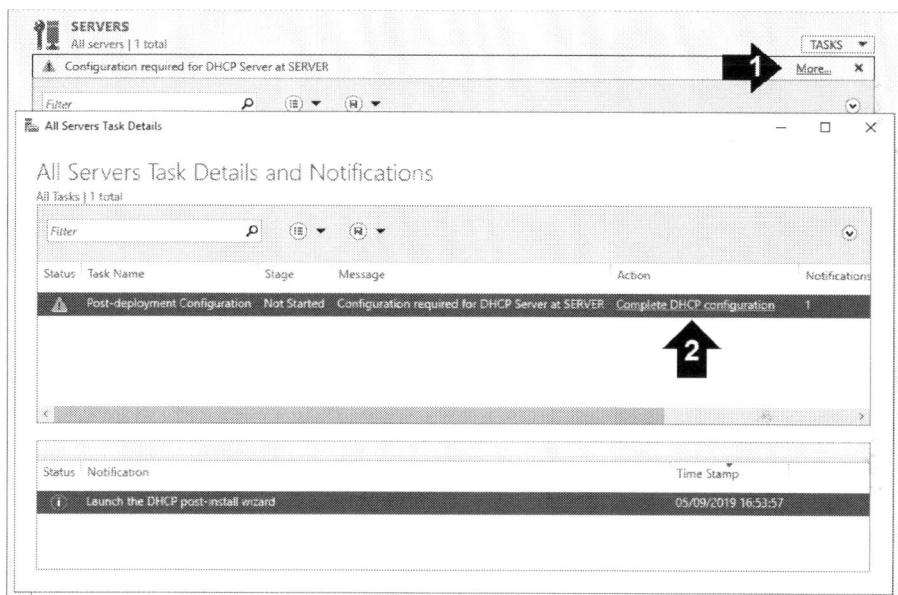

Figure 173: Message about need for configuration

The *DHCP Post-Install configuration* wizard appears. Click **Next** on the first screen and the following one appears:

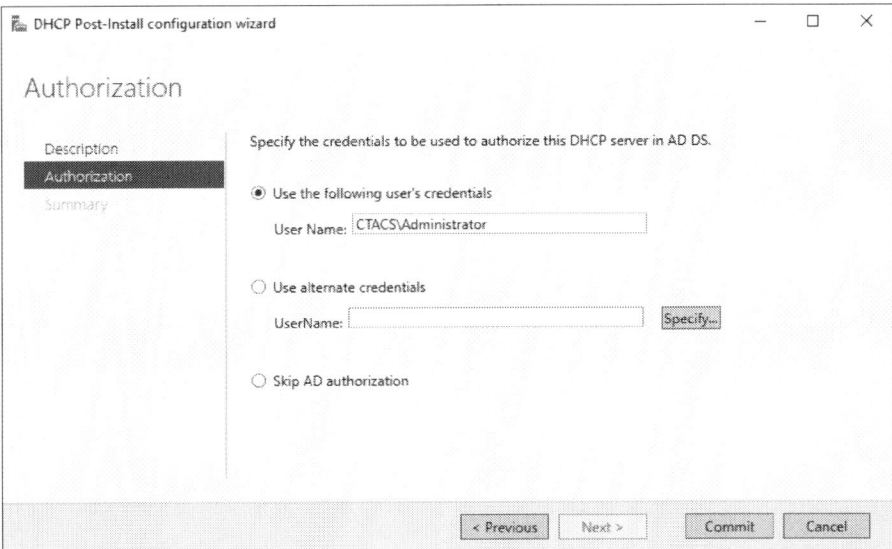

Figure 174: Post-Install configuration wizard

The existing user credentials (*"Administrator"*) are fine so just click the **Commit** button. After a few seconds a *Summary* panel will be shown. Click **Close** and you will be returned to the *All Servers Task Details and Notifications panel*, which you can now close.

The next step is to configure the *IP scope*. Still within Server Manager, click **Tools** followed by **DHCP**. Expand the tree down the left-hand side until it appears as follows:

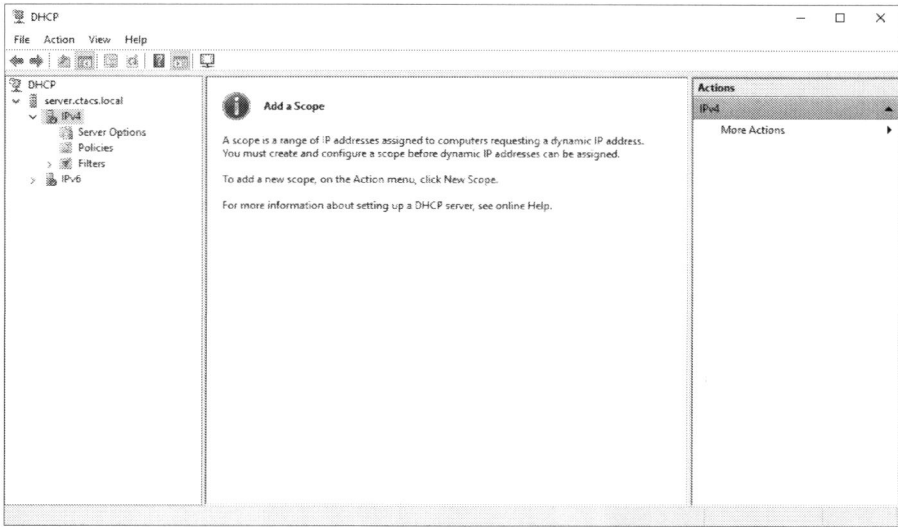

Figure 175: Configure DHCP Server

Right-click on the entry for **IPv4** and choose **New Scope** to start the *New Scope Wizard*. Click **Next** and the following panel is displayed. Give it a suitable name e.g. *clientdevices* and an optional description, then click the **Next** button:

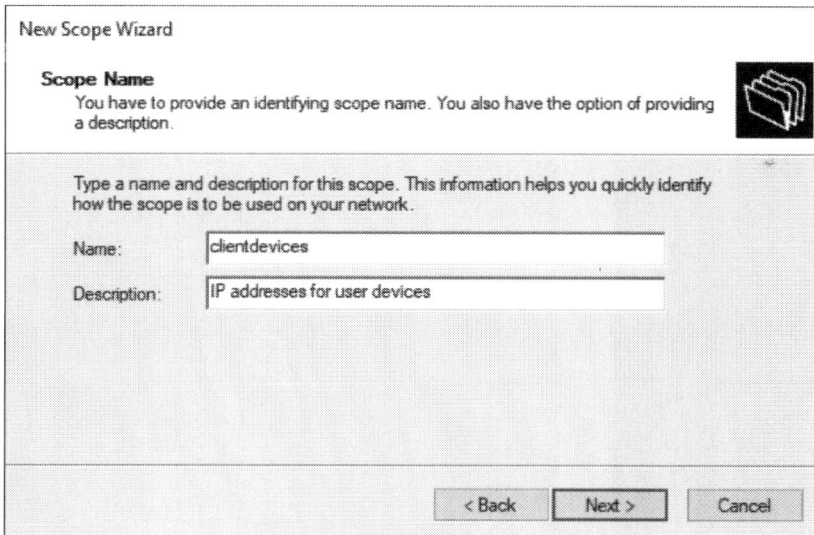

Figure 176: New Scope Wizard

On the subsequent screen enter the addresses according to the scheme you are using. In this example, our server is on 192.168.1.253 and the scope for the workstations will be 192.168.1.50 to 192.168.1.200. Make sure the **Length** is 24 and the **Subnet mask** will automatically change to 255.255.255.0. Click **Next**:

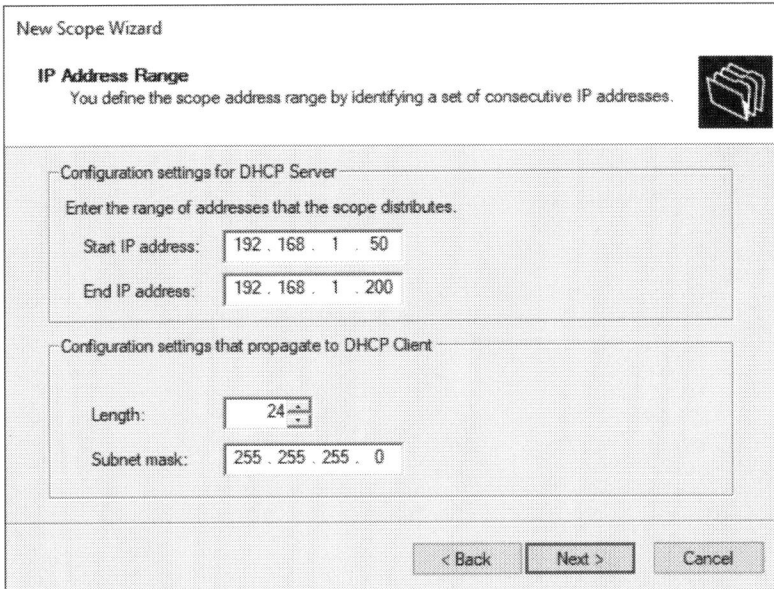

Figure 177: IP address range for DHCP server

The next panel allows you to specify any exclusions (i.e. gaps) in the IP scope. Unless you have very specific requirements you can just click **Next**. The subsequent screen is for specifying how long a lease will last. The default value of 8 days is not a great choice, so reduce it to a single day and click **Next**.

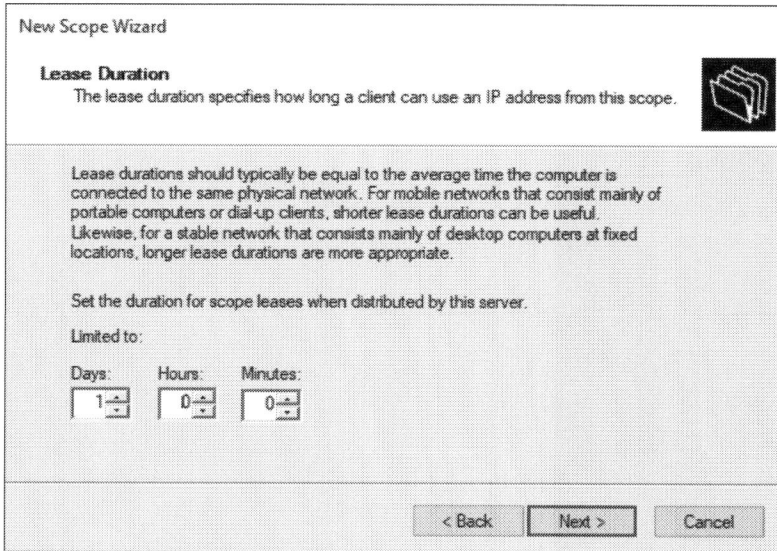

New Scope Wizard

Lease Duration
The lease duration specifies how long a client can use an IP address from this scope.

Lease durations should typically be equal to the average time the computer is connected to the same physical network. For mobile networks that consist mainly of portable computers or dial-up clients, shorter lease durations can be useful. Likewise, for a stable network that consists mainly of desktop computers at fixed locations, longer lease durations are more appropriate.

Set the duration for scope leases when distributed by this server.

Limited to:

Days: Hours: Minutes:
 1   0   0

< Back   Next >   Cancel

Figure 178: Specify Lease Duration

The following screen is concerned with more advanced options. They are of no great importance in a small network so choose **No, I will configure these options later** and click **Next**.

Upon completion, which is a matter of seconds, a confirmation screen is shown. Click **Finish**. The scope now has to be activated. Expand the tree on the left-hand side of the DHCP panel. Currently, the entry for IPv4 will have a blue circle with a white exclamation mark on it. Wait 30 seconds, right-click the new scope that we just created and choose **Activate**. The exclamation mark will be replaced by a green circle containing a white tick mark in it; everything should now be working correctly. You should restart the server at this point.

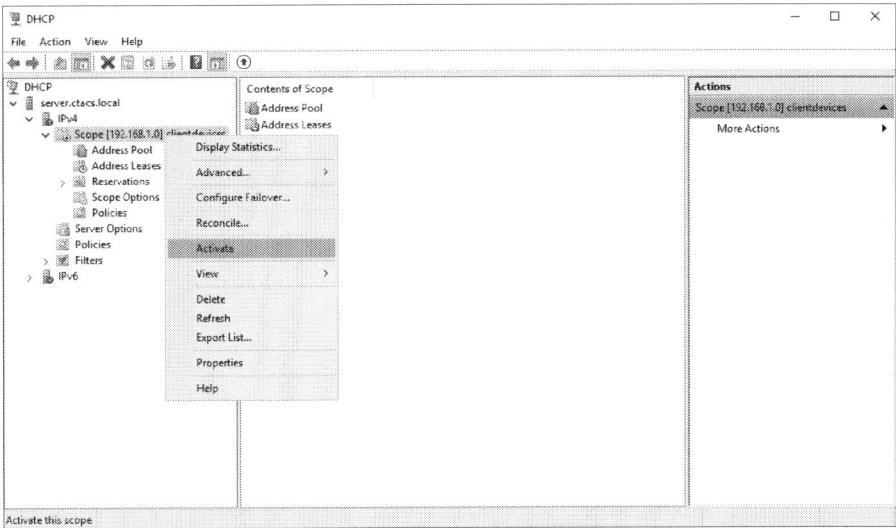

Figure 179: DHCP after configuration

13.10 Multiple Network Adapters (NIC Teaming)

A file server can and ideally should have more than one network (Ethernet) adapter; multiple adapters can be used together in different ways to improve resilience and/or performance using a technique known as *Teaming* or *NIC Teaming* (NIC is short for *Network Interface Card*).

The main network card represents a single point of failure – if it is lost then the server is out of action as nobody can access it. Ethernet adapters can fail, as can the ports on the switch that they are connected to, or the cable may accidentally be pulled out. In this example, a second Ethernet adapter has been installed in the server to improve network resilience; in the event that the first or main adapter fails, it will take over automatically, such that service continues without interruption. Important: before progressing, make a note of the settings of the first adapter, which was given a fixed IP address in section **2. BASIC INSTALLATION AND CONFIGURATION**, as it may be necessary to re-enter them later on.

On the server, launch *Server Manager* from the **Start** menu and click **Local Server**. In the Properties panel locate the *NIC Teaming* entry. Click where it reads **Disabled** and the following panel is shown:

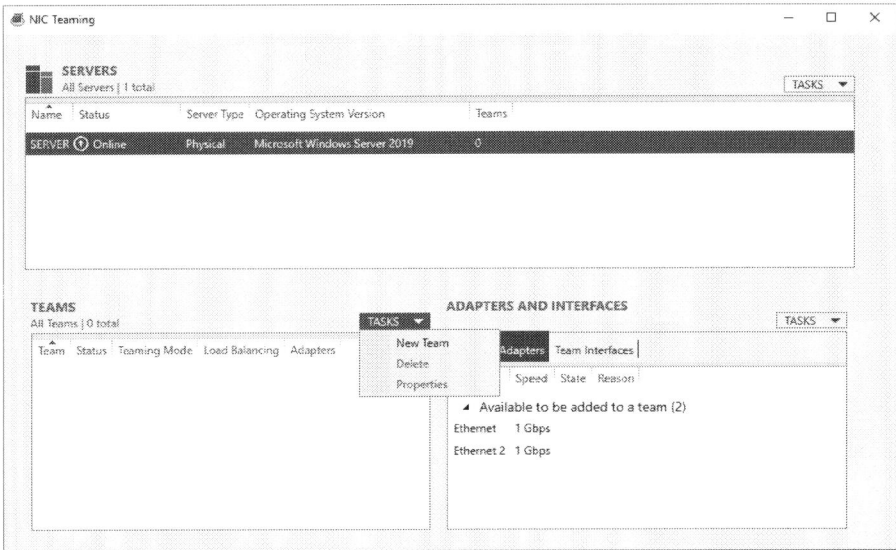

Figure 180: NIC Teaming screen

In the Teams section, click the **TASKS** drop-down and choose **New Team**. On the resultant panel, specify a *Team name* (e.g. *LAN*) and tick the boxes for the network adapters. If you were to just click **OK** at this point, then by default the adapters will be bonded together to double network throughput. However, we need to click **Additional properties** to change the settings: **Teaming mode** should be **Switch Independent**; **Load balancing mode** should be **Address Hash**; **Standby adapter** should be **Ethernet 2** (or whatever your second adapter is called). Click **OK**.

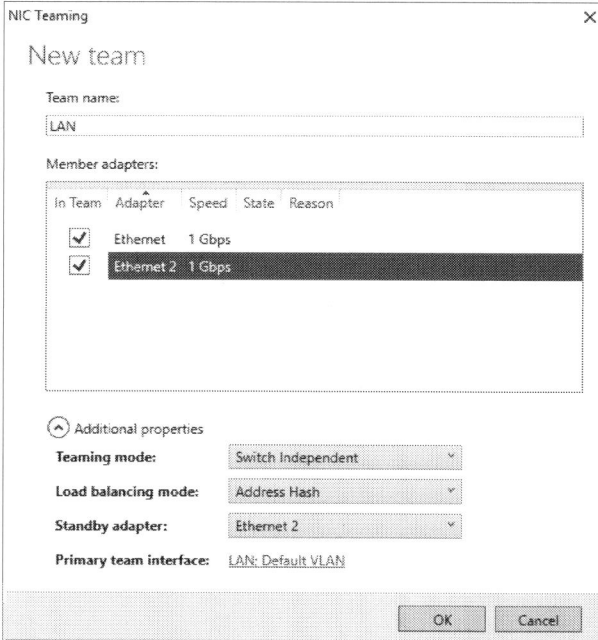

Figure 181: Creating a new Team

The server may take a minute or so to adjust, during which time connectivity may be lost and an error status may be displayed on the NIC Teaming screen. When matters have settled down, it should appear along the following lines:

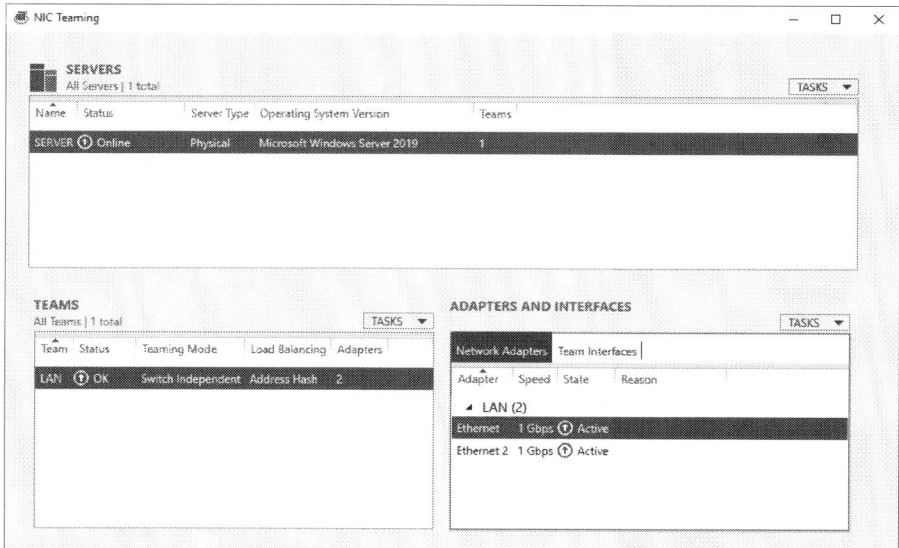

Figure 182: NIC Teaming status

Returning to the Local Server Properties screen within Server Manager – you may need to refresh it - there should now be an entry underneath NIC Teaming for *LAN* (or whatever you named the Team):

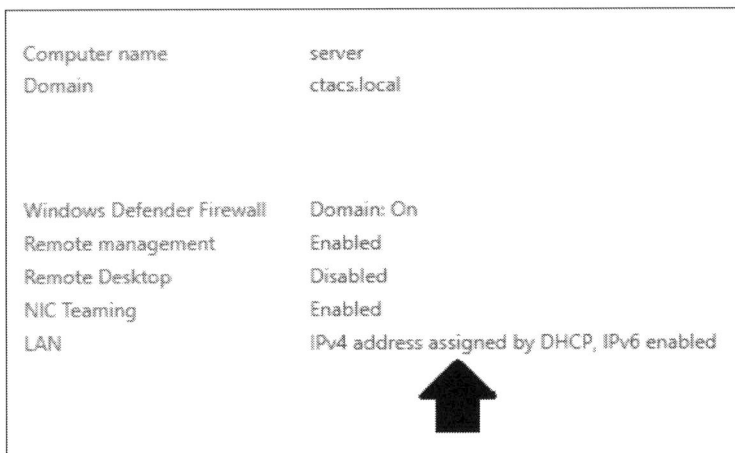

Computer name	server
Domain	ctacs.local
Windows Defender Firewall	Domain: On
Remote management	Enabled
Remote Desktop	Disabled
NIC Teaming	Enabled
LAN	IPv4 address assigned by DHCP, IPv6 enabled

Figure 183: LAN entry in server Properties

What we have just done has implications for the IP address of the server and so we now need to fix matters. Click on the blue writing to the right of *LAN* (as shown above) and it will display the Network Connections. Right-click the entry for the team (*LAN* in our example) and choose **Properties**. Highlight **Internet Protocol Version 4 (TCP/IPv4)** and click **Properties**. Change the entries to be the same as the original single adapter was before beginning this exercise. Again, there may be an interruption to the connectivity whilst this takes effect.

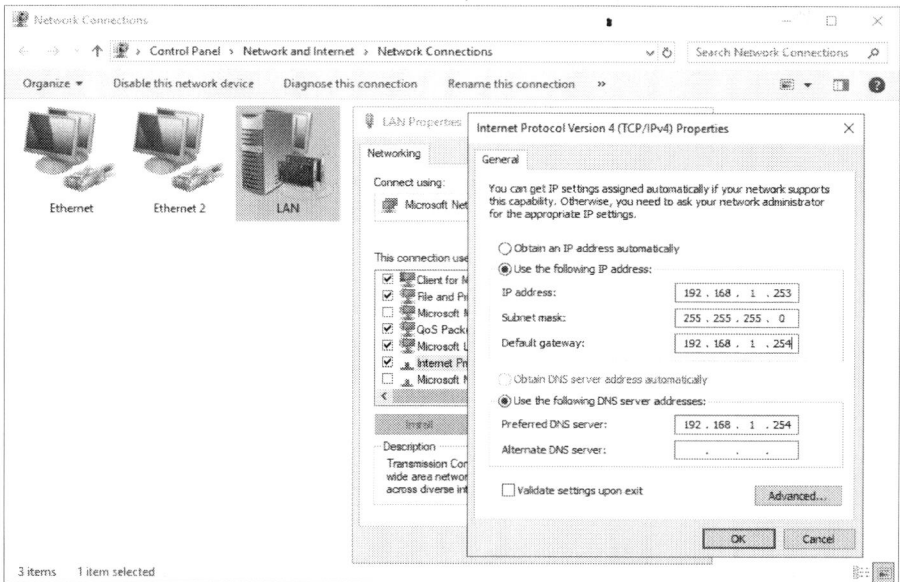

Figure 184: Network Connections

It should now be tested. Remove the network cable from the first Ethernet adapter; the second one should take over automatically and the server still be accessible.

13.11 Adding Additional Servers

Note: this section refers to Windows Server 2019 Standard only. It is not possible to add further servers to a Windows Server 2019 Essentials-based network.

In a small organization, there is typically just one server. However, in a larger organization there may be multiple servers, providing different roles and capacity. Critical to the operation of the entire network is the Domain Controller running Active Directory, which defines every server, computer, user and other resource in the system. If the Domain Controller is unavailable for any reason, for instance, hardware problems or it has crashed, then everything comes to a halt. To avoid this possibility, it is standard practice to have one or more additional domain controllers which can take over and/or share the workload in a larger network. In this example, we will add another server to fulfil this role (and having done so, you can then add further roles to that server if required).

Another scenario is where an existing network is being upgraded with a new server, and it might be desirable to have both running simultaneously to facilitate the migration process.

In this example, we will refer to the original server as *server* and the additional one as *server2*. Using the instructions in section **2. BASIC INSTALLATION AND CONFIGURATION**, install Windows Server 2019 on the second server and add the Active Directory role, to the point where it is ready to be promoted to be a domain controller. Then, change the settings of the network adapter, giving it a static IP address in accordance with your IP scheme. For instance, if *server1* is on 192.168.1.2 then you might choose to make *server2* 192.168.1.3. The *Preferred DNS server* should be changed to explicitly point to the first server – this is very important (the alternate can be set to the loopback adapter, 127.0.0.1). Make sure the two servers can 'see' each other, for instance by use of the PING command.

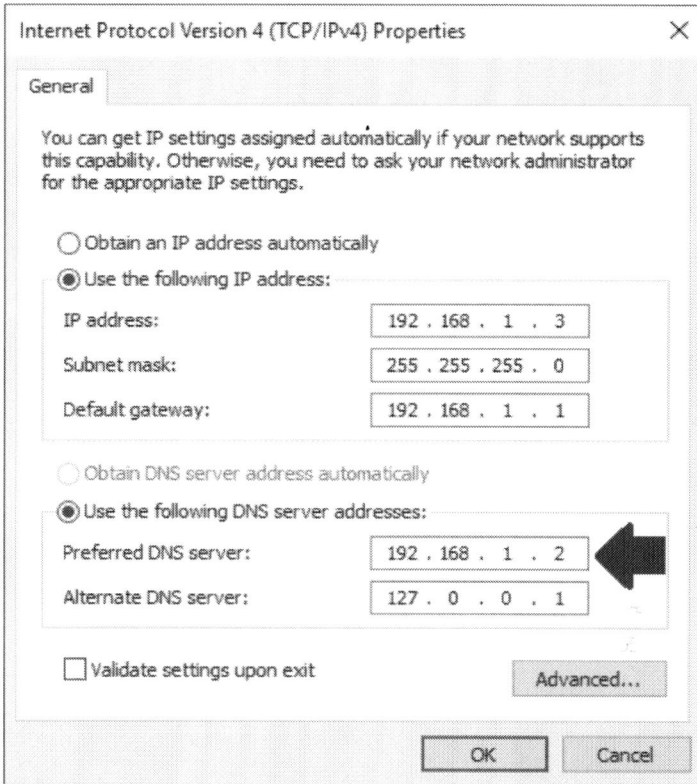

Figure 185: Set Preferred DNS to IP address of the first server

The second server should now be promoted by clicking on the message that appears at the top of Server Manager:

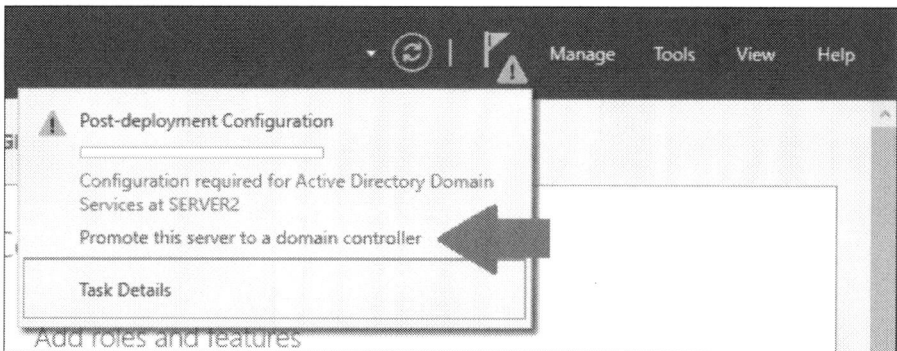

Figure 186: Promote the second server

The *Active Directory Domain Services Configuration Wizard* runs. On the *Deployment Configuration* screen choose **Add a domain controller to an existing domain**. Type in the name of the domain e.g. ctacs.local and click the **Select** button; if it cannot find it, this will almost certainly be due to a DNS error, so check the DNS settings on both servers. You need to supply credentials to affect the change, so click the **Change** button and enter the Administrator account details for this server; it is not apparent, but this should be in the format *domain_name\username* e.g. *ctacs\administrator*. Click **Next** to proceed:

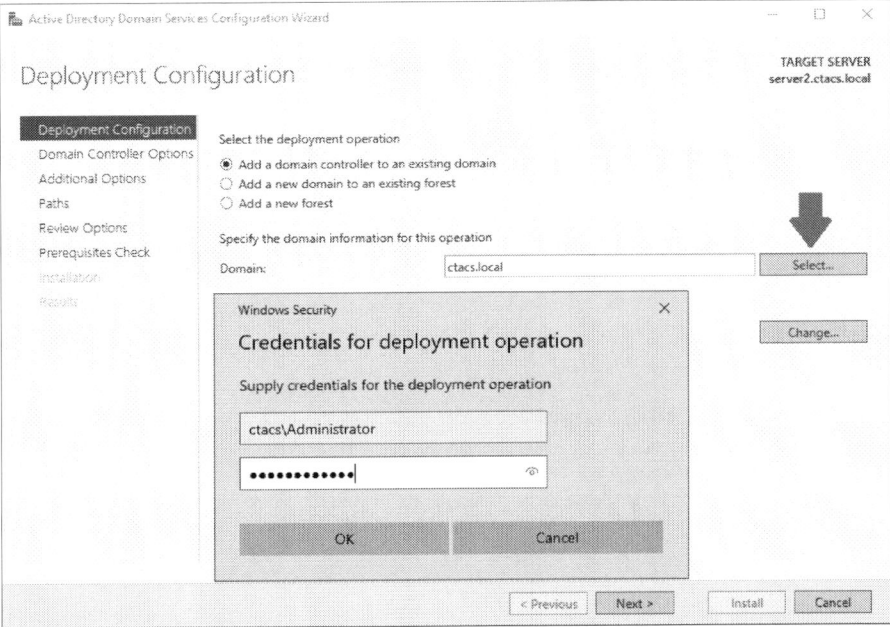

Figure 187: Choose the deployment option

On the second screen, specify and confirm the *Directory Services Restore Mode (DSRM)* password. For convenience, you may wish to use the same password as the Administrator account. Click **Next**:

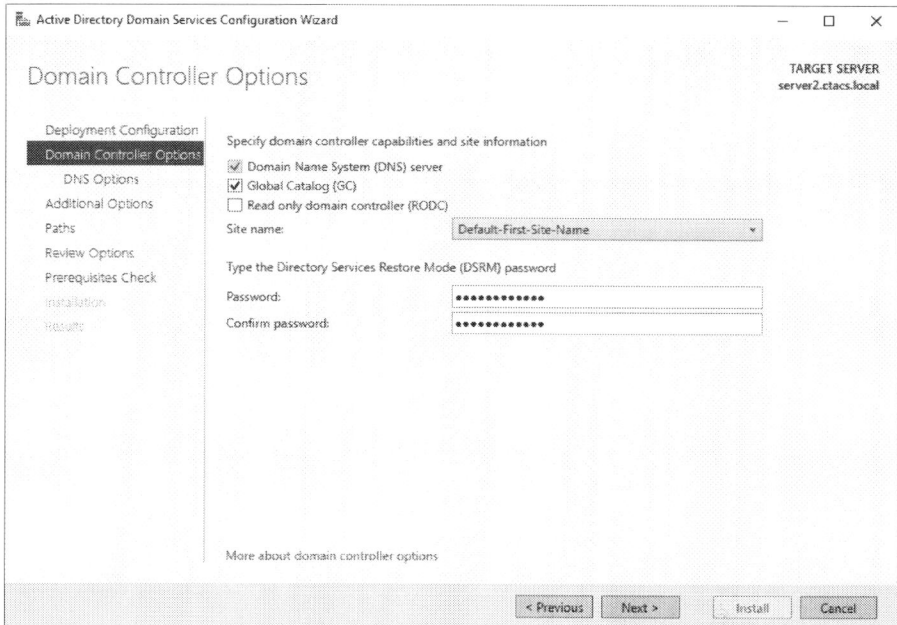

Figure 188: Domain Controller options

You may receive a message that states 'A delegation for this DNS server cannot be created because the authoritative parent zone cannot be found...', particularly if you are working in an environment where DNS is being provided by an all-in-one router. For now, ignore it by clicking **Next**.

On the subsequent *Additional Options* screen, click **Next**. If you receive an error message relating to *adprep*, use the *Replicate from* drop-down field and change the value from *Any domain controller* to the full name of the first server. Click **Next**:

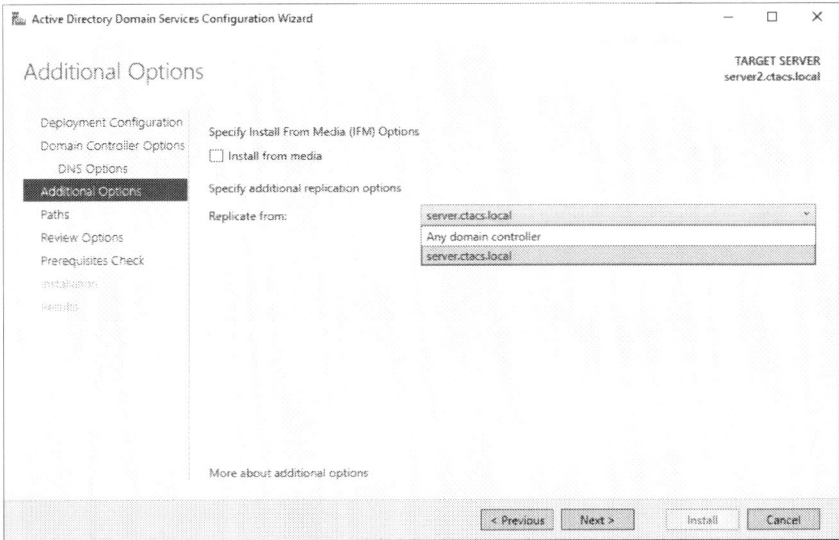

Figure 189: Specify the first server for replication

The next screen is for specifying the location of the database and log files associated with Active Directory; usually you will just click **Next**. There will then be a screen to review the options – click **Next** to continue. The wizard will run a pre-requisites check; there may be some warning messages but provided the *'All prerequisite checks passed successfully'* message is displayed, you can click **Install** to begin the installation proper. Installation will take a minute or so, after which the server will restart.

To prove that things are working, go back to the original server and create a new user using the Active Directory Administrative Center (as described in section **5.2 Creating Users**). Wait a few minutes, go the second, newly added server, and launch the *Active Directory Administrative Center* on it – the newly created user should be listed, proving that the servers are synchronizing.

If you need to add further servers, repeat the above steps for them. These servers can then have additional roles added to them to meet the needs of the organization. If you are using Windows Admin Center (see **12. WINDOWS ADMIN CENTER**), they can be added to it and managed from there.

252

Index